TOGETHER WE ASPIRE • TOGETHER WE ACHIEVE

INSIGHT GUIDES

The world's largest collection of visual travel guides

TRINIDAD & TOBAGO

Edited by Elizabeth Saft
Photography by Junia Browne, Bill Wassman and others
Editorial Director: Brian Bell

APA PUBLICATIONS

L

Part of the Langenscheidt Publishing Group

This is a thoroughly revised and updated edition of a landmark guide to Trinidad and Tobago, the first high-quality publication devoted entirely to the sister islands that have become increasingly popular Caribbean destinations. We hope it maintains the spirit, verve and hard work of the editors, writers, and photographers who originally helped capture the quintessence of the Trinidadian people, their lifestyles and culture, and transformed it into a visual commentary which is both informative and stimulating.

Apa Publications' innovative approach to creating travel chronicles has been honored throughout the world since the company was established in 1970. The first book, *Insight Guide: Bali*, set the precedent for the distinctive style that is evident in the succeeding 200 *Insight Guides*. Apa's concept offered a more insightful look at a country than traditional guidebooks. It called for each title to have clear, frank journalistic writing illustrated with fine photographs.

Heading the team for *Insight Guide: Trinidad and Tobago* was project editor, **Elizabeth Saft**. Before embarking on this project, Saft had just finished a stint in the editorial department of a major New York publisher. By then, she was keen to return to her earlier wandering ways traveling in America, the Caribbean and Europe, and hence welcomed with enthusiasm the opportunity to immerse herself in a culture so richly dissimilar though parallel to her own culture.

Saft

The comprehensive and provocative history section was written by **Kim Nicholas Johnson**, a graduate of the University of the West Indies. Johnson's passion for the culture and politics of T&T has also resulted in the book *Festivals in the Caribbean*, as well as numerous articles in regional journals and papers.

Johnson's involvement led Saft to **Merle Hodge**, whose article "People" is an invaluable aid to newcomers to T&T society. With the disarming straightforwardness of so many of her fellow countrypeople, Hodge gives the lie to stereotypical views of Trinidadians while elucidating the origins of their distinctiveness. Hodge comes well qualified for this project, with numerous scholarly articles to her credit, as well as many contributions to books on T&T and the Caribbean, and a long career of public service in the form of research projects on all aspects of Caribbean culture.

The impressionistic sections on carnival and other festivals were the work of **Molly Ahye**, a Trinidadian who began her career as a dancer. She founded a modern and folk dance troupe and is the author of two volumes on Caribbean dance forms.

Therese Mills, a lifelong resident of Port of Spain and a journalist and editor-in-chief at *Newsday*, brought her considerable knowledge to bear on the Places chapter on Trinidad's capital city. She also contributed the "Roti on the Run" food chapter and to the Travel Tips section.

Clara Rosa de Lima, who has died since the first edition of this book, picked up where Mills left off, covering all corners of the bigger island. Owner of an art gallery in Port of Spain, de Lima was the author of three books of verse, five novels, many magazine and newspaper articles, and a daily commentary on Radio Trinidad.

The "Above and Below the Water" chapter was compiled by **Ian Lambie**, who is as president of the Asa Wright Nature Centre. As a naturalist and nature photographer, Lambie also lectures widely on Trinidad and

Johnson

Tobago's flora and fauna, and breeds fish in his spare time.

The illuminating article on Trinidad and Tobago's musical past and present was the work of **Ernest Brown**, an assistant professor of Music and African-American studies at Boston's Northeastern Univeristy. Widely traveled in Africa and the Caribbean, Brown has previously written articles on jazz and on children's game-songs, as well as on Caribbean music.

Knolly Moses, a *Newsweek* editor, was born and raised in Trinidad and has lived in the United States for more than 15 years. He is widely published in Caribbean and American magazines. "Local tastes" is a subject close to his heart, as food and cooking are a longtime hobby of his. Aptly, he wrote the article "Roti on the Run."

Moses

Photographer **Junia Browne**, an enthusiastic and tireless chronicler of the landscape and culture of his country, made it his mission to ensure that Trinidad and Tobago were beautifully, fairly and thoroughly represented in this book. For over 25 years, Browne has been photographing current events and natural beauties for three local newspapers. He has also acted as chief photographer for the Trinidad & Tobago Tourism Office (TIDCO). Besides contributing a large portion of the photographs for this book, his work has also been published in numerous books and brochures on Trinidad & Tobago and the Caribbean.

In addition to Browne's photographs, many of **Bill Wassman's** images are reproduced in this volume. Wassman is a resident of New York whose work first attracted international attention in *Insight Guide: Nepal*. Wassman spent months poking his Leicas into every part of Trinidad and

Browne

Tobago, gathering mountains of pictures despite incurring misfortune upon misfortune during his long expedition through the landscape, greatest of which was the temperamental behavior of his rented motorcycle. A graduate of Indiana Univeristy in comparative literature and anthropology, Wassman worked as an assistant to photographers Eric Meola and Peter Turner in 1973 and 1974 before establishing his own reputation. He is a regular Insight Guides photographer.

Photographs were also contributed by **John Hill**, an Englishman who has lived in Trinidad since 1979. Trained as an architect, he has been a commercial photographer since 1983.

Photographer **Richard Spence**, a Trinidadian who studied the art in Rhode Island, now works as a photographer in Port of Spain.

Individuals who contributed in one or many ways are **Peter Post**, who edited several pieces; **Zorina Shah**, who worked quickly and thoroughly on "Trinidad"; and **Robert Hadow**.

The book is kept up to date by Trinidadian, **David Renwick**, an established freelance journalist who writes articles for several international publications including the *Daily Telegraph* in London. He was CEO at *Newsday* when originally commissioned.

Lesley Gordon coordinated this update from Insight Guides' London editorial office. The text was proofread and indexed by **Mary Morton**.

A note on language: because Insight Guides are international collaborations, using as many local writers and photographers as possible and selling all over the world, we employ either British spelling or American spelling according to whichever predominates in the destination. This book uses American English.

Wassman

CONTENTS

Preceding pages: coat of arms and motto; tomorrow's cricketing hopefuls.

TRAVEL TIPS

WELCOME

Sir Walter Raleigh envisioned it as the gateway to the gold of El Dorado; Robinson Crusoe sustained himself on the fruits of its earth and sea; 18th-century Europeans traveled thousands of arduous miles in the hope of becoming as "rich as a Tobago planter." For hundreds of years the beauty and fecundity of these paradisiacal islands have entranced and inspired dreamers, visitors and inhabitants alike.

Southernmost of the islands in the Caribbean archipelago, the Republic of Trinidad and Tobago lies only 7 miles (11 km) from the South American mainland, just off the coastal plains of Venezuela. And unlike other Caribbean islands, Trinidad and Tobago are not the remnants of ancient volcanoes but rather the serendipitous result of a gradual and gentle breech between South America and a small, mountainous region on its northeastern coast. This geological fact creates a sea of difference between these two islands and those further north, with a geography, flora and fauna as multiform as that of the great continent.

For eons these islands lay in relative obscurity in an elysian corner of the uncharted world, but in the few hundred years they have been on the European map, the peoples and lands of Trinidad and Tobago have exerted a subtle influence on the culture and history of countries all over the world.

When Trinidad and Tobago were "discovered" by Europeans, the promise they held of riches and beauty brought four of the most powerful nations in the Western world to struggle with one another for control. Kings, Princes and Dukes staked out the islands as their own, and in their greed involved even more distant peoples in their future. The cruel commerce of slavery transplanted the people of many African nations to these islands, and when, only 150 years ago, that practice was ceased, laborers from India, China and the Middle East were compelled by both despair and hope to make new homes in Trinidad.

Indirectly, Trinidad and Tobago were involved in the United States Civil War, and since then the Trini people and their music have filtered northwards to entwine themselves in the growth of the US and its music. Calypso and steel drums have brought their rhythms to folk songs, jazz, big band music, R&B and rock 'n' roll, while hundreds of thousands of Trinidadians have made themselves an integral part of American life.

After so many years of foreign control, those immigrants who made Trinidad and Tobago their permanent home forged an independent and original nation, and since declaring itself in 1976, the Republic has made a concerted effort to consolidate its culture without the constant intrusion of Europe and America. The number of visitors to the islands is increasing but the natural beauty and indigenous culture remain unspoiled. Those who come to enjoy the scintillating beaches and lilting music also discover a land and peoples as diverse as that of countries many times the size, and a population eager to welcome the traveler and the tourist to a unique and vibrant culture.

Preceding pages: a young Carnival beauty; Trinidadian schoolchildren at River Estate in Petit Valley; a Carnival band; bathers in Nylon Pool, Tobago; Tobagonian roadblock. **Left**, Trinidad coastline.

PROVINCE OF CUMANA

BOCAS DEL TRAGO

GULF OF PARIA

LAND of TRINIDAD.

All the Interior is covered

with Impenetrable Woods

When the Meso-Indians established communities in Trinidad, they made it the first settled island in the Caribbean, hunting, fishing and gathering in the swampy coastal areas. Their tools of stone, bone and shell were left behind like fingerprints.

Around 300 BC Neo-Indians of the Saladoid people arrived again from the mainland and their skills were even greater. They could spin and weave, make nicely painted pottery, cultivate sweet potato and cassava and process the latter into a long-lasting bread. These people eventually colonized the lesser Antilles, the Virgin Islands and Puerto Rico, but around the time of Christ they were only in Tobago. The two peoples were joined around AD 250 by the Barrancoid people and Saladoid pottery was replaced by Barrancoid. (The names come from archaeological sites in Venezuela.)

A sharp break occurred around AD 1000 when central and southern Trinidad developed close cultural links with the Paria coast of Venezuela. Tobago and north Trinidad kept their ties with the Windward Islands to the north. Formerly, all of the tribes of Trinidad and Tobago had spoken Arawakan dialects, but after AD 1000, Cariban dialects were probably introduced. And for the next 500 years more immigrants arrived from the mainland to settle on what was then called "Ieri," land of the humming bird, eventually, perhaps to move on up the Caribbean archipelago.

So when Columbus arrived in 1498, who was there? Shebaio and Arawak tribes were on the south coast, Nepoio on the southeast and east coasts, and Yao on the southwest coast. In the northwest were the Carinepagoto who, like the Yao and Nepoio, spoke Cariban dialects, along with the Kalina of Tobago. All in all, they totalled about 35,000.

The Trinidad and Tobago Amerindians were described by the Spanish as well-proportioned and of fairer complexion than the Island Caribs. They went naked but for girdles and head bands, painted their bodies red and wore feathers for decoration. Chiefs wore crowns and ornaments of gold while normal folk contented themselves with beaded decorations of stone, bone and teeth.

Living in villages of no more than a few hundred inhabitants, they moved their bell-shaped thatch houses regularly. Theirs were loose societies, and chiefs, who held little secular power, were easily replaced. This arrangement allowed them to resist the Spaniards much more successfully than the hierarchic Incas and Aztecs of Central and South America, for the death of a chief did not immobilize the tribe.

The main social divisions were between men and women: men cleared the forest, hunted and fished; women planted, weeded, harvested and prepared meals. The economy was based on the shifting cultivation of cassava, maize, tobacco, beans, squash and peppers for food, cotton for clothes and hammocks, and annatto for body paint. They fished, hunted and gathered shells, crabs and turtle eggs. And they traded and made war. Villages fought with one another, formed and dissolved alliances, and captured slaves. Their weapons were darts, stones, bows and poisoned arrows. Yet most war expeditions resulted in no more than a minor skirmish which never interrupted the mutual commence between otherwise hostile villages.

Cannibal culture: What of the notorious man-eating habits of the Caribs, whose very name has given us the world cannibal? Undoubtedly most Amerindian tribes in the region practiced some form of ritual cannibalism, eating bits of the heart of a courageous enemy or a beloved chieftain. Certainly there existed nothing like the voracious flesh-eaters as portrayed in many history books. This scurrilous myth was the creation of Spanish slave traders who sought to justify their un-Christian activities.

In 1510 there were declared to be no peaceful Indians along the coast of Tierra Firme, except in Trinidad. The King of Spain forbade slave raiding from the island. In 1511, Trinidad was categorized as Carib but, following protests from Las Casas, Trinidad was eventually excluded from the list of Carib islands in 1520. In 1532 Sedeno nonetheless asked for permission to catch slaves in Trinidad, for the inhabitants were "Caribs and people who eat human flesh and have other rites and evil customs and are very warlike."

The Amerindians in Trinidad and Tobago participated in a trade network that stretched for thousands of miles to include the three Guianas, northeastern Venezuela and the Orinoco basin. Each tribe had its specialty products which it traded for those of others. Feasts were held for the

Preceding pages: an early British rendering of Trinidad. **Left**, one of the remaining Carib Indians poses for a 19th-century guidebook.

initiation of chiefs or their burials, or as part of war preparations. But feasts also integrated several villages for trade in a fair-like atmosphere where products were bartered: cassava graters for salt, pearls for axes, trumpets for hammocks. The last were produced by a tribe called Lokono, whose villages were found in Trinidad and along the Orinoco. Lokono specialized in trade, traveling hundreds of miles up the river with the wares of other tribes, for water in those days did not separate people but brought them closer.

One particular Lokono village, located on the left bank of the lower Orinoco, was larger than the others because of its admirable position for trade upriver and downstream along the coasts. This "town" was called by its inhabitants "Arucay" and

1498. This was the Admiral's third trip to the New World. Becalmed at the equator, he changed his plans out of desperation and sailed due west and north. It was on this course, just as the drinking water on his ships was about to run out, that they sighted three peaks joined at their base. Overjoyed at their deliverance he named the land "La Trinite," or, Trinidad.

Columbus cruised along the south coast for an anchorage and found one at Punta de la Playa (now Erin) where he landed. His men met only footprints in the sand. He continued along the coast, to the southwestern tip, dropping place names along the way like a god. Next day his ship was approached by a pirogue containing about 20 Amerindians. Men from the two worlds stared at

supplied many a Spanish expedition with food. This earned the Arawaks, as they were called, the title "friends of the Christians." Spanish dependence on the Lokono, and especially those from Arucay, enhanced the latter's economic strength, for they had access to the coveted iron tools. It also exempted Lokono from Spanish slave raiding, so that all Lokono, and other tribes as well, found it expedient to describe themselves as Arawak. A reverse logic worked for the Spanish slave raiders for whom it was convenient to find as few "friends of Christians" as possible, and as many cannibals as there were Amerindians.

Spanish Trinidad: It was a well populated island that Christopher Columbus sighted on July 31,

one another for some time until the Spaniards began singing and dancing on their deck. The Indians let loose a flight of arrows and the Spaniards responded in kind. The Indians approached one of the caravelles and invited the pilot to come ashore, but then lost their nerve and fled. The Admiral departed, never to land again on the island, content with leaving a few more names before heading on to Santo Domingo where he'd deposited settlers on an earlier voyage. En route he espied two islands to which he gave the names "Concepcion" and "Assumpcion." They were Grenada and Tobago.

God or man?: Further Spanish incursions into Trinidad began as a search, in the 16th century, for slaves to work the nearby pearl islands of Cubagua and Margarita. The story is told that once the Indians had grown tired of the Spaniards' burdensome presence, the decision was made to chase them off. The problem was whether these white people could be killed? A skeptical chief named Brayoan devised a plan: they found a Spaniard passing through their lands and offered to escort him. Once the group arrived at a river the Indians courteously offered to take the Spaniard across on their shoulders, but in the deepest part they threw him off and held him under the water until he was still. Then they dragged him to the bank and wept copious tears, apologizing for keeping him under so long. The chief then inspected the corpse; once it was proven to be indeed dead, they knew it was possible to wage war against the Spaniards.

Sir Walter and the Spaniards: Otherwise, Trinidad was used as a starting point for expeditions into Guyana in search of El Dorado – the mythical city of gold – and the first Spanish settlement wasn't established until 1592 by Domingo de Vera at St Joseph. He marked out the sites of the church, the Governor's residence, the Cabildo (town council) and the prison. And so was founded a colony which, for the next two centuries, would be characterized by poverty and anarchy, and which would be repeatedly attacked by foreign adventurers, including Sir Walter Raleigh heading for the mainland in search of El Dorado. Just passing through, he sacked the town and put its occupants to the sword because "to leave a garrison in my back interested in the same enterprize, who also dayly expected supplies out of Spaine, I should have savoured very much of the asse."

Raleigh then freed the Indians held prisoner by the Spaniards, and told them of his "Queene, who was the great casique of the North, and a virgine." Another, less sanguine, invasion, by the Dutch this time, merely took all of the Spaniards' belongings, including their clothes: Trinidad was turned into a nudist colony until clothing could be sent from Margarita.

Missions and malaise: Having staked their claim, the Spaniards then allotted a certain number of Amerindians to privileged colonists in four *encomiendas* (plantations). The failure of these to see to the Indians' conversion led to the setting up of Catholic missions. In 1699 the Indians at Arenales (the site is marked at San Rafael) rebelled and killed the missionaries along with the

Governor and several soldiers who came to restore order. They were pursued by a vengeful army to Toco where, rather than surrender to the Spaniards, they leapt off a cliff to their deaths. By then, however, the missions had fallen foul of the planters who wanted labor, not devotion. They were eventually abolished in 1708, although four survived the 18th century as Amerindian villages: Savana Grande (Princes Town), Guayria (Naparima), Savanetta and Montserrate.

The early Spanish settlers grew tobacco, an Amerindian drug for which Europeans had acquired a taste. It was produced for illegal trade with the Dutch and English. Spanish naval policing (in 1610 a fleet destroyed all foreign ships in the Gulf) and competition from North America

ended that industry. Cocoa became the next major industry, it was cultivated by Indian laborers on the plantations. Then in 1725 a disease wiped out the cocoa farmers, and in 1739 a smallpox epidemic ended all pretense of civilized life: the settlers abandoned the town of St Joseph, and surrendered to a subsistence life in the bush from which they emerged to intrigue against the Governor. The Cabildo even staged a coup in 1745 and imprisoned one Governor until a force was sent to the rescue from Venezuela. Eventually, in 1757, the representative of the Spanish state abandoned St Joseph to set up office at Puerto de España: a fishing village on the coast consisting of about 30 houses.

Left, Sir Walter Raleigh, on his way to El Dorado, sets free five Indian kings. **Right**, Caribbean priests breathe courage into their native subjects.

The intrigues continued but the winds of change had begun to blow, even through the moribund Spanish state, even through sleepy Port of Spain, described in 1777 as "several cannons on a battery, a church, and about 80 houses covered with straw." Trade within the empire was liberalized (though foreigners were still excluded) and under the influence of his French allies, Charles III sought to strengthen the empire's defenses by developing the more neglected provinces. In 1776 Manuel Falquez was appointed Governor with instructions to attract Trinidad Roman Catholic immigrants, especially French planters, by offering land grants and tax incentives. But it was the Africans, whose labor had enriched islands such as Barbados and Haiti, who were really in demand.

The first trickle of immigrants came from Granada, where the French suffered discrimination under a new British Government. One such man was Romme de St Laurent; this energetic planter supported the scheme by lobbying in Caracas and Madrid for its expansion. In 1783 his opinions were embodied in a Cedula of Population issued from Madrid offering very generous terms to planters willing to immigrate with their slaves to this wilderness. Every white immigrant was entitled to approximately 130 acres (53 hectares) of land for each member of his family and half as much for each slave he brought with him, and there were tax exemptions as well. Free colored and free black settlers were granted half as much. The settlers only had to be Roman Catholic and from a nation friendly to Spain.

It is a strange coincidence that Tobago, kicked around between different metropolitan countries for the previous two centuries, was at this time in the hands of the French, who pursued a similar immigration policy to that of Trinidad: a French colony was offering money bribes to attract French settlers from a Spanish colony.

In 1784 there were almost 4,500 non-native people and only 1,495 Amerindians in Trinidad. By 1797 there were 16,000 non-natives, including Europeans, slaves and people of mixed blood, and only 1,000 or so Amerindians. Trinidad was not yet a plantation society based on African slavery in the same way some of the other islands were, but it was getting there, with a slave population that nearly twice outnumbered the freemen.

The man in charge was Governor Don José Maria Chacon, an educated multilingual Spaniard with a black mistress and mulatto children. Chacon set about encouraging new colonists to the detriment of the old Spanish settlers. A decree was passed forfeiting to the Crown lands left uncultivated, for Chacon thought the old Spanish settlers lazy and crooked. His advisers were Spaniards from Spain or the mainland and French settlers, and by 1788 six out of nine members of the Cabildo were foreign. As Trinidad grew less

like the mainland colonies in social structure, Chacon's powers grew more autonomous and extensive and Trinidad's links with the captaincy-general of Venezuela, under whose jurisdiction the island lay, grew weaker. It was as if the antediluvian connection with the mainland, continued in an Amerindian cultural unity and a Spanish administrative unity, had at last been broken. And so the old Spanish and Amerindian society became superseded and its members left the historical stage for new actors to strut and fret.

Building the plantations: Very soon, Trinidad was a colony whose mind and heart were French. French planters filled the important public offices such as the Commissioner of Population, the

Left, slaves landing from the ships. **Right**, a rebel slave complete with musket.

Commandant of Quarters and the members of the Cabildo; the predominant language was French or French patois, and social customs were French as well. This was when Carnival, which lasted then from Christmas to Ash Wednesday, was introduced. And while French and patois would die out in the 20th century, Carnival would grow from an exclusively white festival to one inclusive of all races and classes, providing an idiom for the Trinidad social mind in general and a wellspring of the nation's arts.

The leaders of society were all wealthy white planters, but in the 1790s, as the fortunes of the French Revolution waxed and waned in the Caribbean, immigrants in Trinidad began to reflect the entire ideological spectrum, much to the dis-

claiming equality was seen as a wild revolutionary.

The largest group of immigrants, however, were the African slaves. Roman Catholic, patois-speaking, at first they came with their owners. Some were brought or kidnapped from neighboring colonies. But the development of the colony required more slaves and soon the slave trade was flourishing in Trinidad and declared open to all nationalities in 1790.

It is sometimes argued that Spanish slavery was less harsh than in the French and British islands. The Spanish Slave Code of 1789 was quite liberal. But Spanish laws were implemented in Trinidad by French planters, and the mortality of slaves in Trinidad was higher than the birth rate, especially in the early phase of clearing the land. Yet the

may of the island's Governor and the planters.

More numerous than the whites were the free coloreds, who fled the older French slave colonies such as Grenada, where they had suffered systematic discrimination. In Trinidad, although they were given no official public posts, coloreds faced no public apartheid as in British and French colonies. Some were wealthy slave-owning planters, some were republicans. Most were petit bourgeois smallholders and artisans with no more ideology than a desire for equality. Already they possessed the contemporary characteristics of large numbers, beautiful women and deep conservatism. But they were judged just as the free coloreds of Haiti, and every other colored man

scarcity of slaves, the accessibility of the bush, and the influence of Latin culture, made for a more intimate master-slave relationship than that found in other territories. The issue is clouded, but certainly the Roman Catholic tolerated, even encouraged, much of the Africans' culture in a way not found in Protestant colonies.

British at the controls: For Governor Chacon the 1790s were the worst of times. His nightmare was that of all slave-owners in the age of revolution. He wrote to Madrid: "the contact which our colored people and our Negro slaves have had with the French and the Republicans, has made them dream of liberty and equality." Britain and France were fighting the Napoleonic wars, which often spilled into Spanish colonial territories, especially the poorly defended island of Trinidad. French privateers and British warships battled in the Gulf of Paria, and in May 1796 open fighting broke out in Port of Spain between British sailors from the *Alarm*, which had just sunk some privateers in the Gulf of Paria, and French inhabitants.

Chacon did what he could: he organized a militia, armed a few Amerindians with bows and arrows, and pleaded with Madrid for reinforcements. But when the French Jacobin emissary Victor Hughes offered his assistance, Chacon demurred: "Should the King send me aid, I will do my duty to preserve his Crown to this colony; if not, it must fall into the hands of the English who I believe to be generous enemies, and are more to

be trusted than treacherous friends."

In September 1796 a Spanish squadron of five ships commanded by Admiral Apodaca arrived in Trinidad from Puerto Rico with 740 soldiers, many of whom immediately fell ill with yellow fever. In October Spain declared war on Britain; the *Alarm* incident was mentioned. A corvette bringing money and ammunition from Puerto Rico had been captured by the British who had long set their eyes on Trinidad. On February 16, 1797, their invasion force sailed into the Gulf: 18

Left, a cartload of sugarcane to be used as cattle fodder. **Above**, a type of sugar mill in use throughout the West Indies.

ships to Apodaca's five, 7,000 soldiers to Chacon's 2,000 (most of them deserted, if healthy enough). That night the Spaniards burnt their own ships. The next day they surrendered to the British with hardly a shot. For this Chacon would be later vilified by the Trinidad planters and humiliated by the King of Spain.

The terms of the capitulation offered by Sir Ralph Abercromby were generous: Chacon's soldiers were to surrender and would be allowed to return to Spain – but not to take up arms against Britain; officers in the judiciary and administration were allowed to remain at their posts and Spanish law was to be maintained; everyone, except the prisoners of war, was to swear allegiance to Britain and, having done so, was allowed to retain his property; men of property were allowed to keep their weapons; and those who considered themselves to be citizens of the French Republic were to be given safe conduct to some French, Dutch or Spanish colony. Abercromby next appointed one of his officers, Thomas Picton, as Governor with near absolute powers. "Do justice according to your conscience," ordered Abercromby, and then he left the island. The results were horrendous.

Thomas Picton was a harsh soldier who had been early advised to rule with an iron rod because the island was full of revolutionaries and assassins. Arbitrary imprisonment and execution, judicial torture and mutilation were the hallmarks of Picton's six-year reign, and slaves and free coloreds bore the brunt of it. The blunt soldier with the frightening laugh had overnight become an absolute dictator and a planter; his cruelty was merely the logic of his position.

Picton's transformation was a gradual departure from British policy. When they first captured the island, their aim, apart from the tactical one, was to foster an illegal trade with Venezuela by two methods. First would be to encourage the contraband trade through Port of Spain, up the Orinoco and into Venezuela. The second plan was to encourage the embryonic nationalist revolution on the mainland, knowing that a liberated Venezuela would trade openly with Britain. For a while, Picton diligently assisted the Venezuelan revolutionaries, turning Port of Spain into a den of spies and conspirators, much to the dismay of the Governor of Cumana who offered $20,000 for Picton's head. Picton offered 20 for the Governor of Cumana's.

Praised in 1801 for his "zeal," by 1802 Picton was an embarrassment to the British Government, for he had promoted a slave colony. London wanted a colony of free white settlers. There lay Picton's great mistake, and a Commission was set up to govern the colony. Picton, William Fullarton and Samuel Hood were its three members, but the first two became involved in a sordid feud over Picton's methods of government. The Commission dissolved, Fullarton secured an indictment against Picton for torturing a colored girl, and the problem of how to rule the country was, in 1803, once again painfully raised.

Meanwhile, over in Tobago: In the same year, 1803, a British force took Tobago away from the French without any opposition. Tobago, the region's most knocked-about island, had changed hands for the last time, and Britain's ownership was confirmed in 1815 at the Congress of Vienna,

the sword: as Eric Williams explains, "Trinidad and Tobago went to war." The English landed again in 1639, and again the Indians chased them off. It is believed that Charles I gave the island to his infant godson, the Duke of Courland (Latvia), as a christening present, so another settlement was attempted in 1642, this time by Courlanders. Indians chased them off, along with a party from Barbados. Courlanders returned in 1650, and again in 1654. The Dutch came again and suppressed them. Louis IV of France gave the island to the victorious Dutch, who were expelled by the British, who were in turn driven off by the French, who razed the settlement and abandoned the island.

By 1674, when Tobago was ceded to the Dutch, the island had changed flags over a dozen times,

never to be challenged until Independence. But let us start at the beginning.

At the time of Columbus the island was probably occupied by Kalina Indians, and in the 17th century there was immigration of Kalinas from St Vincent. Although the Admiral had named the island "Assumpcion" in passing, as it were, it later came to be called Tavaco after an Indian smoking instrument, so it is sometimes told.

Whatever the name, it was a nominally Spanish island on which the first British settlers arrived in 1625. The Indians wiped them out, but the British claimed the island anyway. The Dutch landed settlers in 1628, but a Spanish and Indian force from Trinidad invaded in canoes and put them to

and so it continued – Dutch, French, Latvian, English, Dutch, French, English – even the Americans took a chance in 1778 at capturing the half-deserted, undeveloped island which was, for most of the time, just a nest of pirates.

Rum and rebellion: European policy for Tobago was that the island should be "so laid waste as will hinder all settlement," partly to appease other colonies fearing competition. The British began to encourage settlers once again in 1764, and by 1769, 23,000 acres (9,300 hectares) were under cultivation. The colony developed rapidly and seven years after the first shipment of sugar was exported, Tobago was producing 1,200 tons of sugar, 1.6 million gallons (6 million liters) of rum,

1.5 million lbs (680,000 kg) of cotton, and 5,000 lbs (2,300 kg) of indigo. The corollary of this expansion was that by the early 1770s slaves outnumbered whites by 20:1. It was a ratio higher than anywhere else in the British West Indies, and, as a result, Tobago, up until 1774, experienced almost annual slave revolts on a small scale. One rebellion in 1774 brought savage punishments on the rebels, and after that Tobago simmered down for the rest of the 18th century.

The French captured Tobago again in 1781 and proceeded to sponsor immigration from the other islands by offering incentives similar to those offered by the Spanish in Trinidad around the same time. And sugar production began in earnest: Tobago's population rose from 5,084 in 1771 to 15,020 in 1791; 14,170 of these were black slaves. Only five Amerindians could be found. But the black-white ratio had fallen to a less dangerous level, or so the planters thought.

The British and the French made Tobago productive and populous, an exporter of sugar and cotton, at the cost of creating a typical West Indian slave society. Nevertheless, Tobago planters also displayed a remarkable if futile perspicacity. By 1780 they had reduced the ratio of free to unfree by half, and reduced the number of African slaves in favor of Creoles. Then in 1798 a Legislative Committee in Tobago produced a report on the state of the slaves unique for its liberality.

In summary, land was to be distributed to slaves and time to cultivate it allowed, more food was to be given to them, slave imports were discouraged and the Creole population to be increased naturally. Matrimony was encouraged, children and pregnant mothers protected, and midwives paid by planters. And Guardians of the Rights of Negroes were to be appointed in every parish.

The planters were pleased with themselves and confident of their slaves. Early in 1801 Sir William Young, stated that, "here the planters talk of their Negroes as their resort to be depended on against either a licentious garrison, an arbitrary Governor, or the mad democracy of French hucksters." Imagine their surprise when a Christian slave exposed a massive plan for insurrection, scheduled for Christian Day 1801.

Martial law was declared, 200 suspects rounded up, and the whole conspiracy exposed. Slaves from 16 estates were involved. Roger, a driver at Belvedere estate, was the "governor," and Thomas,

Left, a map of Tobago showing British divisions. **Right**, freed slaves celebrate Emancipation August 1, 1834.

a cooper, the "colonel." There were five "captains" on various estates and five "chiefs" in Scarborough. These men had formed companies of slaves and the plan was to set alight five estates, killing any whites who came to control the fire. In the town, the Governor and the Commander in Chief of the garrison were to be assassinated. It was expected that the whole slave population would then arise in revolt. By January 4, 1802, sentences had been handed down and the whole affair finished. For this reason only six rebel leaders were executed. Four other rebels were banished, and the rest sent back to work after a severe flogging. Tobago was quiet for the next 60 years.

The experimental colony: In 1812 it was written, "Trinidad is a subject for an anatomy school or

rather a poor patient in a country hospital on which all sorts of surgical experiments are tried, to be given up if they fail and to be practised on others if they succeed."

The first experiment sought to discover what kind of government the colony should have. The issue had been forced by the Governor who'd replaced Picton, Thomas Hislop. He became embroiled in a struggle with Chief Justice George Smith, an irascible man whose rigorous application of Spanish laws angered the planters. Chief Justice Smith despised them in return. "Generally colonies are peopled by the refuse of the Mother Country," he said, "but Trinidad is peopled by the refuse of the other colonies." Hislop, his Council of Advice and the Cabildo petitioned the King in 1810 for a British Constitution and British laws.

Britain, however, was less willing to grant British laws to new colonies than in the 18th century. London had grown too familiar with the difficulties and obstructions of which West Indian colonial assemblies were capable, but they could not ignore as unanimous a demand as came from Trinidad. The free coloreds also petitioned for consideration on the matter. They were uneasy that a local assembly would merely entrench the power of a small and bigoted elite. Hislop was furious, the secretary of state elated. Smith reasoned that if the free coloreds were excluded from an assembly there would be difficulties, so there could be no assembly. Including the free coloreds, even the wealthiest, was never considered and the matter was closed: Trinidad would be a Crown Colony under direct supervision of Britain. This signaled the beginning of the end of colonial self-government in the British West Indies.

The second experiment faced the problem of development. Trinidad was mostly forest and large slave-owning plantations were rare. The planters wanted more slaves although their number had doubled in Picton's time, but the British Parliament was under pressure from abolitionists to make no extensions of the slave trade. Other sugar colonies agreed with the abolitionists because they feared competition. So Britain suggested a scheme of free laborers, but implemented it halfheartedly. In 1806 the slave trade was prohibited to new colonies and in the following year it was completely abolished. Trinidad never became a mature slave society like the other West Indian territories, although sugar came to dominate land use and exports.

The third experiment sought to solve the problem of illegal importation of slaves. "The poor patient has to go through some very severe operations. She is now actually bound down for a most painful one – a registry of slaves, prescribed by (abolitionist) Dr Stephen." Every slave was to be registered within a month of March 1812 and no unregistered person could be held as a slave. The Registrar was a slave-owner and both he and the Governor, Sir Ralph Woodford, hardly implemented the Order at all. The deadline was ignored or extended and the whole exercise rendered useless. Slave smuggling continued, many brought in as "domestics" from other territories and sold in Trinidad where the prices were high. A new Governor, Sir Lewis Grant, prosecuted many who had illegally imported slaves but too late – only a year before Emancipation in 1833.

A fourth experiment tested whether the harshness of slavery could be ameliorated by legislative measures. In 1824 an Order in Council was passed restricting an owner's right to punish his slaves and giving slaves limited legal, religious and social rights: no more whipping of women; for men no more than 25 strokes; no more Sunday labor; manumission must be facilitated, even without the owner's consent; slave evidence was admissible in court; and a Protector of Slaves was to act on their behalf.

Howls of protest went up from the planters and, as with the Registration Act, the planters subverted the Amelioration Act and made it nugatory. By 1830 this was apparent to the British government and a tougher Order was drawn up. Planter reaction grew hysterical as they resisted with the assistance of officials, especially those in the Cabildo. In so doing they paved the way for the abolition of Spanish laws and the Cabildo in the 1840s. But more importantly, the planters themselves convinced the Imperial Parliament that it was time to end slavery completely.

The Great Emancipation: And so the Act of Emancipation – the "Great Experiment" – was passed in August 1833 to take effect on August 1, 1834. Slave-owners were compensated for their loss of property; field slaves were apprenticed to their former owners for six years, other slaves for four; special magistrates were appointed to administer the system. On the big day, hundreds of slaves assembled in Port of Spain to protest the apprenticeship period. The militia was called out, arrests made, and the most dismal era of Caribbean history came to a close.

Or did it? On June 17, 1837, a Yoruba African called Daaga led a mutiny of liberated Africans from the First West Indian Regiment. The mutineers, under Daaga's inspiration, attacked and fired on the barracks at St Joseph. They then set off to walk back to Africa. After days of skirmishing with the regular forces the rebels were put down, and within a week the whole affair was over, having cost 40 lives, most of them rebels. On the morning of August 16, 1837, Daaga and two others were executed in the mists of St Joseph by firing squad.

But in 1971 another man with flashing eyes and a deep voice, the leader of a "Black Power" movement which had also inspired an unsuccessful mutiny in the army, changed his name from Geddes Granger to Makandal Daaga.

Right, a letter from the Governor of Trinidad is a mixture of fear and paternal reassurance.

THE HISTORICAL SOCIETY OF TRINIDAD AND TOBAGO.

Publication No. 882.

General Hislop to the Under Secretary of State.

Source:- Public Record Office. State Papers Colonial.
C. O. 295/14.

Published by the courtesy of the Master of the Rolls
and the Deputy Keeper of the Public Records.

Private.   Trinidad.
                                      8th January 1806.

Dear Sir

                X   X   X

You will learn from my public dispatches which are forwarded by this packet, of the alarming situation into which the Colony has recently been thrown, and in which it still exists to a certain degree.

Our neighbouring Island of Tobago, is also under Martial Law in consequence of a discovery of an intention to poison the cistern of the garrison. It is also reported that a plan of an insurrection among the negroes in Guadeloupe has fortunately been discovered; and that General Evreux caused six of the Chiefs to be burnt alive. They were said to belong to San Domingo.

I can assure you that our situation is far from being pleasant but I trust that with proper examples in the first instance and a strict observance of discipline in the next, we shall succeed in preserving the Colony from a recurrence of so shocking a state as that from which it has so miraculously escaped.

THE PROBLEMS OF FREEDOM

Apprenticeship of the ex-slaves ended two years before schedule, in 1838, because of the insistence of abolitionists in Britain and the intransigence of the ex-slaves who decided to not work after August 1, 1838. On that day the old society died, and the future offered only the challenge of building freedom.

For the ex-slaves, freedom meant choosing how they wished to live: culturally, socially and, most important, economically. It involved no retreat to the bush – largely the preserve of Spanish-Amerindian peons – and any movements were to the urban areas. Most of all, in an island where labor was scarce, freedom for the ex-slaves meant using their bargaining power to improve their economic conditions, and that they did successfully. The average wage per task throughout the Caribbean was 30 cents; in Trinidad it was 50. In 1841 the planters collectively tried to reduce wages to 30 cents, but the workers withdrew their labor and the planters backed down, scoring a success for Trinidad's first strike.

Planters sought to retain a dependable labor force by allowing ex-slaves to occupy estate huts and provision grounds, but most left the estate anyway. Many settled in or around the towns and a large internal trade network grew up. For others, land was abundant and if they were unable to meet the price they squatted illegally. The Crown showed no inclination to distribute land to the landless, but couldn't stop the squatting.

This pull and tug was interrupted in 1846 when the Sugar Duties Act was passed in Britain, allowing cheaper foreign sugar into the mother country. West Indians howled; many estates were abandoned and wages fell. The industry recovered in a few years but two important changes had been precipitated: first, in 1848 the British Government agreed to sponsor the immigration of indentured laborers from India; and second, the sugar industry would be modernized but in the hands of large British companies.

The 1860s and 1870s saw two important and closely related developments. Under Governor A.H. Gordon, Crown lands were opened up to smallholders. His predecessor, Lord Harris, had sought to prevent ex-slaves from becoming landowners by authorizing the sale of large lots of land

Left, a young indentured laborer from India on her arrival in Trinidad.

only and at high prices. In 1869 Gordon reduced the smallest lot to five acres, the price to £1, and conveyance costs to a minimum. Many of the most intransigent squatters, it was discovered, were willing purchasers, and Gordon also offered land to the Indians who had served their indenture in lieu of a return passage to India.

The second change was the expansion of cocoa cultivation. Completely owned by locals and often in peasant hands, cocoa had always been cultivated in Trinidad in small quantities. When chocolate touched the English sweet tooth in the 1860s, the market opened up, and cocoa blossomed in Trinidad to become the largest export. It was an achievement mainly of the peons, although blacks and Indians later contributed. These peasants bought small plots of Crown land, then cleared and planted them with cocoa. When the trees began to bear they sold the plots to a plantation and were paid for both land and trees. They then repeated the process. Or, the plantation, already owning the land, contracted with peons for its clearance and cultivation. They did so but simultaneously used it for cash crops. At the end the peons were paid for each tree and moved on. Thus the French Creole elite shifted their wealth from depressed sugar to buoyant cocoa, increasing their wealth until the 1920s, when the cocoa market crashed.

Tobago's travail: Tobago, a more classic plantation society than Trinidad, found itself bankrupt on Emancipation Day. "This Colony," stated an 1823 petition, "has now arrived at a pitch of distress of a deeper nature than we can possibly detail." As everywhere else in the British West Indies, in Tobago the labor force lost its tractability once freed, so again the common solution: planters sought to encourage immigration of English convicts, Barbadians, Africans from Sierra Leone, free blacks from America. But wages were too low to be an incentive, half the level of Trinidad, and the treasury could not afford to pay for immigration. A hurricane in 1847 devastated the island and made prospects more grim. Even the British capitalists, usually willing to buy out bankrupt estates at knockdown prices, considered Tobago a bad deal. A different approach was required, and the planters looked to St Lucia and Antigua for inspiration. What they came up with was known as the Metairie System.

It was an arrangement whereby the workers took no pay for their labor but instead shared the

History: 1840–1900 35

crop with the owner. An oral agreement, it worked well enough until, in the late 1870s, the sugar industry declined further. Then planters began to renege on their agreements and the almost feudal relationship showed its cracks.

Riots broke out in May 1876 at Roxborough Estate: there had been fires on the estate – arson by Barbadian workers, it was said. Corporal Belmanna and five privates were sent to arrest the alleged incendiaries but, as the warrants were being executed, the people grew restive. The corporal was knocked down and he shot a woman. She died, and the flame of justice was set alight. The Manager's House was gutted, and the people besieged the Court House. The police released their prisoners, but Belmanna, especially hated by the people, was beaten to death. A warship was sent from Grenada and many constables sworn in.

As the Morant Bay Rebellion did for the Jamaican planters in 1865, the Belmanna Riots scared the Tobago planters into surrendering their self-government in favor of Crown Colony government. So at the beginning of 1877 the 215 eligible voters in Tobago lost their democratic right to elect representatives, and Tobago became a Crown Colony. A Royal Commission was appointed in 1882 to look into the impoverishment of Tobago (and other colonies). The Commission found an empty Treasury, but it was the laborers who felt the pinch hardest.

In 1886 a *métayer*, Joseph Franks, was evicted by a planter from his plantation. The 73-year-old Franks, an ex-slave, took the planter to court, and lost the case. He appealed and, in February 1890, received the judgement of Sir John Gorrie, the Chief Justice of Trinidad. Sir John castigated the planter for his shamelessness and upheld the old man's claim for damages. And the planters raised their tiresome voices in the same centuries-old protests: "…the laboring classes of the Island are in an unsettled state and… this condition of affairs is attributable to an impression which has been created amongst them, with which your Honour's name is unfortunately associated." A Commission of Enquiry was set up to look into the question, and the Chief Justice was reprimanded. What was suggested instead of the Metairie System? More immigration, and if Tobago couldn't afford it, then try to inveigle some Indians over from Trinidad which had by then been wedded to Tobago.

The Commission of 1882 had recommended a federation of St Vincent, St Lucia, Grenada and Tobago to reduce administrative costs and to combat the (fiscal) "evils of isolation," and in 1885 this was effected, although Tobago retained its own bureaucracy. Then in 1886 Britain decided to tack the island on to Trinidad, either as a dependency or as a wholly incorporated ward. Tobago planters opted for the former, demanding fiscal autonomy. As Tobago resisted, so Britain insisted, and in 1889 a union of sorts was forced upon the two grumbling partners, although, again, Tobago retained some autonomous institutions. Eventually, tired of the whole matter, Britain decided to solve the issue by fiat, and in 1897 Tobago was made a ward of Trinidad. A shotgun marriage, yes, but only for the wealthy; for the ordinary people it was a union long before consummated by their migrations and the communities of Tobagonians on Trinidad's north coast.

The arrivants: Labor in Trinidad had always been scarce, but after Emancipation things grew worse, for ex-slaves could no longer be compelled to work 18-hour days. Recruitment agents were sent to the other islands to tell of job opportunities, high wages and cheap land. Many came but few remained on the plantations. And if they brought their crafts and skills, they were still inadequate because planters wanted sugarcane fodder and nothing more. Next the United States was looked at as a source, but the few free blacks who came were even more urbanized. A colony of liberated slaves – Sierra Leone – was turned to and yielded over 3,000 Africans. But although they remained discrete tribal groups – Radas in Belmont, Yoruba and Congo in Laventille – they, too, abandoned sugar. Some Europeans came but they either took overseas jobs or left for America. Portuguese came from Madeira and quickly set up as shopkeepers, as did the Chinese. But eventually the planters found what they were searching for, when in May 1845 a windjammer, the *Fatel Rozack*, docked at Port of Spain, bringing 225 immigrants from Calcutta.

India had a large destitute population willing to immigrate. Largely a British colony, it had a tropical climate, and its people were mainly agriculturalists. Transportation costs, though high, were not prohibitive. Only one problem remained: the first immigrants from India had deserted the estates, in Trinidad. The solution was an indentureship contract which would later be described as "a new system of slavery."

A financial crisis temporarily halted the scheme between 1848 and 1851, after which a steady flow of Indians arrived in Trinidad until the Indian government stopped it in 1917. By then a total of about 144,000 Indians had come to Trinidad. Most of them were from the Gangetic plain, especially the provinces of Uttar Pradesh, Bihar and Oudh. Smaller numbers came from Bengal and the Punjab, and a tiny minority from Madras in the south.

Conditions in India were the main incentives to immigration: there were famines due to a decaying economy and exploitative ruling classes, and dislocation caused by British imperialism. In addition to extreme poverty, there was the savage repression which took place after the Indian Mutiny (1857).

On arrival, immigrants were assigned to a plantation and bound to work for three years. After that, they had to complete a two-year "industrial residence" during which they could re-indenture to any plantation, or pursue another occupation – provided they paid a special tax. Only after five

tured laborers were treated as criminal offenses punishable by imprisonment.

Conditions were wretched. Indentured laborers lived in single-room barrack ranges reminiscent of early slave quarters, cramped and insanitary, and suffered from malaria, hookworm, anaemia and ground itch. Some plantation hospitals were so deplorable that the cure was often worse than the illness.

Perhaps the cruelest cut was the imbalanced sex ratio which made women scarce and generated the notorious 19th-century Indian crimes of passion, when Indian men murdered wives who had succumbed to the enticements or coercion of another man. Between 1872 and 1900, 87 Indian women were murdered, 65 by their husbands.

years was completed did immigrants receive their "free paper." However, they were not yet entitled to free return passage, and first had to remain in the colony for an additional five years. And after 1895 indentureds were forced to pay a proportion of the cost of returning to India.

Cruel conditions: The indentureship "contract" signed in India laid down minimum wages, working hours and working conditions. These were often ignored by planters, especially in the 1880s when the sugar industry almost collapsed. On the other hand, breaches of the contract by the inden-

On the plantations they were an isolated community, desperately poor yet despised by the wider society who thought them amoral, deceitful, revengeful, barbarous and dirty. Their customs were considered "degrading practices," "vile" and "painted devilry." Even the black ex-slaves held the Indians in contempt for their languages, customs, appearance, poverty and their bondage. And yet most remained once their indentureship contracts had expired, perhaps for reasons of both optimism and inertia.

Once released, many Indians remained as laborers on the plantations. Some picked up the crafts they'd practiced in India, while others became petty traders. Moneylending made a few

Above, farm workers breaking cocoa around the turn of this century.

rich but many more subsisted as laborers, gardeners, porters, scavengers, domestics and a host of other menial "coolie" jobs. Most importantly, they became peasant proprietors, growing "wet" rice, sugarcane and vegetables on land received in lieu of a return trip or purchased from the Crown. By 1905 a Labor Committee could find that they "are industrious and useful citizens."

The creation of a peasantry allowed Indians to recreate their customs as best they could, by the last quarter of the century the countryside was dotted with Hindu temples. By then an Indian sense of community with middle-class leadership had been formed. In 1897 the East Indian National Association was created to protest the discrimination suffered by Indians, and in 1898, the Indian

The English on the islands were Protestant, often born abroad and employed by the state. Conflict between the two groups took the form of local versus foreign whites, or merchants and planters versus government officials, but most consistently it was French lined up against British, the latter wanting to Anglicize the colony in language and manners, the former wanting some say in government policies. Otherwise the two groups were very similar in their outlook, and by the end of the century their antagonism appeared to have been a storm in a teacup.

Yet this sparring had important consequences. First was the creation in the 1850s, under the Anglicizing Governor Lord Harris, of a series of free (primary) Ward Schools and (teacher train-

AVENUE OF PALMS, QUEEN'S PARK, SAVANNA.

Kohinoor Gazette was published – the first Indian newspaper.

Creole contradictions: At the top of Trinidadian society there were the whites, the ruling class who controlled the wealth and power. Yet whites did not form a single homogeneous group, but were divided between English and "French Creoles." Today "French Creole" refers to any white person whose family has been resident in Trinidad for some generations.

In the 19th century it was a different matter. The French Creoles then were Roman Catholic, French speaking and descended mainly from Royalist French settlers. They were racially exclusive and saw themselves as an aristocracy.

ing) Normal Schools. Second was the fact that when, in the 1880s, the Government sought to abolish the black Carnival because of its rowdiness, the French Creoles protested. Finally, there was established a tradition of French Creole opposition to government, a tradition which produced men like Philip Rostant and Captain Cipriani.

When Lord Harris's Normal Schools began taking in graduates from the Ward Schools, most black children remained outside of those doors, but for a few of the brightest the state-funded Ward Schools provided the means of social mobility. They could, on graduation, study to become teachers in the Normal Schools and make the first faltering steps out of manual labor. Thus

38

was begun the formation of an educated black and colored middle class. A smaller group of fortunates won free places in the secondary schools, which qualified them to become junior clerks, journalists and store assistants. And every few years one of these sons of the respectable working class won the College Exhibition Scholarship to study abroad, whence they returned doctors and lawyers to the man. Two notable 20th-century exceptions read literature and history: they were V.S. Naipaul and Eric Williams.

But it was the teachers who formed the backbone of this class, producing even at an early stage men such as John Jacob Thomas, a philologist of international repute.

Among the Indian community, largely ignored or smallholders alongside the Mestiso-black peons known today as "cocoa payols." Even within the black community there were discrete groups: those who spoke French patois and the immigrants who spoke English, the "Americans" (demobilized US soldiers in the Company Villages), the demobilized soldiers of the West Indian regiment, and the freed Africans who numbered about 8,000. In common they held their poverty, lack of education and exclusion from political power.

Yet Trinidad was a rapidly urbanizing colony, and Port of Spain at the turn of the century contained a quarter of the population. The urban black plebeians were found in various menial jobs, as domestics, messengers, washerwomen, longshoremen, and petty traders. Many practiced

by the state, the Canadian Mission began to set up schools in 1868, creating a parallel Indian middle class in embryo.

The largest sector of the population was the black laboring classes, however. Predominantly rural, they worked as agricultural laborers, small farmers and tradesmen. In the sugar industry they were replaced by Indians in the fields but kept many of the skilled jobs in the factories. In the Northern Range, shaded by immortelle trees, they worked on cocoa estates as laborers, contractors,

trades as artisans, carpenters, masons, tailors, printers and merchants. Many were periodically or permanently unemployed and they all lived in overcrowded, squalid barrack houses in the city or the labyrinthine hills of Laventille and Belmont, racked with dysentry, malaria, sometimes cholera and smallpox, camping, as Earl Lovelace puts it, "on the eyebrow of the enemy." This group exhibited the symptoms of urban unemployment: juvenile delinquency, vagrancy, prostitution, and petty crime. They also practiced African and syncretic religions, indistinguishable in respectable eyes from the illegal obeah (witchcraft) of slavery times. It was a tightly packed community with an exuberant demi-monde and intense loyalties.

Left, urban blacks enjoy Port of Spain's largest park around 1903. **Above**, young farm hands pause in a cornfield.

The years of revolt: The closing years of the 19th century saw the various classes and the factions within them stretching to adjust to the new places they now occupied in the society. In some cases the exercise was painless. The French Creole elite and the British governing class grew closer, with only two slight obstacles to the process. The first was a land distribution policy of Governor Gordon (1866–70) who allowed the peasants to buy plots of Crown land – the planters were displeased. Second was the impartiality of Chief Justice Gorrie who reformed judicial procedure to make the courts more accessible to the lower classes – even the Governor didn't like that.

Things went differently for the lower-class blacks, the Indians and the rising middle class. The blacks, and in particular the urban working class, felt the brunt of upper-class fear and loathing from the long end of a police baton, wielded more often than not by "Barbadian rowdies," according to J.J. Thomas, "whose bitter hatred of the older residents had been often brutally exemplified." The law interdicted lower-class music and religion, frowned upon their sexual mores and language, and punished even trivial offenses with stripes.

The most outrageous were the *jamets*, described in the *San Fernando Gazette* as "hordes of men and women, youthful in years but matured in every vice that perverts and degrades humanity, (who) dwell together in all the rude licentiousness of barbarian life." The *jamets* had taken over the Carnival celebrations in recent years with sexual horseplay, gang warfare, ribald songs and drumming. At the Canboulay procession on the Sunday before Carnival Monday, gangs tramped around with lit torches (Canboulay from the French *cannes brulées*, meaning burning canes), singing and dancing and challenging rivals to duels in *kalenda*, a traditional martial art performed with sticks.

In 1877 the Inspector-Commandant of Police, Captain Baker, decided to destroy the *kalenda* gangs and reform Carnival. The next two years he clamped down and in 1880 called on all marchers to surrender their torches, sticks and drums. Taken by surprise, they complied. The following year, in 1881 he armed the force with clubs and tried the same tactic, but the *jamets* were ready with bottles and stones and sticks, and a riot started. The Governor conciliated the revelers and confined the police to barracks until things cooled down. Three years later the Canboulay was made illegal and warfare erupted in San Fernando. Two gangs laid siege to the police station; police shot into the crowd leaving two dead and five wounded. Thus

ended the *jamet* Carnival, and the respectable classes joined the fête once more. Noticeably, throughout it all, the French Creoles, despite their high moral tone, criticized Baker's high-handedness and condemned any intention on the part of the Government to ban Carnival.

A similar fate befell Hosay, a Shiite Muslim festival in which bands of masqueraders, carrying a large ornate tomb, reenact a famous battle of Islamic history. Despite its origins, this celebration was mainly supported by Hindus, and by the 1870s it had become "a sort of national Indian demonstration." Gatka – an Indian martial art with staves – was performed and Hosay bands from different estates competed with one another. In the 1880s the festival grew more riotous, more a demonstration of class and ethnic solidarity, because of worsening conditions in the sugar industry. In 1884 regulations were passed to exclude Hosay bands from San Fernando and Port of Spain and to stop the *jamets* from joining the festival as they were accustomed to doing. The bands ignored the order and the police opened fire, killing 12 and injuring 104. After that the festival became a more domesticated affair.

The emergent middle class also sought changes, but politely, in the reform movement begun in the 1880s by Philip Rostant, a white French Creole journalist. Rostant organized meetings and a petition in favor of elected members for the Legislative Council, but the Colonial Office in 1889 rejected the idea. Thereafter the banner was carried by black and colored professionals such as C.P. David, Henry Alcazar, J.S. de Bourg and Emmanuel Lazare. The reform movement appeared a useless passion, the suffrage sought was exclusive and the tactics used were courteous, but the Secretary of State for the Colonies, Joseph Chamberlain, put an end to the matter in 1895 by refusing point blank. In 1898 he also abolished both the Borough Council and the unofficial majority in the Legislative Council.

Nevertheless, the reform movement was not simply sound and fury, and in years to come some of its members would engage in black nationalist and working class politics, foreshadowing key developments of the 20th century. In 1897 Walter Mills, a druggist, formed the Trinidad Workingmen's Association, and in London a Trinidadian lawyer, Henry Sylvester Williams, formed the Pan-African Association which opened enthusiastic branches at home in 1901.

Right, the French aristocracy watches while slaves enjoy their own festival.

Amazing scenes were witnessed in Port of Spain on Monday, March 23, 1903, when the Red House, seat of government in the colony, was burnt to the ground in the course of a riot over water.

In the previous months, the government had announced its intention to control the wastage of water by installing a metering system in houses (for the wealthy were known to bathe indulgently), and by visiting homes to cut off the water supply to leaking taps. The culprits were unrepentant: "We know that rheumatics is the only evil resulting from the use of these baths," com-

threw a rock, and a rain of stones fell on the building; Governor Maloney hid with one official and the rest fled. The Red House was set alight, and the RPA leaders of the crowd decamped; the hidden official escaped, disguised as a policeman but the Governor had to be escorted by the police, under a shower of stones, away from the conflagration. Firemen came to the rescue, but were repelled by the crowd. The Riot Act was read and the police fired into the crowd and charged with bayonets, leaving 18 dead and 42 wounded. And the Red House was burnt to the ground.

Fig 10.2 *Crowds gathering in Port of Spain during the protest against new water charges. Later the same day the Red House, the large building on the right, was burned down.*

plained one writer. Besides, government inefficiency was thought to be the cause of much wastage anyway. But the underlying issue was really the middle-class demand for a more representative and less high-handed government.

The objectors forced the government to postpone its water legislation in 1902, then again in February 1903, and yet again on March 16. Leading the struggle was the Rate Payers Association (RPA), a middle and upper-class group led by reform agitators of the 1890s. This time, however, they were supported by the lower class.

Tension mounted. The RPA leaders were denied entry to the Council Chamber in the Red House, and the crowd outside roared. A woman

An investigative Commission absolved the police, and found the riots unrelated to the issue of representative government. Joseph Chamberlain, the Secretary of State for the Colonies, was more perceptive. He told the Governor to begin talks for the restoration of the abolished Borough Council, and in 1913 it was agreed that an elected Council would be created.

Ten years on – the franchise that eventually arrived was limited, but on the Borough Council local politicians now had a platform. Significantly, in the waiting the RPA disappeared but the older Trinidad Workingmen's Association (TWA) grew in the struggle only to lapse once the 1914 franchise excluded its members.

War and oil: It was in the same year Europe entered World War I that the first oil refinery in Trinidad was opened at Pointe-à-Pierre.

The history of the oil industry in Trinidad dates from 1857 when the first oil well in the world was drilled by the Merrimac Oil Company at La Brea in Southern Trinidad. The company folded soon after that pioneering effort and two other 19th-century outfits were no more successful. Then in the 1890s the internal combustion engine became a commercial proposition. Things were never the same again.

The oil industry was pioneered by an Englishman called Randolph Rust who had migrated to Trinidad in 1881. Rust sought to explore for oil in the Guayaguayare forests with local backing.

become interested. In 1910 Trinidad Oilfields Ltd was formed, to be joined in 1913 by United British Oilfields of Trinidad and Trinidad Leaseholds Ltd.

Drilling for oil in those days was hard work. The fields which were found in Guayaguayare, Palo Seco, Rousillac, Siparia, Erin and Tabaquite had to be wrested from dense jungle through which heavy equipment was dragged. It was, in Rust's words, "one terrible fight against nature." Blowouts, gushers, fires, explosions, all of these were common occurrences and as late as 1929 a fire killed several people near Fyzabad. It was one of the last, however, and technology and safety standards improved rapidly thereafter.

The dockworkers' strike: World War I revolution-

None was forthcoming, so he obtained Canadian capital and the first well was drilled in 1902, followed by eight others in the next five years. He lobbied tirelessly, in Port of Spain and London, for government support, and in 1905 an engineer was sent from England to prospect for a British company. His successful drilling prompted a conference at 10 Downing Street with the Governor of Trinidad and representatives of the Colonial Office and the Admiralty in 1909. The Navy, which was converting to oil-powered ships, had

Above, the original Red House; and **left**, the beginning of the water riot that left the Red House in ashes and 17 people dead.

ized Russia; in Trinidad and Tobago changes were less spectacular but important nevertheless. The war years and after were hard, inflation was high, especially for basic foods, and wages remained low. The diet of the laboring classes became, in the words of the Surgeon General, "somewhat deficient in protein." A strike in oil and asphalt in 1917 resulted in imprisonment for the leaders and for a Seventh-Day Adventist who had displayed a placard saying "Awake ye Stevedores and be men." The East Indian Destitute League was formed only to have its founder deported in 1918; Indian immigration was curtailed because of agitation against it in India.

Government drafted the infamous Habitual

Idlers Ordinance (although widespread opposition delayed its passage until 1920) in an attempt to keep the Indians tied to the estates. The Colonial Secretary thought that the law went "considerably beyond anything in the UK, in that it makes the mere fact of refusing to work and being without visible means of subsistence a punishable offence." It was eventually passed anyway. It tells much of the society that in 1911, the year of Eric Williams' birth, £62,000 were spent on education, and £66,000 on the police, £18,000 on prisons, and £4,000 on the local military.

The British West Indian soldiers had fared no better in Europe. As good British subjects, they'd volunteered to fight for the Empire, but the British Government refused to let blacks serve, and only

Taranto, Italy, for demobilization under a South African camp commander. There they were made to wash linen and clean latrines, and work for labor units, because "the men were only niggers." When they refused to do it, several were court-martialed and sentenced to from 15 months to three years. In postscript some West Indian soldiers created the clandestine Caribbean League, which advocated economic, social and political reforms for the West Indies. The League was reported to the authorities and disbanded, and its members closely observed on returning to their islands. But ideas leavened with experience cannot so easily be set aside, and the soldiers, especially Captain Arthur Andrew Cipriani, returned home to make their mark on the times.

when King George V interceded did the War Office agree to a West Indian contingent. They formed a separate regiment, not part of the British Army, with lower pay and lower allowances; and only those of "unmixed European blood" were eligible for commissions. Furthermore, perhaps to preserve them from acquiring a taste for white blood, they were excluded from actual combat with Europeans.

Some were sent to Egypt where a few, briefly, saw action against Turkish troops; most performed labor services, like the others who'd gone to Europe, digging trenches and carrying ammunition. November 11, 1918, and the war ended. The British West Indian Regiment was sent to

In July 1919 there were anti-black demonstrations in Britain, and news of this inflamed the returned soldiers. British Honduras saw rioting. In Trinidad, soldiers boycotted the victory celebrations held on July 19, and a few British marines from the *HMS Dartmouth* were attacked. White businessmen requested arms from the Governor. They also sought the suppression of the paper which informed the public of conditions in Britain. The *Argos* was a paper for the colored middle class which, along with Marcus Garvey's paper, *Negro World*, advocated race pride.

In 1918 the TWA had come under new and more radical leadership: James Braithwaite and David Headley, two dockers influenced by international socialism; J.S. de Bourg from the reform movement; and Howard Bishop, a journalist. From early 1919 the revamped TWA had participated in agitation for high wages, supporting a wave of strikes throughout the island. Workers on the railways, city council employees, electricity and telephone workers, and laborers at the Pitch Lake, all called strikes in 1919. But it was the laborers at the Port of Spain docks who changed the tempo.

Called the "scum of the wharves" by the *Trinidad Guardian*, the dockers were the most well-informed and cosmopolitan workers in the colony. Many had traveled abroad as sailors, and all had access to smuggled literature and new ideas. In November 1919 they went on strike. Led by the TWA, the dockers demanded wage increases. When

The same day, around noon, the *HMS Calcutta* steamed into the harbor, and the tide of conciliation turned to one of repression. The government, backed up by the British troops and a white volunteer force of colonial vigilantes, cracked down on the strikers. Ninety-nine people were arrested, 82 imprisoned and four leading TWA members deported.

On December 6, a crowd attacked the government wireless station in Tobago with bottles and stones. But it was already too late for that kind of behavior – the troops had imposed order next door the day before. Emboldened, the police fired on the crowd, killing one and wounding six. The marines came soon after to mop up.

Rise of the Captain: The immediate outcome of

the shippers refused to negotiate, they walked off the job. The shippers brought in scab labor, and on December 1 the dockers retaliated: they smashed warehouses, driving off the scabs. Then they marched through the city, closing businesses and encouraging other workers to join them, and the workers throughout the colony downed their tools in support. Even the black police, thought the Governor, "could not be relied upon." He formed a conciliation board which, on December 3, offered the dockers a 25 percent wage increase.

Left, sailboats at anchor in Port of Spain harbor and, **above**, a passenger ship steaming into port while dockhands and greeters watch.

the 1919 dockworkers' strike, which had almost become a general strike, was repression. The government passed the Strikes and Lockouts Ordinance, and the Industrial Court Ordinance, which made strikes illegal. The *Trinidad Guardian* expressed "profound gratitude." The government also wrote to the TWA threatening deportation for anyone who started strikes. Next the Sedition Ordinance was passed which banned Garveyite and socialist literature, and saw to the closure of the *Argos*. A Wages Committee, set up when conciliation was necessary, recommended a minimum wage of 68 cents for men and 45 cents for women. The government threw out the report.

Although a Colonial Officer had described the

dockers as "the most gentlemanly rioters I have ever heard of," the planters revived a fear which had possessed them since the 18th-century Haitian Revolution: the fear of a black millennium. People spoke of a secret organization led by six foreigners, dedicated to the destruction of organized Government, and the "elimination of the white population."

Out of this turmoil rose the Captain. Arthur Andrew Cipriani was born in 1875 to Albert Cipriani, a white planter of Corsican stock and with blood ties with the Bonaparte family. Arthur lost both parents by the time he was seven, and was brought up by an aunt. He left school at 16, distinguished only by atrocious handwriting. His next 25 years were equally unremarkable, divided between managing cocoa estates and horse racing.

A few months before his 40th birthday, World War I broke out. Cipriani lobbied for a West Indian contingent and eventually found himself a Captain in the British West Indian Regiment, stationed in Egypt. There he earned the respect of his compatriots by defending them against army racism. He wrote letters, sent off protests, argued at court martials, and continued to do so until demobilization. By the time Captain Cipriani returned to Trinidad in 1918 he was loved as a man of the people, both because, and in spite of, his white planter background.

Captain Cipriani, who retained his army title, joined the TWA in 1919 and became its president in 1923. The organization had shifted its focus from trade union struggle to political agitation; and Cipriani, the white planter who sided with the "unwashed and unsoaped barefooted men," was seen to be the perfect man for the job. In 1925 he won a seat in the first Legislative Council elections – despite a limited franchise – on a platform favoring workmen's compensation, an eight-hour day, abolition of child labor, compulsory education, competitive examinations for entry into the Civil Service and repeal of the Sedition Ordinance. He kept the seat until his death in 1945.

Cipriani was autocratic but an effective speaker and under his joint leadership with Howard Bishop the TWA grew, boasting 33,000 members in 1928. Although the organization was predominantly urban, black and strongly influenced by Garveyism, the TWA also attracted support from the Indians. Sarran Teelucksingh and Timothy Roodal, two Indian leaders elected to the Legislative Council, joined the TWA. Krishna Deonarine, later known as Adrian Cola Rienzi, was president of its San Fernando branch in 1925, years after he became Uriah Butler's emissary.

Cipriani sacrificed trade unionism on the altar of reformist politics. Worsening economic conditions in the 1930s made many followers disillusioned with his limited ambition "to propose and oppose legislation." Two incidents foreshadowed this. In 1931 the government proposed a Divorce Bill which was hotly opposed by the Roman Catholic French Creoles. The TWA was neutral but Cipriani broke ranks in favor of the French Creoles. Howard Bishop criticized him in the *Labour Leader*, the TWA organ. The paper was closed in 1932. Then in 1932 came the Trade Union Ordinance which gave limited rights to trade unions. After two years of consultation with the British TUC, Cipriani decided not to register the TWA as a union; the Association was renamed

the Trinidad Labour Party. Again his colleagues grumbled; having given a colonial people an awareness of politics, Cipriani's star began to fall.

Cultural evenings: The 1930s began with dark clouds on the horizon. The world economy was depressed, and Fascism ascendant. In Trinidad unemployment rose and planters tightened the screw, lowering wages and extending tasks. In Tobago the peasants, "wrestled with the earth with their bare hands for sustenance." So wrote their poet, Eric Roach, of a people who were "like figures in bas-relief, half-emerged from the heavy clay of our tragic past.

In this context a cultural movement was started by men such as C.L.R. James, Alfred Mendes,

Albert Gomes and Ralph de Boissiere, men influenced by World War I and the Russian Revolution.

"Those were the two events in our lives at that time which drove us into writing about our islands," recalls Mendes. This marked the beginning of West Indian creative writing. The movement began around *Trinidad*, a magazine started in 1929 by James and Mendes. It folded after two issues, for the colony was just a small, philistine backwater. Then the 20-year-old Albert Gomes brought out *The Beacon* in 1931, editing and financing it through 28 issues for three years.

The Beacon published fiction and poetry, cultural criticism, political analysis and historical essays. In their "barrack yard" literature *The Beacon* group celebrated urban lower-class life for its spontaneity, and criticized the respectable classes for their hypocrisy. Nor were they merely middle-class romantics, and so *The Beacon* group also condemned the exploitation of the laboring classes.

As Gomes described it, *The Beacon* was, "the debunker of bourgeois morality, obscurantist religion and primitive capitalism." And inevitably the magazine came under attack from the establishment: the police harassed its leading writers, and businessmen organized advertising boycotts. It folded before the end of 1934. (That was a bad year for culture, for the Government passed a law to censor calypsos). But in its short life *The Beacon* did its job well; it created the beginning of a Trinidadian literature, and politicized men who would play leading roles in times to come.

Before the storm: A Commission of Enquiry found working class housing in Port of Spain, "indescribable in their lack of elementary needs of decency." Conditions were worse in the rural areas where in places 80 percent of the population was infested with hookworms. From the late 1920s onwards, prices climbed with unemployment, but workers earned less in 1935 than in 1929. Like a bad joke, the Wages Advisory Board found that workers' needs were lower in 1935 than in 1920; malnutrition was epidemic. Life was even harder in Tobago, and the poet Eric Roach remembers "clinging to life by the skin of our teeth ...(although we) did not realize our hardship because we knew nothing else."

By 1934 the National Unemployment Movement (NUM), formed by Jim Headley, Dudley Mahon and Elma François, was organizing hunger marches in Port of Spain. But it was the Indian

sugarworkers who started the ball rolling. In July 1934 sugarworkers from San Fernando to Tunapuna demonstrated against their desperate situation. A hunger march fought its way from Caroni to Port of Spain, attacking bosses and policemen, burning buildings, and looting shops. Just outside the city, a police barricade halted the marchers and a delegation of "leaders," all unknowns, went to parley with the Governor; Cipriani's organization was by-passed. The situation was defused, but only for the moment.

The torch passed to workers at the Apex Oilfields. In March 1935 they downed tools and tramped to Port of Spain, protesting low wages and harsh conditions. Cipriani had sanctioned no such action, but the workers went ahead under the leadership of John Rojas and Buzz Butler, a fire-and-brimstone preacher with a pronounced limp and a loud voice. The two broke with Cipriani, and from then on Butler began mobilizing oil workers in the South.

Bertie Percival, a friend of Butler, was an Apex worker with a talent for public speaking. He gave a speech in Port of Spain about conditions at Apex, and was invited to join a new organization, formed by Elma François, Jim Barrat and others, called the Negro Welfare, Cultural and Social Association (NWA). It was the successor to the NUM. Denouncing Cipriani as "Britain's best policeman in the colonies," the NWA saw to mobilizing workers in the north and establishing links with Communist organizations around the worlds. When in 1935 Fascist Italy invaded Abyssinia, the NWA organized large demonstrations in support of the Africans.

Social explosion: Oil was important. Trinidad supplied most of the British Navy's fuel, and the oil companies made large profits in the colony. White expatriate staff, some South African, lived luxuriously. Black workers, however, were treated shabbily. Their wages lagged behind inflation, the bosses were insufferably racist, workers were liable to instant dismissal and a blackballing system made it difficult for a man dismissed by one company to find employment with another. There was no compensation for industrial accidents. Yet the oil workers were a concentrated modern industrial proletariat, better off than sugarworkers, and easier to mobilize.

Tubal Uriah "Buzz" Butler was a Grenadian who came to Trinidad in 1921 to work in oil. In 1929 an industrial accident lamed him and, unfit for oil work, he turned to the Moravian Baptist Church. After the Apex strike of 1935 Butler left Cipriani's TLP to form his own party, the British

Empire Workers (BEW&CHRP). By the early months of 1937 he was moving up and down the southlands, holding meetings, opening and ending each one with a hymn, rallying workers for the "heroic struggle for British justice for British Blacks in a British colony." Butler had indeed become the "Chief Servant."

On June 18, 1937, having exhausted the "prayers, petitions and bootlicking tactics of a suffering class," oil workers at Forest Reserve began a sit-down strike for better wages and working conditions. Police swarmed into the area.

On June 19, the strikers were dispersed and, at 5.30am, two oil wells at Apex oilfields were set on fire. The authorities thought it was the call to strike; more police were sent to the area. That

real signal, for there was no turning back. Later when 40 policemen attempted to recover the charred corpse, the crowd repelled them with bottles and bullets, killing another policeman.

On June 20, a platoon of the policemen attempted to clean out Fyzabad but the strike had moved to other parts and the operation had to be aborted. At Point Fortin, on June 21, the police fired on strikers, killing three and wounding four. The strike moved on, closing down San Fernando and Ste Madeleine, shutting off the power station. At the telephone station, the strike met with police who killed two and wounded eight. Another siege left one policeman dead and four civilians wounded. Yet the strike grew, closing Waterloo Estate, Wyaby Estate, Woodford Lodge (one dead,

evening a warrant for Butler's arrest was issued and a group of policemen traveled to Fyzabad to apprehend him. There they found Butler addressing a large crowd. The police closed in on Butler. He asked that the warrant be read. Lance-Corporal Price tried reading it, but the crowd grew restive. An officer held Butler by the arm and the crowd set on the police, chasing them off. Corporal King, a plainclothes officer, tried to arrest Butler. King was one of the most unpopular policemen around and the threatening crowd closed in on him. He ran into a shop and trying to escape, jumped from a high window. His leg was broken in the fall and, utterly helpless, he was set alight by the uncontrollable crowd. That was the

two wounded) and receiving succor from the NWA in Port of Spain where shops closed. At Rio Claro and Dinsley, work stopped on the estates; police killed one man. That was June 22, the same day that *HMS Ajax* steamed into Port of Spain. *HMS Exeter* arrived the following day and by July workers were returning to work. On July 6 the *Trinidad Guardian* reported that the strike was finally over.

While the marines were mopping up, the Governor and the Colonial Secretary tried to appease the masses. A Mediation Committee was set up and public workers were granted an eight-hour day and a new minimum wage. Both officials castigated the employers for their rapacity: "tact and sympathy (would be) a shield far more sure than any forest of bayonets to be planted here," stated the Governor. "Industry has no right to pay dividends at all until it pays a fair wage to labor," added the Colonial Secretary. For this the Governor was recalled to London and forced to resign in December 1937, and the Colonial Secretary was transferred in 1938. The Forster Commission of Enquiry submitted a tough law-and-order report in February 1938. However, the Moyne Commission, which investigated conditions in the whole region, produced a report so damning that its publication was delayed until after the war.

Hold the fort, for we are coming!: Butler got the ball rolling, but after June 19 he was in hiding, and so he remained until he emerged straight into the

arms of the police and two years' incarceration. The man who held, or rather built, the fort in Butler's absence was Adrian Cola Rienzi.

Born Krishna Deonarine, the grandchild of indentured laborers, Rienzi left school at 14. In 1925 he was a solicitor's clerk and the President of the San Fernando branch of Cipriani's TWA. Already this young man took sufficient interest in world politics to be considered by the Governor as having "markedly seditious views." Deonarine

Left, a woodcarving of Uriah "Buzz" Butler conveys the ferocity of the union organizer. **Above**, Adrian Cola Rienzi, who continued Butler's work in a more moderate vein.

was unimpressed. He organized protests, formed a Young Socialist League and became President of the Indian National Party. Frustrated in Trinidad, he changed his name to Adrian Cola Rienzi (fair skinned, he hoped to pass as Spanish) and migrated to Ireland where he joined the Sinn Fein Movement, and studied jurisprudence. Then on to London where he qualified as a barrister, came under the watchful eyes of the police, and tried unsuccessfully to go to India. Frustrated again, Rienzi returned to Trinidad where he was refused admittance to the Bar until he promised to "not indulge in agitation."

Maintaining links with Butler, he gave advice, and when the strike started he operated as Butler's emissary. After the strike subsided, Rienzi was approached by a deputation of black oil workers who asked his assistance in forming an organization. Presently a group of sugarworkers approached him with the same request.

In September and November were registered, respectively, the Oilfield Workers Trade Union (OWTU) and the All Trinidad Sugar Estates and Factory Workers Trade Union (ATSEFWTU). Rienzi was the President-General of both unions. Oil and sugar, African and Indian, had joined hands.

In the north, Rienzi and others organized the Transport and General Workers Union. And there were others: the dockworkers formed a union, as did the building workers and the Public Works workers. By the end of 1939 there were 12 unions, and labor was finding its voice.

All this was in keeping with numerous official recommendations which considered unions to be the best protection against social anarchy. But neither government nor employers were convinced of that, and the police relentlessly harassed the unionists.

When Butler was released from prison in May 1939, he was given a hero's welcome and an executive post as General Organizer in the OWTU. Butler's combative messianism and Rienzi's organizational discipline didn't mix, however. And when Butler began urging workers to go on strike in defiance of Executive decisions, he was expelled from the union. Four months later he was once again arrested for sedition and this time kept behind bars for the duration of the war. Rienzi, for his part, continued working with the trade unions until 1944 when he withdrew from the movement, fulfilling his own prophecy: "individuals are subordinate to the movement, they play their role, then take their exit, to be succeeded by others; but the movement itself goes on."

The years of World War II, coming on the heels of the Butler riots, marked the end of one era and the birth of another. The Government locked up Butler and prohibited Carnival in its war effort. The people were skeptical. "This war with England and Germany, going to mean more starvation and misery," sang the Growling Tiger: "But I going plant provision and fix me affairs, and the white people could fight for a thousand years." He couldn't have been more wrong. For Sir Winston Churchill had leased parts of the West Indies to the United States in return for 50 old destroyers.

Spain and the United States. In response, the Germans infested the Gulf of Paria with submarines. But most importantly the Americans provided well-paid jobs for tens of thousands, and in Trinidad life changed. The Yanks paid high wages, and the people lost their servility. The Americans labored bareback, swore, got drunk and brawled, and white respectability crumbled. Nightclubs and calypsonians prospered, and their music grew more risque. Nor was it all hunky-dory: the racist arrogance of the American soldiers irritated the population, and the defection of many of the local

In Trinidad, the Americans chose the North West peninsula (Chaguaramas) and the Valencia district (Waller Field), and a reluctant Governor Young was eased out of public office. The world of a small colony shifted orbit.

In his memoirs, the calypsonian Raymond Quevedo, also known as Attila the Hun, recounts: "We had been seeing them for months past around Macqueripe, Chaguaramas and Scotland Bay. They had been depth-testing, mapping, measuring, surveying and engineering. But now they had arrived officially." Huge military bases were built where the Americans tested their carriers and airplanes, formed their Atlantic convoys, and filtered the movement of Latin Americans to

women to the Yanks rubbed salt in the wound.

Glory days: VE Day arrived on May 6, 1945, and music filled the streets of Port of Spain. But now there was a new sound. Formerly, until Carnival was prohibited in 1941, the bands tramped the streets to the thumping of bamboo pipes. Tamboo bamboo these bands were called, and they'd come into being after drums were outlawed in the 19th century. On VE Day, however, there was a ringing, clanging, booming melody being hammered on metal pans: out of the slums of eastern Port of Spain the first steel band emerged.

Andrew Beddoe and Winston "Spree" Simon of John John Band (now Carib Tokyo); "Fisheye" Olivierre and Neville Jules of Hell Yard

Band (now Catelli All Stars); Ellie Manette of Oval Boys (now Petrotrin Invaders): these and a host of others had collectively fashioned a new music during the war years. In the 1940s and 1950s the steel band movement grew, gaining important patrons such as Beryl McBurnie, Canon Farquhar and Lennox Pierre, and new innovators such as Bertie Marshall, Anthony Williams and Rudolph Charles. But those years of the steel band's adolescence were difficult ones. The movement was pioneered by lower-class men, direct descendants of the *jamets* of the 1880s, who faced all the hostility of respectable society. "Steelband fanaticism is a savage and bestial cult and it must be completely wiped out," wrote one correspondent to the *Trinidad Guardian*, and the police

continuous practice (no seasonal bands, these) welded them into tightly-knit units: Desperadoes, Casablanca, Invaders, Destination Tokyo, Renegades, Red Army. And when bands met, a hell of bottles, stones, machetes and knives broke loose.

Steel band warfare continued sporadically until as late as 1960, but a winding down of the violence began in 1950 when Invaders and Casablanca ended their feud, the T&T Steel band Association was formed, and the Spree Simon Benefit Performance, attended by the Governor, was mounted. The following year a tour was organized by the Association, and the Trinidad and Tobago All Steel Percussion Orchestra performed at the Festival of Britain. "If you let this movement die," cautioned a recently returned

backed up this attitude with batons, staging regular forays to disperse practicing steel bands.

Nor were the steel band men angels. Wilfred Harrison, a stalwart from the early days, recalls that "they were difficult boys and I renamed the band 'Desperadoes' ... they were famous for their 'action.' The steel band, which then numbered about 20, was supported by numerous strong robust dangerous men who were respected in the community." They had inherited a violent rivalry from the *kalenda* (stick-fighting) days and their

Left, mounted police watches over a public gathering. Above, pre-fabricated houses being assembled on an American base.

academic, "then you drive a nail in the coffin of our aspirations." The passionate speaker was Dr Eric Williams.

The cultural efflorescence of the early 1930s preceded the labor riots of 1937. Similarly the nationalist movement of the late 1950s was led by an artistic exuberance of which steel band was only a part. There was also the growing confidence and professionalism of the calypso, as practiced by such men as Attila the Hun, the Roaring Lion, King Radio, the Mighty Spoiler and Lord Kitchener. Beryl McBurnie opened the Little Carib Theatre for folk dance performances, and in literature Samuel Selvon and V.S. Naipaul, though abroad, immortalized the language and characters of Trinidad, while Edgar Mittelholzer, in Trinidad, explored their human comedy.

Birth of parliamentary politics: In 1946 and 1950, the first two rowdy elections were held under universal suffrage, and all of Trinidad's anarchic individualism came to the fore. Thus in 1950, 141 candidates vied for 18 seats. Ninety were without a party. It was the heyday of the independent politician, men subject to no party discipline or program, and who offered the moon to an ignorant electorate, from higher pensions to more scholarships, cleaner water to a "better" Carnival. One candidate vowed to abolish dog licenses while another promised to "demobilize unemployment."

These rum-and-roti politicians exploited every possible division of race, class and culture to

capture votes: Butler and Rojas relied on the black trade union block; Victor Bryan on the eastern peasants; the Sinnanan brothers wooed the Indians; and Bhadase Maraj manipulated "his" Hindu Maha Sabha; Norman Tang remained absolutely inscrutable so as to offend no one; and Ajodhasingh was renowned as being a mystic masseur. Some candidates weren't above using obeah (witchcraft) in their causes.

Much of the to-do of these first two elections was reported by a journalist, Seepersad Naipaul, who had married into a well-known political family, the Capildeos. Years after, Seepersad's son, Vidiadhar, would relive his childhood memories to produce two brilliant satirical novels on the elections: *The Mystic Masseur* and *The Suffrage of Elvira.*

There was a left-wing United Front (1946) and a Caribbean Socialist Party (1950), but both fared badly. All eyes focused on two men: Butler and Albert Gomes. Butler, released from gaol in 1945, challenged Gomes in his St Ann's seat in 1946 and lost. On the industrial warpath again, Butler's popularity rose amongst workers, and he won in the south in 1950, when his coalition party held more seats in the Legislative Council than any other. Yet none of the Butlerites were nominated by the Governor onto the Executive Council. "Political blasphemy," accused Butler to no avail. The man who held the limelight was Albert Gomes.

Albert Gomes, the leader of *The Beacon* group in the early 1930s, was a Portuguese of immense girth and over 200 lbs (90 kg) in weight. After the 1937 riots he, along with Quintin O'Connor, built the Federated Workers Union, and went into politics as a City Counsellor. In that forum he bitterly attacked the colonial government and Cipriani, and defended the rights of the common people. He supported the steel bandsmen, the calypsonians, the Shouter Baptists and many other plebeians who felt the heavy hand of the government. One of his famous tactics was to make a scene in the Council meeting until he had to be ejected. When the police came to take him away, he prostrated himself on the floor from where he, all 15 stone, would have to be carried. "But the Captain (Cipriani) had reckoned without a technicality... The Standing Orders... did not provide against my immediate return once I had been evicted," Gomes gleefully recalls. "I, therefore, promptly returned."

When Gomes was elected to the Legislative Council and nominated to the Executive Council in 1946, his radicalism evaporated and he broke with his erstwhile comrades. "In different positions," he explained, "we were bound to assert different claims." In 1950 he was elected again, and this time was nominated to be Minister of Labor, Commence and Industry. He was easily pulled over to the side of the government, for the Constitution provided for only a partly responsible cabinet system: five elected representatives were put in charge of ministries at the Governor's discretion. There, in that Executive Council dominated by Britain's representative, Gomes spent his time implementing a policy of "industrialization by invitation" by restraining union demands and encouraging foreign investment. "O what a awful thing," sang the Roaring Lion, "to see Gomes in a lion skin." And although he contested the 1956 and 1961 elections, Gomes, like Butler, found himself swimming against the nationalist current, doomed to failure.

Williams the Conqueror returns: The pace of life quickened in 1956. In the south, George Weekes, a young trade unionist, was elected President of the key Pointe-à-Pierre branch of the Oilfield Workers Trade Union. The British oil company, Trinidad Leaseholds Ltd, was bought by the American Texaco. "Money start to pass, people to bawl," sang a new calypsonian. "Pointe-à-Pierre sell the workmen and all." The singer, using the sobriquet Mighty Sparrow, won both the Calypso King and the Road March competitions that year with a calypso titled "Jean and Dinah." He instantly became the hero of the black working

Queen's Royal College. Then, on his second try, he won the House Scholarship which took him through until, on his third try, he won the Island Scholarship in 1931. By then, as a footballer, he had already suffered the ear injury which would eventually render him close to deaf.

In 1932 Williams left for Oxford to read history, determined to follow in the footsteps of some of the teachers whom he admired. One of his tutors at college, C.L.R. James, had gone to England a few months earlier, hoping to make his way as a writer. James stayed with a Trinidadian cricketer, Learie Constantine, and worked as a cricket correspondent. He soon became well-known as a Trotskyist and Pan-African speaker. He was to produce several important books, in-

Campaigning in Woodford Square, 1956

class, second only to another man, Eric Williams, who also made his debut in 1956 but on the political stage.

Eric Williams was born in 1911 to a declining lower middle-class family. ("Family fortunes were reflected in the descent from the water closet to the cesspit.") Yet they were ambitious, and little Eric was rigorously drilled to win whichever scholarships were for the taking. At Tranquillity Primary School he won the Government Exhibition which funded him through five years at the

cluding *A History of Negro Revolt, Minty Alley, The Life of Cipriani, World Revolution* and *The Black Jacobins.*

Williams, meanwhile, pursued his academic career single-mindedly, studying throughout the "excessively long vacations," and graduating with first class honors. The chairman of the board of examiners asked about his interest in colonial history and Williams replied that he could not see the value of study unless there was that connection with the environment. Two years were wasted trying for an All Souls Fellowship at Oxford, and then Williams decided to undertake a research degree in history. The topic he chose, on James' advice, was the economic factors underlying the

Left, soldiers enjoying the perks of the Yankee dollar. **Above**, Eric Williams addresses a class at the University of Woodford Square in 1956.

abolition of slavery. In 1939 Williams went to the United States to take up a post at Howard University. James, who had arrived in America the previous year, was engaged in leftist politics.

In America, Williams expanded his doctoral thesis into the book, *Capitalism and Slavery*. A research grant allowed him some Caribbean travel, out of which came the radical book *The Negro in the Caribbean*. He began working part-time with the Washington-based Anglo-American Commission, an organisation set up by the two countries to encourage Caribbean cooperation, in the early 1940s and received his full-time appointment in 1944. He maintained his university connections, however, and continued giving guest lectures. In 1948 he was put in charge of the Commission's

pices of the progressive Teachers Educational and Cultural Association, Williams lectured on a wide variety of topics: West Indian history, the sugar industry, the development of small scale farming, education in the Caribbean, John Locke, Rousseau, Toussaint L'Ouverture, Carlyle, Aristotle. But the lectures were always variations on a single theme: "the defense of the national interests against colonialism." And Williams, now dubbed the "Third Brightest Man in the World," drew ever larger crowds which spilled out of the public library into Woodford Square. There they heard the words of the "Doctor" over a loudspeaker, and were mesmerized by his eloquence, uplifted by his scholarship, and fired by his passion.

The first months of 1955 were quiet. The Politi-

research – a post tenured in Port of Spain, Trinidad. He severed his ties with Howard University and returned home.

University of Woodford Square: Williams had always been interested in education. After discussions with John Dewey, he submitted a memorandum on the proposed West Indian University to the Committee on Higher Education. But this interest really made an impact in the sphere of adult education after he'd been transferred to Port of Spain. He started the *Caribbean Historical Review*, wrote a weekly series on Caribbean history in the *Trinidad Guardian*, and gave public lectures in the early 1950s, at the Trinidad Public Library facing Woodford Square. Under the aus-

cal Education Group, a nucleus of committed supporters, had secretly crystallized around Williams to promote his entry into politics, and a People's Education Movement was formed from the teachers' association to sponsor his lectures. On June 21, Eric Williams' contract with the Caribbean Commission expired and was not renewed by the Commission. For hours that evening he told the public of the injustice of his dismissal.

Williams vowed, "I am going to let down my bucket where I am, right here with you in the British West Indies." A new series of lectures was started, and so was founded a new politics based on public education and nationalism. A speech on constitutional reform ended with a call to sign a petition; within weeks the embryonic party had collected almost 28,000 signatures. The cocky self-assurance of a brilliant academic had captured the black middle class and proletariat. "Now that I have resigned my position at Howard University in the USA," the Doctor promised them, "the only university in which I shall lecture in future is the University of Woodford Square and its several branches throughout the length and breadth of Trinidad and Tobago." "Master! Giant!" shouted the people.

In April 1955, elections were postponed from September 1955 for one year. On January 15, 1956, the Inaugural Conference of the People's National Movement (PNM) was held. And in September 1956 elections finally took place.

French Creoles, the Hindus, the trade unionists, the independent politicians, the newspapers, and the Roman Catholic Church.

The PNM's greatest threat, however, was the People's Democratic Party (PDP) led by Bhadase Maraj. Thought by many to be little short of a gangster, Maraj was nevertheless the President of the Maha Sabha, an orthodox Hindu association, and leader of the sugarworkers' union. He was viewed by rural Indians as their equivalent of Williams: a man whose achievements had elevated the entire ethnic group. And Maraj, accustomed to racial politics, categorized the PNM as "Pure Negro Men."

Williams used a divide and conquer strategy against the PDP. He wooed the Muslim Indians:

There were independent politicians, but only 39 of them this time. There were seven parties. Although there were few differences between their programs, the parties all varied in style and tone, and all came to be seen as representing different social groups. The PNM emphasized morality and discipline, intelligence, nationalism and modernity, and was considered by all to be a "black people's party," versus the rest. Riding a wave of black nationalism, the PNM attacked the

Left, the first Trinidad and Tobago Cabinet of 1962 (Eric Williams is third from left in front). **Above**, young girls at the festivities welcoming Queen Elizabeth in 1983.

labeled the PDP a racialist party akin to the Hindu Maha Sabha in India, thus alienating Muslim, Christian Indians and reformist Hindus from it; and attacked it as a Brahmin (high caste) party linked to big business.

The results of the elections surprised everyone familiar with Trinidad's politics. The PNM, an organised political party, won the majority of elective seats, 13 out of 24; from the polling results it seemed that even some of the French Creoles had voted PNM. The PDP won five, the Butler Party two, the TLP two, and the independents two. Many looked on it as "Trinidad redeeming itself," and the Governor decided to give the winning party a working majority: the Legislative

Council also contained four nominated members and two officials; the PNM was allowed to nominate two, and the rest were chosen from people not hostile to the party. A constitution which Williams had inveighed against was invoked to give the PNM a chance to effectively govern. The black intellectuals came to power, prompting the Mighty Sparrow to sing:

Well the way how things shaping up
All this nigger business go stop
I tell you, soon in the West Indies
It's please, Mister Nigger, please.

Survival of the fittest: The years leading to independence in 1962 were acrimonious ones for the country. Peace offerings were made to the French Creoles by the PNM, who nominated two white members to the Legislative Council, and the trade unions were conspicuously ignored. Not just an olive branch, this was part of the government's continuation of Gomes' industrialization by importing foreign capital. Williams wooed the Indians as well as the Creoles but with little success. The whites and the Indians came together to form the Democratic Labor Party (DLP) which bitterly and without respite attacked the government. The West Indies Federation, set up in 1957, held its elections in 1958. The DLP won six seats, the PNM four, and political tone sank to an even lower level. Williams was furious, C.L.R. James was invited to Trinidad and put in charge of *The Nation*, the PNM organ, and the nationalist strug-

gle intensified. A strike in the oil industry in 1960 had businessmen clamoring for government intervention. Williams folded his arms and turned away, saying "Industrial democracy is based on the right of workers to withhold their labor by way of strike, even if the community is thrown into turmoil." Britain was criticized for giving Chaguaramas to the Americans, and Williams demanded it be returned to Trinidad, calling the lease "a callous anachronism." A demonstration was organized for April 22, 1960. Rain fell bucket-a-drop, but it couldn't deter the thousands who marched behind the Doctor.

Meanwhile, the DLP leadership had slipped from an ailing Maraj to Dr Rudranath Capildeo. As a youth Capildeo was frail, sensitive and

volatile, tormented by his family life. Although, unlike his cousin Vidiadhar Naipaul, the boy had difficulty with English, he was bright. In 1938, he won the Island Scholarship and left to study medicine the following year. His career in England was also marked by loneliness and uncertainty, but in 1941 he graduated with first class honors in mathematics and physics, and in 1944 was elected President of the Men's Union. In 1945 he returned home to teach. Soon, however, he fell afoul of the Director of Education and Capildeo packed his bags and returned to England. By 1950 he had his doctorate and was a lecturer at the University of London. In the next few years he studied law, visited Trinidad, and took up a post as the principal of the Trinidad Polytechnic under the PNM government. In March, 1960, he accepted the job of leader of the DLP. "Trinidad's Most Educated Man" had come to match knowledge with "The Third Brightest Man in the World."

The DLP began campaigning against a blistering PNM attack. Trade unions demonstrated for the PNM, and the *Trinidad Guardian* complained of the "hooligans." Williams turned a blind eye: "March where the hell you like," he said. They thought he meant "mash up what the hell you like." PNM supporters went on a rampage, looting Indian and French Creole homes and businesses, slashing car tires, breaking up DLP meetings. Capildeo called for "bloodshed and riot, revolu-

alliance of 10 British islands, unwilling to financially assist the smaller islands. They were further repelled by Trinidad's proposals for a highly centralized Federal Government; the capital site was to be in Trinidad; the Federal Prime Minister, Grantley Adams, was Barbadian. A Jamaican referendum in September 1961 decided that the island would no longer participate in any Federation and would move towards independence alone. Hearing this news, Williams refused to saddle his country with the poorer islands. He ignored his objectors and decided that "one from ten leaves nought." Trinidad and Tobago would also move to independence alone. It was a bitter defeat for Pan-Caribbean idealists. "Federation boil down to simply this," rhymed the Mighty Sparrow: "Is

tion or civil disobedience." On October 15 he told a large crowd to "arm yourselves with weapons in order to take over this country." His French Creole supporters quietly withdrew. Violence erupted in the east; one man was killed and a state of emergency declared. In December 1961, with the country teetering on the brink of a racial war, elections were held. The PNM won 20 out of 30 seats. Even Tobago turned to the PNM.

The West Indies Federation became the next bone of contention. The Jamaicans were unenthusiastic about the idea of an economic and political

Left, a military regiment salutes the national flag of the Republic of Trinidad and Tobago, **above**.

dog eat dog and survival of the fittest."

Initially, the move to independence saw the DLP and the DLP still at each other's throats. The PNM drafted an independence constitution, but the DLP were critical; they wanted certain safeguards against political interference from the Elections Commission and the Judiciary. Williams turned a deaf ear. Tensions mounted again in the country. Then, at the last moment, the PNM conceded to many of the opposition's demands. Everyone heaved a sign of relief, and at midnight, August 31, 1962, the Union Jack was lowered for the last time in 165 years: Trinidad and Tobago had become a sovereign state, fully equal in the community of nations.

After independence, the DLP accepted its fate of permanent opposition; Capildeo, while still leader of the party, returned to his post at London University. Williams discarded the University of Woodford Square, and parliamentary politics declined.

The "industrialization by invitation" strategy followed by the PNM entailed restraining trade unions, and encouraging foreign investment. Williams had invoked a militant nationalism amongst the black working class before the 1961 elections, but after 1962 these same people de-

James, who was in Trinidad to report on a cricket match, was placed under house arrest; and the Industrial Stabilization Act (ISA), which made striking virtually illegal, was rushed through Parliament in 24 hours. It was all unnecessary: the following year the PNM won the general elections once again, and all candidates from the newly formed Workers & Farmers Party, including C.L.R. James, George Weekes, and Basdeo Panday, lost their deposits.

Development still seemed to elude Trinidad and Tobago. The favored manufacturing sector

cided to translate independence into terms meaningful to them. A rash of strikes against foreign-owned companies prompted the government to set up a Commission of Enquiry into Subversive Activities in 1963. In 1964 the Minister of Finance observed "a developing strike consciousness" which threatened the confidence of investors. In 1965 sugarworkers went on strike, against the orders of their leader, Bhadase Maraj. They appealed to the sympathetic leader of the OWTU, George Weekes, for assistance. A confrontation within the trade union movement loomed, and the government acted fast. The Subversive Activities Commission released its report; a state of emergency was declared in the sugar areas. C.L.R.

didn't perform as expected, unemployment rose, oil prices stagnated, and foreign capital was not coming in as fast as profits were being exported. Independence made the poor poorer and the rich richer. The poorest 20 percent received 3.4 percent of the total wealth in 1957 and 2.2 percent in 1970; the wealthiest 10 percent increased their share from 33.3 percent to 37.8 percent in the same period. Fourteen years of PNM rule had left the "massas" still in control of the wealth. Youths who had benefitted from the PNM's expansion of secondary education were joining an already saturated job market by 1968. The clerical jobs for which they had been trained were not available to blacks, however.

In April 1969 transport workers downed tools in contravention of the law. A confederation of radical groups, the National Joint Action Committee (NJAC), joined the fight. The police moved in and the union was defeated. But the workers had flexed their muscles. Three man-days lost in strikes in 1967 grew to 17,568 in 1968, 19,972 in 1969, and 99,600 in 1970.

Black power: On Carnival Monday 1970, there appeared on the streets masquerade bands, which almost seemed to be demonstrations, portraying topics such as The Truth About Blacks, King Sugar, and 1001 White Devils. The more sensitive noses smelled a storm, and the PNM thought to formulate a program "to achieve dignity and self-respect for the numerically dominant groups."

black. After an hour they left to tramp around the city some more, denouncing the exploiters. That day cabinet met in emergency session and on the following morning the leaders of the procession were arrested. Taken to court and refused bail, the protestors were supported by a crowd of thousands chanting "power!"

The leaders were released from jail on March 4, and a disheveled generation took to the streets, marching into Shanty Town, a ghetto of cardboard and tin shacks. The movement swelled to over 10,000 and several black power groups addressed the crowd. The following day, when Geddes Granger, one of the leaders, came up for trial for behaving without decorum near a place of worship, a massive crowd assembled. Suddenly

On the anniversary of an earlier protest against racial discrimination in Canada, the Sir George Williams University incident, the NJAC took 200 marchers into Port of Spain where they tramped around for hours. They halted at the Canadian High Commission and scuffled with the police, then moved on to the Royal Bank of Canada to scuffle again. Then they went to the Roman Catholic Cathedral on Independence Square. Inside the Cathedral, the demonstraters made speeches from the pulpit and draped the statues in

Left, the President's residence, Port of Spain.
Above, the Oilfield Workers' Trade Union building in Fyzabad with its statue of Buzz Butler.

people were running everywhere and batons were swinging. Into downtown Port of Spain the surging crowd went.

Throughout the next weeks, the Black Power Movement trudged all over the country during daylight. The movement held enthusiastic meetings at Woodford Square, renaming it "The People's Parliament." At night, however, the movement showed its teeth; businesses and banks were bombed. Under pressure, the government offered concessions: unemployment relief, small businesses, a Commission of Enquiry into Racial Discrimination. "We do not want crumbs," replied the movement, "we want the whole bread." Then the steel band movement joined the ranks.

Tobago sponsored a rally, and the Deputy Prime Minister, A.N.R. Robinson, a Tobagonian, resigned from Cabinet. "The law will have to take its course," announced Williams, and the police swung into action. When the police shot Basil Davis, a young Black Power activist, the movement brought 60,000 people to his funeral. "By God we will fight fire with fire," declared Geddes Granger. "This is war." The movement identified Williams with the "exploiters."

The island-wide unrest culminated in a series of wildcat strikes. Oilfield workers, postal workers, water and sewerage workers, civil servants, government workers, all were being swept along by the movement. On April 19 the sugar-workers walked off the job, and planned to march into Port

Meanwhile, in Port of Spain, there was some burning and looting. One man was killed in clashes with the police, and a dusk-to-dawn curfew was imposed. The rebel soldiers eventually surrendered to the police. When everything subsided, the jail was held 87 soldiers and 54 militants.

After that, Black Power, a movement that contained much of the theatrical, lapsed into cultural concerns: African names and dashikis and pyjama suits in public; Afro hairstyles and an emphatic brogue; redemption songs from a new breed of political calypsonians, and musical extravaganzas. Even Eric Williams occasionally surrendered his jacket-and-tie in favor of hot shirts and colorful scarves. But the movement had succeeded in politicizing a generation and remov-

of Spain on April 21. As in 1965, they called on George Weekes of the OWTU for assistance. Transport workers in another radical union planned a demonstration, also for April 21.

On April 20 a state of emergency was declared, and in the wee hours the NJAC leaders were arrested. Sugarworkers were routed by the police, and the Regiment was called out. A section of the soldiers, led by Lieutenants Raffique Shah and Rex Lassalle, rebelled and took over the army camp at Teteron. A convoy of the rebels then set out for the city. The Coast Guard had a different idea: from their boats they shelled the road and blocked the rebels' passage with landslides. Some took to the hills, most remained at the army camp.

ing the grossest forms of racial prejudice, especially in employment.

Unconventional politics: The Public Order Bill was introduced by Attorney-General Karl Hudson-Phillips on August 7, 1970. A draconian piece of legislation, it prohibited marches and public meetings, unless authorized by the police, and unlawful oathtaking, inciting a racial hatred and subversion. The Bill also gave the police wide and arbitrary powers of search and entry, and "suspected persons" could be restricted in their movements. Only the Catholic Church endorsed it, and the Bill was withdrawn. Hudson-Phillips offered his resignation, but Williams didn't accept it. Most of the Bill's provisions, however, were eventually slipped into the statute book piece by inconspicuous piece.

But that was only one part of the confusion surrounding the elections which were due in 1971. A.N.R. Robinson, the PNM renegade, took to wearing gold chains and Nehru shirts, and formed the Action Committee of Dedicated Citizens (ACDC). The ACDC formed a merger with the DLP, now led by Vernon Jamadar. Bhadase Maraj protested: he should be the one to replace Capildeo. So he formed a new party, calling it the Democratic Liberation Party, to have an identical acronym.

Then there were the groups advocating "unconventional politics" and calling for a boycott of the elections. The first of these was NJAC. But NJAC's brand of revolutionary politics became identified

paign. Then there was the Tapia House Movement, a collection of intellectuals led by Dr Lloyd Best. Often capable of a witty turn of phrase, Best nevertheless aroused no public enthusiasm.

As the elections approached, the "no vote" campaign won a last minute convert in the form of A.N.R. Robinson. The ACDC/DLP merger collapsed, and both parties called on supporters to join the boycott. As a result only the PNM, Bhadase Maraj's DLP (which offered no program), and an obsure African National Congress participated in the 1971 elections. The PNM, supported by 28 percent of the electorate, won all 36 seats. Those who questioned the results, mostly OWTU and NJAC leaders, were detained under a new state of emergency. And a Commission of Enquiry was

in the public mind with anarchism and violence and tiring marches in the hot sun. Left of NJAC's radical black nationalism stood the Union of Revolutionary Organizations (URO). This confederation contained a fluctuating membership mostly of NJAC renegades, some of whom Lloyd Best described as jumping "from the frying pan into the frying pan." Consequently, its tone varied at times from pink to scarlet, from vaguely left to orthodox Communist. URO's vital contribution to the times was to spearhead a "don't vote" cam-

Left, a stream of Black Power demonstrators crossing the flyover into Port of Spain. **Above**, protestors chant slogans downtown.

set up to look into Constitutional Reform.

Peace, bread and justice: On September 29, 1973, at the 15th Annual Convention of the PNM, Eric Williams shocked everyone by announcing his decision to retire. He told the party to choose a new leader by December 31, claiming weariness, his daughter's pleas, and his desire to return to academic research. Two contenders offered themselves for the post: Karl Hudson-Phillips and Kamaluddin Mohammed. Hudson-Phillips was the more popular. The decision was to be made on December 2. Instead, that meeting was manipulated into asking Williams to change his mind. He did so, and Hudson-Phillips was left with nowhere to go. He never forgave Williams.

Bhadase Sagan Maraj died in October 1971. An unlettered, violent man, he had made mischief amongst the Indian community for 25 years. As Leader of the Opposition, he made deals with the PNM and vilified his own party. As President of the sugarworkers' union, he fêted with the bosses and intimidated workers who tried to go on strike. Maraj was given to displaying guns in public and flashing large rolls of dollars. So it was that when this picaresque, dangerous man died, everyone knew that big changes were in the air.

In the vacuum created by Maraj's demise three men came to the fore: Basdeo Panday, George Weekes and Raffique Shah. George Weekes was born in 1921 in the northern village of Toco, son of a village schoolmaster. He traveled widely

when he was an officer in the Caribbean Regiment, and was influenced by Social Democrats. Returning to Trinidad, he worked in oil and became a member of Butler's union. Eventually he joined the OWTU and successfully led a group of "rebels" to remove John Rojas. In those days Weekes was a PNM supporter, but by 1966 he had become involved with C.L.R. James and the Workers & Farmers Party. Shortly before the elections that year he persuaded a young barrister, Basdeo Panday, to abandon his doctoral scholarship and join the party. Recently returned from England, Panday had studied drama, then law, then politics.

Raffique Shah had been one of the leaders of the 1970 mutiny. Sentenced to 20 years' impris-

onment, he appealed and was set free in 1971 on grounds that he had not received a fair trial. In 1972 the new Islandwide Cane Farmers Trade Union needed a leader, someone well-known who could unite the scattered cane farmers against the old farmers' association identified with the PNM. ICFTU's talent scouts eventually settled for Raffique Shah and Winston Lennard. By 1974 ICFTU had the support of the cane farmers and was fighting for recognition from sugar producers. Simultaneously, Panday was fighting for wage increases for sugarworkers, and Weekes was fighting Texaco for wage increases. Despite some hostility between Shah and Panday, a meeting between the three unions came up with a proposed rally. The meeting ended and members were walking out when Basdeo Panday suggested they call the rally a United Labor Front.

Over 30,000 turned up to hear the militant words of the trade union leaders who all vowed to continue their struggles. The ULF launched a campaign of public meetings. A religious march for bread, peace and justice was planned for Tuesday, March 18. The day arrived, thousands came, and the procession was led by religious men and the trade unionists. The police had a different idea: they told the marchers to disperse, and immediately clouded the air with tear gas before wading into the panic-stricken crowd, swinging truncheons. All the leaders were arrested for participating in an illegal march, and the day went down in history as Bloody Tuesday.

But the ULF couldn't be stopped so easily. On January 4, 1976, a Conference of Shop Stewards of the four unions (oil workers, sugarworkers, cane farmers and transport workers) passed a resolution: "Be it resolved that the ULF, while not sacrificing the unity it represents, takes all necessary steps to bring into being with all speed a party of the working class…" Thus came together as motley a collection of leftists, radicals, trade unionists, and black nationalists as can be imagined, all under the leadership of Basdeo Panday.

Elections 1976: There were 12 parties and six independent candidates. Many of them merely provided a little comic relief. Dr Ivan Perot offered himself as a man "younger and better looking" than Dr Eric Williams; the two DLPs squabbled shamelessly and bitterly. The main challengers to the PNM were the ULF, A.N.R. Robinson's DAC, and Lloyd Best's Tapia House Movement.

The surprise came from Williams. He campaigned against his party and called five PNM candidates "millstones" with a total lack of awareness. He became the PNM's most severe critic, stealing much of the other parties' thunder. "Heads will roll," promised Williams. Lloyd Best thought that the bottom had dropped out of the 1956 bucket; Robinson thought that the party was over. Williams just laughed: he was already planning for the 1981 elections, while a Carnival atmosphere pervaded the crowds who moved from meeting to meeting.

The campaign had little violence, but polling was low and many, perhaps most, voters fell back into the racial voting patterns of the 1960s. The ULF won 10 seats, the PNM won 24, and the DAC won the two Tobago seats. According to Hector McLean, PNM Minister, his party's 20 years of success was because "the other side too stupid. We are winning by default." After elections the ULF made desperate attempts to prove him correct. Panday was voted out as leader of the party by the Central Committee and Shah put in his place.

The reins of the party changed hands several times in the next few months, and the *Trinidad Guardian* asked, "are we to resign ourselves to having a new Leader of the Opposition every morning?" For a while there were even two ULFs. But Panday had always been the main vote catcher, and when the dust finally cleared he emerged as the leader of the ULF and Leader of the Opposition.

Tobago breaks away: Four years after 1961, Tobago was considered a PNM stronghold. For the next 15 years, however, Crusoe's Isle, as Tobago came to be called, languished in its beautiful, idyllic, neglected state, lacking in social amenities. Even administrative facilities were absent, and to obtain land titles, birth and death certificates, planning approval Tobagonians had to travel to Port of Spain. By 1976 Tobagonians had grown to resent their step-sister status, and, unencumbered by racial considerations, they voted the PNM out.

The DAC victory in Tobago annoyed Williams; he blamed it on a desire of secession. "If you want to go, go," he fumed, "whatever used to be said in the past, we don't live in any world of true eternal love. The greatest thing today is the divorce celebration."

In 1957 Williams had felt a need to "insist on the development of Tobago virtually as a self-contained unit." Robinson quoted him in order to table a motion in Parliament "that all proper and necessary steps be taken to accord to the people of Tobago internal self-government in 1977." New laws were drafted and eventually passed, despite

Left, the young Eric Williams. **Right**, the writing on the wall in Tobago.

Opposition complaints, to provide for a Tobago House of Assembly which would replace the County Council. In the interval, the PNM won a large majority in the County Council elections, and they expected to control the House of Assembly. As such, the powers granted the House were wider than the County Council's had been, although narrower than Robinson's proposals. As a result, the Tobago House of Assembly today is a unique administrative arrangement in Trinidad and Tobago, a form of self-government with responsibilities issued to the House by the central government. These include infrastructure and tourism – in fact, everything except national security.

The Assembly elections, held in November 1980 were contested with enthusiasm. The DAC

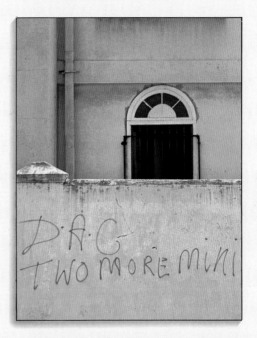

took eight seats, the PNM four, and the DAC House of Assembly and central government settled down to wrangle over financial matters.

Money no problem: It was the best of times, it was the worst of times. In 1974 the oil-exporting cartel, OPEC, hiked up the price of oil to astronomical heights. Trinidad and Tobago's economy ballooned. The visible balance of trade changed from a deficit of TT$188,638 in 1973 to a surplus of TT$387,872 in 1974 and TT$2,158,368 in the peak year of 1980. Over 90 percent came from petroleum exports, production of which was in the hands of US companies. Through taxation the government coffers filled up, and in 1977 Eric Williams announced that "money is no problem."

The government invested lavishly in many costly and ambitious projects. Wages increased, inflation increased, public and private expenditure increased, import bills increased, and millionaires were made overnight as oil money lubricated a freewheeling economy. Every street had its chicken and chip outlet, every home a video; no road without its jam, no big shot without his house in Miami. On the other hand, productivity fell, agriculture disappeared, and inefficiency and corruption clogged the arteries of society. The massive Special Works Program for the unemployed burgeoned into the flaccid Development and Environment Works Division. Trinidad plunged into an obscene and philistine materialism. "Check out their house, and look," lamented

Derek Walcott, "you bust your brain before you find a book." By 1980 social commentators were complaining, from their TT$500,000 homes, that the oil boom was the worst thing ever to have happened to Trinidad and Tobago.

All of this was not lost on the Doc, however. For although he was an arrogant man who turned off his hearing aid at the first sound of an opposing voice, he knew of his contribution to the mess. Intolerant of criticism, over the years he'd surrounded himself with mediocrities whom he despised. Black Power shook him and he'd thought to resign. The oil boom offered a solution to the underdevelopment which seemed so intractable. He brought more technocrats into the govern-ment, hoping they could deal with the problems of near-paralytic inefficiency. They proved to be no more competent, and a lot less entertaining than the mediocrities. So by 1981 the economy was even more skewed, the society even more materialistic than before. In 1962 Williams had written: "The pronounced materialism and disastrous individualism have spread to all parts of the fabric of the society." After 25 years in power he knew that the fabric had all but disintegrated, leaving only the materialism and individualism. In March 1981, a month when sugarworkers, hospital workers, and (O, hard heart of History) teachers, demonstrated around Parliament, Williams ceased taking his diabetic medicines and dismissed his domestic servants. He slipped into a coma and, on March 29, quietly abandoned this world.

"We must do better": Petro-dollars fed the worst aspects of the picaroon society. But they also allowed some positive developments. For one, it must be said that if there was much vulgarity in those years, Williams' Caribbean regionalism was something to be proud of. Thus, for instance, Trinidad and Tobago lent more money to insolvent Caribbean governments than did any other country, including the United States with its well-publicized Caribbean Basin Initiative. Then there was the equalizing impact of wealth: blacks, browns, whites and Indians were no longer inevitably separated by disparities of income, occupation or residence. Consequently, race relations became more relaxed. Finally there was the rising status of women: increased secondary and higher education, and a job market which accepted everyone, allowing women an independence never before tasted. Significantly, the nine women who contested elections in 1966 had increased to 26 ten years later.

The most visible development, however, was the creation of a new political party by one-time PNM Attorney-General Karl Hudson-Phillips. A catch-all for disillusioned PNMs, ambitious Indians, and dissatisfied businessmen, the new party called itself the Organisation for National Reconstruction (ONR): its symbol was a steel beam. With seemingly inexhaustible funds, the ONR launched a PR campaign modeled on US practices, against corruption and inefficiency. "We must do better," was the ONR cry.

Meanwhile, leadership of the country and of the PNM had fallen to George Chambers, a former Minister of Finance. Chambers' low key style and lack of Williams' brilliance left many people unimpressed. Others saw his informality as a step towards a regeneration of the party, however, and his campaign of heckling and insinuation set the tone for the fight.

From the media coverage, these two appeared to be main contenders, but there were other important parties. NJAC had changed its mind about "conventional politics," and roamed the country holding meetings and painting ominous graffiti in red, green and black. They drew moderate crowds of curiosity seekers in the urban areas. Their message was a mild "black" nationalism (stretched to include Indians), and a humanist "philosophy of man." "Let the people decide," was the NJAC cry.

And then there was the coalition National Alliance, consisting of the ULF, Tapia and the DAC. Lloyd Best called it the "party of parties," which represented the three "tribes" of Trinidad & Tobago: Indians, blacks and Tobagonians. The Alliance's program was, like NJAC's, a mild nationalism and, like the ONR's, a promise to be more efficient. So Best's response to the ONR slogan was: "You can't do better than Best."

The campaign resembled Carnival even more than ever with its *picong* ("stinging" from the French piquant, and referring usually to an absurd, boastful heckling). The ONR got the worst of it, however, and was successfully labeled a big business party of authoritarian bent. People hadn't

forgotten Hudson-Phillips' Public Order Bill of 1970. The PNM told the public, "don't worry about the inefficiency and corruption, the bad roads and the electricity blackouts, because we guarantee your democratic freedoms."

The results were a foregone conclusion: The PNM won for the sixth time with 26 seats. There were some upsets, though. The ONR, which received the second highest number of votes, but no seats. The ULF lost two seats to the PNM, and won eight. The DAC won the Tobago seats. Trinidad had decided to give Chambers a chance. That year the price of oil dipped, and the balance of trade showed a deficit for the first time since 1974.

Captain... the ship is sinking: In the 1980s oil prices fell and the government's purse contracted.

bago: Indians, blacks and Tobagonians. The Alliance's program was, like NJAC's, a mild nationalism and, like the ONR's, a promise to be more efficient. So Best's response to the ONR slogan was: "You can't do better than Best."

Immediately after his re-election Chambers began an austerity drive with the slogan, "Fête over, back to work." The timing was unfortunate, coming shortly before Carnival, and many people laughed, "the fête now start." The new stress on productivity temporarily brought the employer class back into the PNM fold and out of the ONR camp. But in next to no time it became clear that the government was unable to discipline workers, and corruption and inefficiency continued.

Local government elections, hitherto ignored, in 1982 gave the opposition parties a chance to rally their forces. A tentative "accommodation" was arranged between the ULF-DAC-Tapia Alliance and the ONR, and they went in to do battle. Of

Left, former two-term president Noor Mohamed Hassanali. **Above**, a view over Port of Spain with the "twin towers" complex in the background.

120 seats, the accommodation picked up 66, leaving 54 for the PNM, and none for NJAC. It was a shot in the arm for the opposition which got another fillip in 1984 when, despite a strenuous PNM effort, the DAC won 11 of 12 seats in the Tobago House of Assembly.

Since then, the opposition parties have been forced into unity by deteriorating social conditions. As state revenue fell with the price of oil, so did unemployment rise; as the trade unions retreated and wages shrank, so did inflation grow, especially since the TT dollar was devalued by 25 percent in 1985. Crime increased and the police seemed hardly able to check it. The expensive and ambitious education system failed to live up to its early promise.

Meanwhile, the ULF, DAC, Tapia and ONR papered over their differences and, in September 1985, merged around a common "Platform For Democracy." Robinson was the political leader, and Hudson-Phillips and Panday his deputies, in the National Alliance for Reconstruction. But a trade union-based ULF and a big business ONR shared an uncomfortable bed.

On December 16, 1986, the National Alliance for Reconstruction won a landslide victory, taking 33 out of the 36 seats in Parliament, the first time since 1956 that the government of T&T had changed hands. A.N.R. Robinson became the new prime minister and Chambers lost his seat as leader of the PNM to Patrick Manning. The victory of the NAR was greeted by spontaneous widespread celebration throughout T&T with the party trying to make as much as possible of their mandate, mobilizing public support, they organised an environmental clean-up campaign.

The alliance, however, did not last very long and, by 1988, many of those formerly associated with the ULF denounced their own government and re-grouped as the United National Congress (UNC), which became the official opposition in Parliament. Also, Robinson was becoming increasingly unpopular.

This inspired the radical Muslim group, the Jamaat-al-Muslimeen, to think it could rally public support by arming itself clandestinely and storming into Parliament on July 27, 1990, holding Robinson and several leading ministers hostage. Twenty-four people were killed during the insurrection, one of them a government minister. The lone TV station was also occupied and the Jamaat leader, Yasin Abu Bakr, announced he had taken over the country. Pinned down by the army and police in both places, the group eventually released the hostages and surrendered. They were charged with a number of offenses, including treason and murder.

Their defense was that they had no charges to answer, because of the amnesty given by acting president, Emmanuel Carter, who had been head of state at the time. All 114 Jamaat members were freed when the High Court and Court of Appeal accepted that claim. However, the Privy Council in London ruled the amnesty invalid in late 1994, though it said the rebels should not be re-tried. The Jamaat and the government have since been suing and counter-suing each other for damage done during the violent insurrection.

A.N.R. Robinson and the NAR never fully recovered from the Muslimeen assault and the PNM successfully returned to power in December, 1991, regaining 21 of the 36 seats in Parliament. The UNC captured 13 and NAR retained only two, both in Tobago. Robinson held on to his Tobago East seat but resigned as NAR leader.

New broom: Patrick Manning was determined to prove himself equal to the task of being the third PNM Prime Minister. He wisely retained the essentials of economic and social policy that helped make the NAR so unpopular but were necessary for Trinidad and Tobago's survival.

Manning openly courted voters, when test cricketer Brian Lara was hailed as a national hero the government rewarded the young sportsman with gifts including half an acre of land. Port of Spain became home to the headquarters of the 25-nation Association of Caribbean States (ACS). This grouped the existing 14-nations Caribbean Community and Common Market (Caricom) with the Spanish-speaking Caribbean Basin countries in Central and northern South America.

But the voters' remained unimpressed and the early election called in 1995 resulted in a dead heat between the two major parties. The NAR and UNC formed a coalition under the leadership of Basdeo Panday. A.N.R. Robinson – recalled to the leadership of the NAR months before the election – became the de facto deputy Prime Minister until 1997, when, following the retirement of President Hassanali he took over as head of state.

As the first Trinidadian Prime Minister of East Indian descent, Basdeo Panday walked a political tightrope. He was careful to include several MPs of African descent in the Cabinet and the majority of ambassadorial appointments went to leading Trinidadians of non-East Indian descent.

Right, cricketer and national hero Brian Lara, courted by politicians.

Trinidadians may be the most heterogeneous people on Earth. For they are a people in a sense that other societies which contain multi-racial populations are not. The favorite national myth is that Trinidad and Tobago is a paradise of inter-racial harmony, and T&Ters view with self-righteous horror the ugly racial strife that seems endemic to other countries. Race is mentioned casually and openly in daily conversation, and Trinidadians appear unconcerned when racial stereotypes and differences are discussed. The truth, however, is infinitely more complex than either of these two extremes. Trinidadians do not, today, fight pitched battles race against race, but neither can the question of race be too glibly glossed over.

There is a nation of Trinidad and Tobago with a central core of culture in which all the races participate, and there is a significant percentage of the population which is of mixed race. But history has not succeeded in melting the peoples down entirely – either culturally or genetically – into one homogeneous block; and so, in Trinidad and Tobago, race is very much an issue, albeit an issue so subtle that it is not likely to assail the attention of the visitor.

Trinbagonians: Who are the Trinidadians and Tobagonians? The term "Trinidadian" will be used hereafter to refer to the combined peoples of the two islands, at the risk of causing offence to the Tobagonian sector of the population. The relationship between the two parts of the country is a thorny problem yet to be solved, and reflected in the clumsy name that they continue to tote around. Groups in Trinidad and Tobago have been agitating for the adoption of a composite name – proposed are "Trinago" and "Trinbago" – which would suggest integration and allow "Trinagonian" or "Trinbagonian." In the meantime "Trinidadian" tends to be the most used umbrella term.

The first people, of course, to inhabit the country were Amerindians, who migrated from the South American continent, discovering the Caribbean centuries before Christopher Columbus. As elsewhere in the region they were all but exterminated in the onslaught of European colonization. There is a tiny handful of people in Trinidad calling themselves "Caribs," and there are many among T&Ters whose physical features suggest an Amerindian admixture in their ancestry. The Amerindian strain has fed into the pool, but is no longer a distinct racial presence.

Most territories of the Caribbean bear the mark of one European culture, at most two. The European element of Trinidad and Tobago hails from no less than three main sources. Spanish, French and British have all, at one time, ruled these islands, and in addition to these three major groups

of European settlers there were minority groups of Portuguese, Italians and others.

But the bulk of the people of Trinidad and Tobago today are the descendants of Africans and Indians brought to work in the sugarcane and other plantations, the Africans transported by force and enslaved, the Indians arriving under a system of indentureship not too far removed from slavery. Together the Indians and Africans constitute upwards of 80 percent of the population. Within the last century Trinidad has received, and continues to receive, immigrants from China and the Middle East who come as traders.

The ethnic groups that make up the population of Trinidad and Tobago all arrived, then, under

Preceding pages: two faces of Trinidad; floral hats and parasol on Republic Day. **Left,** Rastafarian welcome. **Right,** two spectators.

different circumstances. They came from different roots, thousands of miles apart; they came for different reasons, and they came to different roles. Inevitably they continue to be different from each other in many ways.

Plantation legacy: Whites in Trinidad and Tobago remain a privileged minority, fairly aloof from the rest of the population. They live in affluent suburban settlements or on large inherited landholdings scattered around the country, and a few still earn an income from large estates passed on by their forebears – relics of the plantation system.

Whites are the traditional "aristocracy" of the society, who for centuries controlled the resources and reaped the benefits of all economic activity.

society in Trinidad and Tobago are the traditionally upper-class pursuits of water sports (yachting, boat-racing, windsurfing, swimming), lawn tennis, golf, cocktail and dinner parties, or simply meeting at their exclusive clubs.

And it is whites who have kept alive in Trinidadian society European artistic traditions such as ballet and opera. The major national festival of Trinidad and Tobago – Carnival – has its origin in a European celebration (French, to be exact), and although it has been developed to its present state by the African population, white Trinidadians continue to participate in some measure in Carnival activities. Indeed, the most widely-acclaimed Carnival artist to emerge in recent times is a white man, Peter Minshall.

Although today members of other groups have emerged to share the "commanding heights" of the economy with the old masters, whites remain the owners and managers of major business concerns – manufacturing, hotel industry, banking, the import and distribution trades.

Some whites work in education, in religious orders which function as the old "prestige" schools originally founded for white and mulatto children, and in the new private schools set up for the still predominantly light-skinned children of today's upper classes. All in all, the white Trinidadian is a white-collar worker. A white street cleaner, or chambermaid, or bus conductor would be a decided oddity. The recreational activities of white

The diet of white Trinidadian families differs from that of the rest of the population for economic reasons, for example in terms of the balance of the various food groups. The poorer masses of the country consume a great deal of carbohydrate and fairly small amounts of the more expensive foods such as meat and dairy products. The diet of the people of Trinidad and Tobago is also greatly influenced by North American tastes, and this influence is more marked in households which can afford to buy the imported foods associated with American eating patterns.

But basic tastes in food preparation common to the bulk of the population are shared by whites, for a large element of what we see as the cuisine of Trinidad and Tobago emerged out of the kitchens of European settlers where African cooks combined their own inherited ideas about food with Spanish, French, Portuguese and British ways of cookery.

African echoes: Next in order of arrival were the Africans. Alienated from the land by the experience of slavery, the African population has tended to gravitate towards urban centers, though the population of Tobago is almost entirely African. (Tobago was a separate entity and developed apart from Trinidad until less than a century ago when the two islands were unified. The smaller island does not have the same history of multiethnic immigration).

Blacks engage in a wide variety of occupations,

It was the Africans who forged the calypso-steelband-carnival arts, and they remain the chief proponents of this aspect of the vibrant Trinidad and Tobago culture.

It was they, too, who perfected the "lime," and this item has no translation because the concept belongs exclusively to this part of the world. To those who disapprove of the activity, liming means loitering, as in groups of aimless men standing around at street corners or sitting on a culvert watching the world go by. It means pointedly not doing anything too purposeful, or serious, or strenuous, whiling the time away in the company of cronies, talking or not talking, drinking or not drinking, playing all fours; going in a gang to the beach, to a party, to a cricket match…

but shy away from agriculture. Black businessmen are also thin on the ground. The Afro-Trinidadian is a salaried worker – menial, semiskilled and skilled. For years the Civil Service was monopolized by this ethnic group, which still occupies nearly the whole of its upper levels. There is also a class of black professionals: doctors, lawyers and other university-trained people. The means of social mobility for the African population has always been education, rather than the route of entrepreneurship, the pattern for other ethnic groups.

Left, alluring legacy of European settlement.
Above, Scouting, Trinidad style.

The *joie de vivre* of the Afro-Trinidadian is proverbial, and the duty of enjoying all that is put on Earth for God's children to enjoy is taken very seriously indeed.

It is black Trinidadians who expound most readily upon the theme of how their "carnival mentality" is a barrier to the progress of their race, and how the other races are doing well because they are not given to spreading joy, etc… But the attitude of the Afro-Trinidadian to the life-styles of the other groups is ambivalent: it wavers between admiration and mild scorn for those who seem to spend so much time working and saving up that they miss out on living.

The staple of the black population is rice, a taste

acquired from the Indians. Whereas in the rest of the Caribbean, African people make extensive use of root vegetables and green bananas, in Trinidad and Tobago these take second place to rice. Blacks retain a taste for the salted meat and fish which were an essential part of the food rations given out to their enslaved ancestors on the plantation. Today salted beef and pork and dried codfish are mainly used as flavoring for other dishes – rice-and-peas, stewed peas, *callaloo*.

The family patterns of Africans in Trinidad and Tobago, as in the rest of the Caribbean, do not adhere too strictly to the official norms of marriage and the partriarchal family. Common-law unions are prevalent, and women have a great deal of authority in the context of the family. A large

Practically every known sect of Christianity claims a portion of the black population: Roman Catholic, Church of England, Church of Scotland, Methodist, Moravian, Seventh-Day Adventist, Pentecostal, and more. A recent development in Trinidad and Tobago is the "Black Museum" movement, that is Africans turning to Islam, but in their own Muslim organizations, not as part of the established Indian Muslim community already present.

An indigenous population: The mulatto did not come, of course, as an immigrant arriving from distant shores, but as a racial type produced on Caribbean soil, being the offspring of African and European.

There are very many people of mixed blood in

percentage of households are headed by women. Extended-family habits are still alive, mainly among the lower classes. Promotion into the growing middle class generally means adoption of the life-style beamed out from American television, which includes the restricted nuclear family pattern. The more affluent people become, the less use they have for the larger family.

New religions were developed by the African population on Caribbean soil. These religions combine elements of Christianity with African religious practices and beliefs. But Trinidad and Tobago is officially a Christian country, with the Catholic Church being particularly powerful, so the syncretic sects are severely frowned upon.

Trinidad and Tobago. But they do not, by and large, constitute a separate group. They are culturally, black Trinidadians. Within a "black" family, complexions may range from black to palest brown, reflecting miscegenation somewhere along their ancestry. But there is a group of brown Trinidadians who have to be viewed as distinct from the mass. They are the heirs of the original "middle class" of the Caribbean – a privileged, carefully inbred social class.

This group has a very strong sense of being an elite. It jealously guards its racial "purity" – members choose only mates of the same color or lighter. There is not much to distinguish them, in terms of life-style, from the whites. Indeed, in the popular mind, whites and upper-class mulattoes are lumped together under the loose label of "French Creoles," although many families in this class bear Spanish, Portuguese, Scottish, or English names. The designation "French Creole" has to do with the fact that in the 18th century whites and mulattoes were attracted to Trinidad from the French Caribbean by enticements such as grants of land, and soon became a powerful economic and political force in the century.

Eastern elements: The East Indian presence in Trinidad and Tobago is one and a half centuries old, but is already the largest single group in the Republic, claiming over 40 percent of the population. The majority of Indians still live in rural communities, and farming remains their chief

fabric of life in Indian communities for generations. Inevitably, the life-style of Indian Trinidadians has been and continues to be affected by the influences which prevail in the society, namely the culture of their African counterparts, as well as the essentially Western-oriented education system and mass media. But there remains a core of cultural traits which constitutes a distinctive Indian way of life.

A minority of Indians have been Christianized, notably by the Presbyterian Church. But the religions which the Indian immigrants brought with them, Hinduism and Islam, remain firmly in place. The majority religion is Hinduism, and both religions have very strong organizations which, like the Christian churches, set up their own schools.

occupation. With increased access to secondary and tertiary education, however, Indians have entered the clerical and professional fields once occupied almost exclusively by Africans. Small and medium businesses are owned mainly by Indians, and a few Indian concerns have grown into major business enterprises.

Indians brought to Trinidad and Tobago a relatively intact and functional culture which adapted itself to the new environment and shaped the

Left, a black-German-Portuguese man outside a Portuguese church in Arouca; an Indian shopkeeper. Above, an East Indian West Indian at the turn of the century; and today.

Eastern religions may be said to have gained, rather than lost ground, for today they enjoy an official recognition not accorded them during the colonial period. Marriage ceremonies, for example, were not recognized. In Trinidad and Tobago major Hindu and Muslim festivals like Phagwa and Divali are now public holidays.

Indian family organization in Trinidad and Tobago has been eroded somewhat by Westernization. The traditional status of the Indian is challenged by near universal education to secondary level and by the influence of the media. But extended-family networks are stronger than in the African population. Many Indians live in large, multi-generation households, of the type made famous by V.S. Naipaul, although the patterns of authority which previously obtained in such households may not be operational today. But even where Indians split off into nuclear family households, there remains a strong bond of responsibility towards the larger family, which may include economic cooperation.

Indian food, of course, is quite distinctive. Among their standards are eggplant, a string bean known as *bodi*, tomatoes, green mangoes, potatoes, a variety of spinach known as *bhaji*, split peas, chick peans and pumpkin. A favorite seasoning is curry, in addition to other spices such as cumin seed, saffron and massala. Rice is basic to the Indian diet, and so is roti – a flat, supple bread that is eaten with vegetable or meat preparations.

Indian Trinidadians are as fond of the game of cricket as their African compatriots. A favorite form of recreation, too, is going to the cinema to watch movies from India. Indian music and dance are also greatly appreciated and there are highly accomplished Trinidadian Indian musicians, dancers and singers, some of whom are trained in the ancestral country.

Trading places: The Chinese and Lebanese came as traders, and remain largely engaged in commercial activity – small trading and big business. The Lebanese are a tightly-knit urban community, whereas the Chinese are scattered all over the country: the "Chinese shop" is an institution in rural communities.

Both groups are relative newcomers and tend to keep active links with their countries of origin, so that items of their material culture are ever present. In the home of a Chinese family one is likely to be surrounded by Oriental decorations and kitchen utensils. Because they are recent immigrants, Chinese and Lebanese cultures remain fairly closed – practiced "privately" while participating in the common culture of the country. But there is a greater level of integration on the part of the Chinese than the Lebanese and there has been some intermixture of Chinese blood with that of Africans and Indians; many people in Trinidad and Tobago bear no fewer than four different racial strains in their blood.

The mixing of races is part of the reality of Trinidad and Tobago, but what is the real nature of relations among the various peoples?

Status and stereotypes: Race relations in Trinidad and Tobago are defined by the old hierarchy of white down to black, and by the newer and more volatile current of mistrust which runs between the two largest groups in the country: the Africans and Indians.

Europeans constitute a very small minority in Trinidad and Tobago – less than 1 percent – but they retain their economic supremacy and attendant prestige. Today, the traditional attitudes towards white people have been reinforced by the impact of the foreign (mainly American) media. Moreover, deep in the ethos of the Indian population of Trinidad and Tobago is the great esteem which their ancestral culture accorded the Aryan racial type of northern India.

Thus it is that the physical features of the Europeans are the yardstick against which Trinidadians evaluate beauty and worthiness in general. At the lower end of the scale of desirability lie dark skin and kinky hair; at the top, pale skin and straight hair. It stands to reason, then, that great approval also accrues to the physical features of the Chinese, the Lebanese, the light-skinned Indian, the mulatto (or "Spanish") and the "mixed" (provided one part of the mixture is light-skinned).

There are many manifestations of this race-and-color scale of assessment. For years, a Trinidad and Tobago beauty queen was, by definition, a white or pale-skinned woman. The Black Power movement of the 1970s made some inroads into changing that tradition, and today it is more politic to choose a queen of the indeterminate khaki mix (not too pale, but not quite black, either) that is becoming the ideal physical type in Trinidad and Tobago.

When, for bureaucratic purposes, black Trinidadians are called upon to identify their race (e.g. in passport applications, I.D. documentation, census exercises), many choose to write the ambiguous "mixed."

Black men on the rise up the social ladder acquire light-skinned, straight-haired wives as part of the trappings of promotion, and certain high-visibility "women's" jobs – bank teller, air hostess – until recently were filled only by light-skinned types.

Class consciousness: Race relations are far from ideal. Trinidadians mix at school and at work, but not too much at play. "Integration" is involuntary – T&Ters interact when thrown together, not, generally, by choice.

Perhaps the maximum interaction among races is to be found at the top of the pile, where money and paleness of skin unite into one melange of whites, mulattoes, Lebanese and successful Chinese. The commercial giants who have emerged in the Indian population do not appear as yet to

Right, woman from Port of Spain, Trinidad.

78

have been integrated socially into this set. This might be explained by one or all of a number of reasons. The Indian's base is rural, whereas the elite described above is urban. The Indian's cultural identification and sense of responsibility to family or clan do not predispose him to shift allegiance to another group.

Then there is what Trinidadians call their "middle-class," which in their vocabulary may stretch from professionals to civil servants to well-paid skilled workers (especially in the wake of the oil boom). This group, like the mass of the working and peasant population, is largely African and Indian. There are practically no lines of communication between this block of the population (middle and lower classes) and the light-skinned

upper class, and the current feeling between them is standard: the latter views the former with condescension and some apprehension, while the other views its superiors with a mixture of deference and resentment.

Racial stereotypes die hard, as do derogatory racial epithets. The African is a "nigger," the Indian a "coolie"; but these are the two most extreme of racial insults. The names used for other ethnic groups are far milder in their import.

Chinese is abbreviated, almost affectionately, to "Chinee." Middle-Eastern people, who are mainly Lebanese, are casually lumped under the term "Syrian." Mulattoes are described as "red" which is not as flattering as "fair" or "fair-skinned."

Curiously, there are no traditional insult-words for whites: in the 1970s, the era of Black Power, Trinidadians adopted from Black America the term "honky."

Education and economy: Africans and Indians constitute the bulk of the population, and relations between them are uneasy. This fact does not preclude healthy relations at the personal level: firm friendships between individuals and families, communities in which the two races not only live side by side but actively cooperate, and the miscegenation which has produced a whole new race, the "Dougla."

But there exists a fundamental mistrust between Indians and Africans in the mass, a rivalry that dates from the Indian's arrival to replace the African as plantation worker in the wake of Emancipation. Each has traditionally accused the other of wanting to "take over" the country, and the two groups monitor each other's numbers with mindful apprehension.

Since the beginning of party politics in Trinidad and Tobago in the era leading up to Independence, major political parties have been formed along lines of race (Indian and African) and elections clearly perceived as a struggle for African or Indian supremacy. For the whole of this period – 30 years – it is the African-based party which has held sway. Partly because of this, but also because the Indians suffered a serious lag in access to education under the colonial regime, the Civil Service has until recently been an African preserve. Indians, then, seemed excluded from the running of the country.

On the other hand, Africans perceive Indians as taking over the economy of the country, because Indians are so visibly engaged in business activity, ranging from the selling of vegetables by the roadside to ownership of the sophisticated hardware store, whereas Africans have chosen a different route to success, the way of education.

What has perhaps exacerbated relations in the past few years is that the Indians have now caught up in education. With the increase in oil revenue, the incumbent government was able to dramatically increase educational facilities, notably at secondary level. This has given the Indians a new ubiquity which disturbs their African counterparts: the Indian who was once safely tucked away out of sight in the canefield, the rice patch or the family vegetable garden, is now turning up everywhere, in every kind of job. Africans feel upstaged, threatened and Indians feel their resentment. The situation produces foolish muscle-flexing on both sides.

The juxtaposition of two different cultures has been an inevitable source of friction. The original encounter between Africans and Indians was the classic case of "host population" versus immigrants with a foreign, therefore disturbing, culture which (as is the case in such situations) the immigrants showed no inclination to relinquish in favor of the culture of the hosts.

But, in addition, in Trinidad and Tobago the host population had no strong sense of its own cultural identity. The circumstances under which Africans had been brought from their ancestral land made cultural continuity very difficult. Africans from different cultures had been mixed together, languages forgotten, religions garbled – even the African's name was erased. Africans

refusal to be assimilated, tended to be interpreted by the Africans as arrogance. Africans take a dim view of the Indian population's continuing emotional relationship with their ancestral land – Trinidad and Tobago has been brought to the brink of war by the spectacle of Indian Trinidadians cheering on a cricket team from India playing in Trinidad against a Trinidadian team! And Indian music on the radio and Indian movies on national television were until recently a great affront to the rest of the population; but this is changing, and it is in the area of culture that the Republic is experiencing a shift from confrontation to interpenetration.

Racial mosaic: The fact that the different ethnic groups of Trinidad and Tobago have some fairly

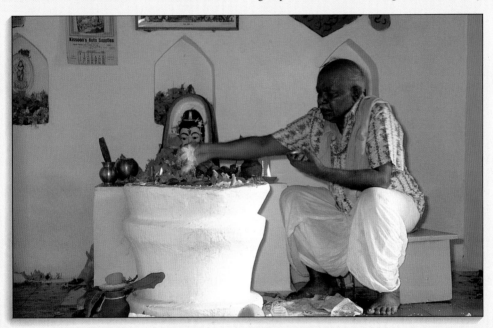

now practiced a new culture that was decidedly African-based, but the official, approved culture was European, and the way of life of the black population was not even seen as "culture." The attitude of the Afro-Trinidadian to his own culture was one of rejection, at best ambivalence. Salvation lay in being assimilated into the white man's culture.

The confidence of Indians in their own culture, the strength and the cohesiveness which this culture gave to Indian communities, the Indians'

<u>Left</u>, a smile as good as gold. <u>Above</u>, an offering is made on a small Hindu altar in the Ramgoolie Temple, Trinidad.

distinct cultural traits does not pose any real threat to the concept of nationhood. "Cultural pluralism" is a term which has entered the vocabulary, and although race relations are not exemplary, Trinidadians set great store by their multi-ethnic image. At the heart of the mosaic, however, is a growing area of shared culture which makes it possible for T&Ters to coexist without major explosions of antagonism.

Creole conversation: There is, on the one hand, the shared language. In all the Caribbean territories Creole (or hybrid) languages have developed out of the meeting of European and African. They are the achievement, in the first instance, of Africans, who in each society developed a lingua franca which allowed communication between themselves and the Europeans, as well as among the Africans themselves. According to one theory, Africans transported to Trinidad and Tobago took the vocabulary of their European overlords and poured it into the mold of a standard West African syntax, retaining some words from their own languages. As Africans lost their own languages, what would have started out as a pidgin for basic communication grew into a language capable of the whole range of expression.

The vocabulary of Trinidad and Tobago Creole is mainly English-derived but it also contains words which can be traced back to languages spoken in West Africa, among these Twi and Yoruba. But Trinidad also spoke French (and its

Trinidadian mythology have French-derived names: *lajablesse, soucouyant, Papa Bois, lagahou.*

Traces of Spanish in the everyday language are relatively sparse, given Trinidad's proximity to Latin America. Words for some of the dishes introduced by the Spaniards are derived from their language – *pelau, sancoche, pastelle*. And there is the terminology surrounding the activity known as *parang* (Christmas music) which is moving into the general vocabulary. Some fruits are called by their Spanish names – *sapodilla* and *granadilla.*

And today people in Trinidad and Tobago of every racial type use some Hindi words as part of their everyday speech. Non-Indians living in inte-

Creole counterpart) for about one hundred years of its history, so there is in the everyday language a large stock of French vocabulary and French constructions using English words.

Trinidadians will say "It making hot," as the French say "*Il fait chaud*"; and the expression "It have," meaning "There is or are" is from the French "*Il y a.*" T&Ters retain many French names for the native vegetation of the country – *balisier* (wild banana), *pomme cythere* (golden apple), *pomme rac* (otaheite apple), *cerise* (a cherry-like fruit). Damaging gossip is *mauvais-langue*; a female crony is a *macommère*; a term of endearment is *doo-doo*, from the French *doux* meaning "sweet"; and the spirits who people

grated rural communities have used Hindi expressions for a long time, and know a great many more of these expressions than the average Trinidadian. But today some Hindi vocabulary has become the common property of all.

Hindi has mainly provided words to do with food, cooking, clothes, religion and family. In the markets the Hindi *beigun* is steadily replacing "melongene" as the word Trinidadians use for eggplant. Indeed, the vegetables in Trinidad and Tobago are largely grown and marketed by Indians, so their Hindi names are passing into the vocabulary: *bhaji, bodi, aloo*. Some names of commonly-known Indian seasonings are *geera, massala* and *amchar*, and Trinidadians know that *roti* is baked on a *tawa*, and more and more people are becoming familiar with the cooking process known as *chungkay*. The orhni, the sari and the dhoti are articles of clothing familiar to all. Terms for the two major religions practiced by Indian Trinidadians are household words – from Hinduism: Phagwa, Divali, Ramleela, puja, deya, Lakshmi; from Islam: Ramadan, Eid-ul-Fitr, Hussein. And Trinis know that the members of the Indian extended family (including grandparents and in-laws) are called by names such as *agee, bhowji* and *dulahin*.

The Amerindians have also made some mark on T&T language, again in the form of words for food – cassava, balata, roocoo, tatoo – but also in the wealth of place names they have left behind.

names abound in Trinidad which is itself a Spanish name. Some of the Spanish place names are San Rafael, Las Cuevas, Sangre Grande, Sangre Chiquito, San Fernando, El Soccorro, Los Iros. Part of the legacy of French language are place names like Blanchisseuse, Sans Souci, Matelot, Champs Fleurs, Lopinot, Petit Bourg and L'Anse Mitan. These are some of the ingredients that go into the common language – basically a Caribbean Creole, but given its distinctive character by the special blending of peoples that took place only in Trinidad and Tobago.

A common accent: Creole differs from Standard English in its syntax – the linguists have found a common syntax across Caribbean Creoles and have traced it back to the West African family of

Trinidadians use the language of their Amerindian predecessors daily in every part of the country when they speak of Tunapuna, Mucurapo, Guayaguayare, Naprima, Curepe, Tacarigua, Carapichaima, Maitagual and many othes.

Indeed, all the place names bestowed by the various groups must be considered as part of the common language of the people of Trinidad and Tobago. English place names are not predominant – they are to be found in greatest concentration on the smaller island of Tobago: Scarborough, Roxborough, Plymouth. Spanish and French place

Left, an elder of the Creole village of Blanchisseuse. **Above**, three schoolgirls.

languages. The intonation of each Caribbean Creole is distinctive, and so is the pronunciation of individual sounds (specifically vowels) from Creole to Creole. So there is an unmistakable Trinidad and Tobago "accent" common to all people, of every ethnic classification, and they use this accent even when speaking Standard English. What is significant is that older Indians sound markedly different from the younger generation Trinidadians: the full acquisition of the common language was not an instant process but one which has taken several generations.

A most interesting indicator of the extent to which Trinidad and Tobago Creole (or, strictly speaking, Trinidadian Creole) has been shaped by its polyglot population is the fact that the Standard Creole of the smaller island, Tobago, is not quite the same as that of Trinidad, and has been found to have striking similarities with Jamaican Creole. Tobago is at the southern end of the Caribbean chain of islands and Jamaica is pretty near the top – the two are separated by over 1,000 miles (1,600 km) of sea. But they are both different from Trinidad in that on both islands Africans constitute the majority of the population.

Rather than a separate, hermetic language, Creole can be seen as positioned at one end of a continuum which shades into Standard English at the other end. Where on the continuum Trinis pitch their language (i.e. whether they use pure Creole, pure English or some combination of the

that the great majority of people do not fully possess Standard English and, for many of those who do, it tends to remain a language written rather than spoken. But Creole is inevitably one of the media through which people receive communication. It is the language of calypso, for example, and the calypsonian is one of the most influential and important communicators in the society.

Jean-Paul Sartre wrote in *Black Orpheus:* "The specific traits of a society tally exactly with the untranslatable expressions of its language."

To the extent that Trinidadians share a common code of communication not quite the same as any other, to the extent that they share their own set of untranslatables, they share a common culture, which encompasses all races within the society.

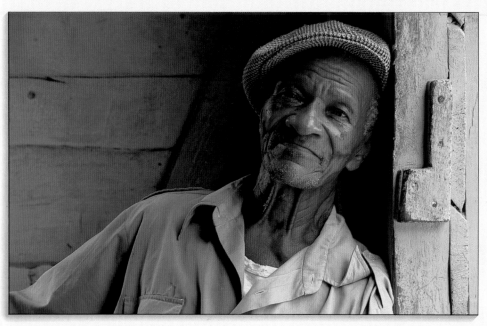

two) depends on situation, mood, topic, listener, level of education and class consciousness. And during the course of one conversation (or better still, one argument) speakers are liable to touch every part of the keyboard.

There is a certain amount of controversy over Creole, its validity, its propriety, whether it is a language or not, or just "bad English." But meanwhile everybody gets on with using it, including many who think that they are talking English all the while. Since the vocabulary is mainly English, people can be vague about where Creole ends and Standard English begins.

Creole is used actively or passively by all the people of Trinidad and Tobago. It is safe to say

Food is another area where T&Ters share and share alike. There is a long-standing Creole cuisine which incorporates African and Amerindian elements with contributions from each of the European cultures (whose cooking is fairly different one from the other).

The Chinese influence has also gone into the standard diet: every self-respecting cook can make chow mein, and delicacies such as wontons have become part of snacking habits.

The American fast-food industry is a feature of the landscape today, and has made all T&Ters (or the children, at any rate) eaters of chicken-and-chips, hot-dogs and hamburgers.

But what makes the diet of Trinidad and Tobago distinctive among Caribbean diets is the addition of the Indian influence. Already mentioned is the preference for rice over what is called the "ground provisions" or root crops. The Indian roti is a real rival to American-style fast-foods, and standard snack-foods are Indian: *channa, kurmah, polorie, bara* (served as "doubles"). Curry is taken very much for granted as one of the everyday options for food preparation and there is a very high level of tolerance for hot pepper. (For details on local cuisine, read "Roti on the Run" on pp. 155–160.)

The merrymakers: There are three tangible areas in which a shared culture has developed – language, food and music. T&Ters, of course, share a great many other institutions which are not

necessarily of their own making but which also constitute common ground – cricket, American soap-operas and the latest in Western fashion.

The subjective characteristics which the people share are, of course, harder to pinpoint. Are there any attitudes, values or behaviors which distinguish Trinidadians from other peoples? Is there a "Trini" personality that cuts across race? Here we have to rely, in part, on the image thrown back by other people's perceptions – how Trinidadians are seen, in particular by their sisters and brothers in the rest of the Caribbean.

<u>Left</u>, a smile from Charlotteville, Tobago. <u>Above</u>, jammin' during Parade of Bands.

There is, first of all, the perception of Trinidadians as a people whose lives are a permanent "fête" (this being the word for T&Ters brand of partying) and, the corollary of this assessment, that they are not terribly serious.

One cannot deny the element of hedonism in their make-up – T&Ters are not in the habit of apologizing for it. It has its source in the cultures of certain of the peoples who settled here, the Africans and the Latin peoples – Spanish, French and Portuguese, and it has been transmitted in the course of time to the whole population.

Trinidad and Tobago is the Caribbean country in which Carnival is the most highly developed. Indeed, there is nothing in the rest of the Caribbean with which to compare the Trinidad and Tobago Carnival. One has to go further afield, to Brazil, for example, another African-Latin culture, to find anything like its peer. Carnival in Trinidad and Tobago is a "season" which lasts for two to three months. It follows hard on the heels of the Christmas "season" which consists of a two-week run-up to Christmas Day peppered with *parang*, office Christmas parties, school Christmas parties and Christmas parties held by every self-respecting organization in Trinidad and Tobago, then a one-week binge stretching from Christmas Day to New Year's Day.

In addition, Trinidad and Tobago has a full calendar of public holidays which, along with weekends, give scope for serious fêting and liming throughout the year. There are no fewer than 15 public holidays in Trinidad and Tobago, mainly long-standing Christian holy days to which have been added Hindu and Muslim days of observance, and dates which commemorate events in the political evolution of the country.

It is perhaps more accurate to say that there are 13 public holidays, because the two days of Carnival on the road have never been declared official holidays. This is a curious carry-over from the colonial era, when the authorities and the upper classes viewed the street festival of the black mob with decided repugnance and would not dream of dignifying it with official recognition. In an 1833 newspaper Carnival was described as: "the shameful violation of the Sabbath by the lower order of the population, who are accustomed at this time of year to wear masks and create disturbances on a Sunday." (*Port-of-Spain Gazette*, January 22, 1833.)

Today, Carnival has active government approval and sponsorship, but Carnival Monday and Tuesday are still officially working days for government employees. Suffice it to say that on these two days the state of the nation is such that it is only the essential services which actually keep on working. Hence there are 15 holidays.

Trinidad and Tobago stop work to celebrate: New Year's Day, Carnival Monday, Carnival Tuesday, Good Friday, Easter Monday, Corpus Christi, Eid-ul-Fitr, Labor Day, Emancipation Day, Independence Day, Republic Day, Divali, Christmas Day and Boxing Day.

Trinis earn the accusation of being unserious partly because they respond to hardship, repression and disaster with a determination to continue enjoying life. In 1970 Trinidad was the stage of a major popular upheaval, the Black Power movement. When the authorities imposed a dusk-to-dawn curfew for a period of time, Trinidadians

gathered indoors before the mandatory hour and held all-night "Curfew fêtes." When the oil bubble burst and the economy crashed, bringing widespread retrenchment, unemployment, inflation, shortages, poverty – all the problems associated with a dire economic slump – a new kind of fête began to be advertised on the characteristic large posters that are always to be seen around the country proclaiming where the upcoming action is: people began to throw "Recession fêtes." Come hell or high water, Trinidad and Tobago will go down fêting. It is one way of coping with existence: who is to say that it is not a valid one?

For another feature of Trini personality which might contribute to a general impression of

unseriousness is the decided irreverence of the Trinidadian, his refusal to be too impressed by anything or anybody, including himself. An important part of the tradition of calypso is what is known as *picong*, or sniping satire against individuals and institutions great or small. In the calypso tent, no personage, no office, no august creation of human beings is sacrosanct. There is no telling where the calypsonian will strike, and he strikes with exquisite humor, on behalf of all – Trinis cheer and egg him on.

This function of the calypsonian has spilled over into the phenomenon of the weekly newspaper. Weeklies proliferate in Trinidad and Tobago today and are read far more avidly than the traditional dailies. A major part of the attraction of the weeklies is their practice of punching holes in public figures.

Constantly exposed to the wider world through the multiple arms of the media, Trinidad and Tobago has the highest density of newspaper production in the English-speaking Caribbean. For a population of just over 1 million, there are three dailies, a fluctuating number of weeklies, and innumerable perodicals put out by political and other organizations. Trinidad has three television channels, plus cable TV and 11 radio stations.

Trinidadians have always done a fair amount of traveling to other countries. Thus there is in the Trinidadians an almost metropolitan sophistication, with some of the negative attributes of metropolitan behavior.

The "Trickidadians": The experience of growing up in a multicultural setting, and the continuous exposure to international currents, make the Trinidadian an eminently flexible person, able to adapt to a variety of situations, able to continually absorb new experiences and learn new roles. Trinis sometimes are referred to as "Trickidadians" by other Caribbean people, for what may be perceived as chameleon behavior.

Their adaptive nature also reveals itself in a great capacity for imitation, and very successful imitation at that. An important aspect of what Carnival is about is the temporary borrowing of another persona – one may be, for two days, a king or queen, a devil, a commando.

It may be said that Trinidadians are entirely too eager to mimic, and that they are a nation of copycats. Amazingly, though, their flair for imitation does not appear rob them of their originality or creativity.

Left, echoes of Asia at Icacos. **Right**, a young Paramin boy.

On a Saturday afternoon walk through the streets of any working-class neighborhood of Port of Spain, you may well run into a steel band rehearsal underway in one of the many tin-roofed, dirt-floored pan yards that dot the city. These sessions are a study in discipline and determination. Though the majority are unable to read music, the 30 to 100 members of a steel bank practice for hours, week after week, without pay, until they have memorized an astonishing repertoire. Steel bands pride themselves on being able to play any kind of music – from Mozart to the Mighty Sparrow.

When the rehearsals are through and the band takes the stage, stand back. This is a revolution in sound. The steel drum, an entirely new concept in musical instrument invented in the last one hundred years and having impact on the musical mainstream, was first fashioned in Trinidad from cast-off oil drums in the 1930s. Only Spree Simon, Ellie Manette and a few other musicians in Port of Spain originally saw their potential as music makers, but now steel bands move young and old, Trinidadians and foreigners, and their sound symbolizes Caribbean culture all over the world.

Music in Trinidad is not a spectator sport. Calypsonians and pan (as steel drums are familiarly known) players do not perform for a politely quiet audience. The risqué lyrics of musician Sparrow, pretending to report the Queen of England's point of view regarding the intruder who entered her bedroom – "he was longer… stronger," are conducive to free-spirited involvement. The insistent rhythms of an impromptu party band, beating dustbins, bottles, and tin cans demand that you participate.

Audience response and involvement is a characteristic of black music all over, and the ultimate source of this aesthetic is Africa. Though no one ethnic group can claim exclusive credit for Trinidad's musical heritage, it is from Africa that much of Trinidad's music springs, evolving over the past 500 years into a spicy international potpourri.

Afro-European synthesis: In Trinidad, as in the rest of the West Indies, music and culture are dominated by an Afro-European synthesis. The first musical result was *parang*, Spanish Christ-

mas carols introduced during Trinidad's days as a Spanish colony (1498–1797). In towns like Lopinot, Arima and Rio Claro, the descendants of the first Spanish-speaking peoples in Trinidad maintain the *parang* tradition, and the continual movement between Trinidad and Venezuela, 10 miles (16 km) away, helps reinforce the tradition. Recently, many young people, searching for their roots have become involved with *parang*, sparking a renaissance of the old tradition. The lyrics and stringed instruments used in *parang* – guitar, cuatro, mandolin – are the Spanish contribution,

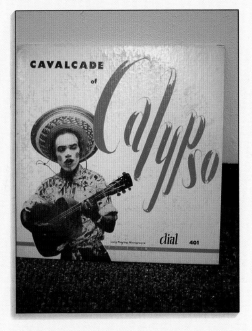

while Africa adds the call-and-response performance style and the incredible rhythms which transform maracas into a solo instrument.

The *parang* season stretches from the last week of November through the first week of January. At night, groups of musicians and singers show up unannounced on friends' and relatives' doorsteps, playing music, singing and asking to be let in. Once admitted, the music continues, African style, until dawn, with breaks only for rum, food and coffee.

Parang is only one of several Afro-European syntheses in Trinidad, the best known of which hybrids is calypso. Like African folk songs, calypsos are repositories of history, reminders of

Preceding pages: pan men play Panorama. **Left,** Carnival musicians. **Right,** an American calypso record from the 1950s.

moral values, and broadcasts of social commentary and news. Calypso combines the African traditions of lively rhythm and an improvised, tell-it-like-it-is attitude sung with European languages, scales and musical instruments.

Steel drums, another Afro-European synthesis, originated when African-style percussion bands, beating brake drums, bottles and other odds and ends, switched to oil drums, which had the potential for sounding more notes. Steel drums are tuned to a chromatic, European scale and, from the beginning, their repertoire has included calypso and classical music. A steel band is an orchestra of many moods. It retains its rhythmic punch when playing calypso, but shimmers like steel when tackling Tchaikovsky.

he had built for his tune and building an entirely new house."

After influences from Africa and Europe, the most important musical traditions come from India. East Indians are now the most populous group in the country, having in the 1970s surpassed those of African descent.

Tassa drumming, which accompanies the street parades of Hosay, a Muslim festival, is one of the most important contributions Indians have made to Trinidadian music. Its rhythms knock down the walls between Muslim and non-Muslim Afro-Trinidadians, who are drawn to the drumming and join the processions through Port of Spain. Many non-Muslims have become excellent tassa drummers, creating an Afro-Indian style of music.

Personal stamp: Purists might recoil at the thought of classical music being played on instruments for which it was never intended, but that doesn't bother Trinidadians. In fact, steel bands have popularized the classics, transforming them into music with mass appeal unmatched in many European countries. Furthermore, when steel bands play classical music, they do not feel bound by the European ideal of faithfulness to the score. Instead, steel band arrangers, like jazz musicians, see the score as a point of departure and strive to put their personal stamp on a composition. Bertie Marshall explains: "I felt that when I was arranging a particular classic that I was imposing myself on the composer. It was like taking the foundation

The common point which made such a synthesis possible is the integral nature of drumming to many religious celebrations and social activities, both in Africa and India. The felt need for drumming is so strong that in the 1880s, when the British banned drumming, Africans and Indians rioted, fighting the police in the streets on several occasions.

Even today, drumming is an integral part of many social activities in Trinidad and Tobago, from the rites of the African Shango religion to boxing matches. When a boxer from the tough Laventille Hills area fought for the Commonweath light-heavyweight crown, his fans of all races were at the ringside, urging their man to victory by singing and beating drums and ringing cowbells.

Pervasive pan: A ride in a Port of Spain taxi is more than a trip across town. Many cab drivers have expensive, almost disco-quality sound systems in their cars, making a ride a musical journey through calypso, steel band, reggae, soul, or the classical traditions of India and Europe. The music never stops. As necessary as a full tank of gas, these contemporary work songs fulfill the same function that the singing of the cane cutters did 100 years ago.

In Trinidad, good musicians can be found in unlikely places. For example, in the United States, insurance agents are not known as a musical lot, but every year in Trinidad the staff and management of the American Life and General Insurance

companies. Jazzman Andy Narrell popularized the steel drum in the United States. More recently, Lionel Richie's "All Night Long" continued the tradition of borrowing from Trinidadian sources. And any time an American advertiser wants to conjure up images of sun, sea and Caribbean romance, steel drums appear on the score.

Calypso's roots: Calypso put Trinidad and Tobago on the world music map, but controversy surrounds its origins and even the word itself. Some argue that the correct name for calypso is *kaiso* – a Hausa word meaning "bravo" and this name is used in Trinidad today alongside calypso. Some trace the word to the French *carrousseaux*, a drinking party, the Spanish *caliso*, a tropical song, or the Carib *carieto*, also a topical song. The

Company draw hundreds to their talent show. In dazzling costumes, they perform the songs and dances of a host of countries: Trinidad, Africa, India, Spain, Mexico, Venezuela and the Caribbean. Obviously, they know about a lot more than underwriting.

Steel bands exist in countless countries around the world – even the US Navy has one. In the 1960s, when Chubby Checker urged his listerners to "limbo lower now; how low can you go?" he meant the limbo, a Trinidadian folk dance that has entered the repertoire of many American dance

Greek goddess Calypso was "she who conceals," and calypso songs excel in shrouding their point in cleverly double-or-triple-edged lyrics.

The situation is complicated by the fact that several ethnic groups in Trinidad had song forms which merged to create calypso. What is clear is that the roots of calypso reach deep into Trinidad's past and that calypso resulted from a synthesis of the songs of several vastly different ethnic groups, although the dominant elements are African.

The slaves that French planters brought in the 1780s carried with them a tradition of improvised song which is the main ingredient in what we now call calypso. From the beginning of slavery in

Left, a *parang* group at practice. **Above**, old folk songs are part of the oral history.

Trinidad and Tobago, slaves were assigned land on which they cultivated their own food in a communal fashion. Gangs competed with one another to accomplish the most, led by singers with such names as Elephant, Trumpeter, and Thunderer, the forerunners of today's Growling Tiger, Lord Invader, Mighty Duke and Black Stalin. The job of the early slave singers was to improvise songs of praise or scorn to inspire their work gangs to surpass all others.

At night, after the day's work was completed, the lead singer of the most productive group exalted his group's achievements and condemned the inadequacies of other gangs.

These songs of self-praise and scorn for others gave rise to the *picong* (or *mépris*) tradition of

the music accompanying the *kalenda*, an acrobatic dance with sticks popular with slaves from Trinidad to New Orleans. The *kalenda* is really a thinly-veiled version of the African martial art of stick fighting, and it is always accompanied by singing. The *kalenda* songs became a major force in Trinidad culture, especially after Emancipation.

Carnival and *kalenda*: The 1838 Emancipation Act changed the country's cultural life forever. No longer confined by slave society, the creativity of the Africans blossomed. They expropriated Carnival, transforming it from a series of bourgeois balls to a raucous street party, enlivened by African drumming and filled with ribald masqueraders mocking high society. Forced to censor their songs and behavior during slavery, the freed

 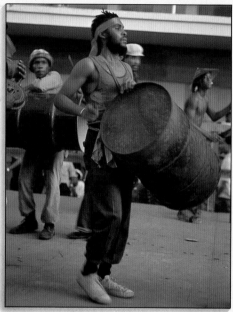

improvised verbal dueling which is a respected talent in calypsonians today. Africa, where songs of ridicule are a powerful mechanism of social control, where royalty never appears in public without its praise singers, is the source of the widely practiced art of extemporizing song texts and music.

In Trinidad these traditions were adapted to local conditions. In the 1780s, a famous French slaveholder, Pierre Bergorrat, held court like a king in a cave near Diego Martin and had slaves sing his praises and damn his enemies in verbal duels. Bergorrat crowned his favorite singer "Gros Jean Master of Kaiso," the first calypso king.

Similar verbal duels were an essential part of

Africans made songs of praise, scorn and social comment a Carnival institution. *Kalenda* and masquerade bands, with their lead singers praising their own members and denigrating the opposition, roamed the streets ready to do verbal and physical battle.

In this period just after Emancipation, Carnival tents of bamboo and thatch were first erected to provide practice space for the neighborhood bands at the beginning of the Carnival season. These tents became local night spots where anyone was free to drop in and observe the performances. The Carnival tents and masquerade bands forged a link between calypso and Carnival that is still strong today.

Freed slaves for the most part remained landless, and therefore flocked to the cities in search of employment. At the same time, the colonial government encouraged immigration from other Caribbean islands, and continued to do so until well into the 20th century. The competition for the necessities of life intensified. People divided themselves along ethnic lines and attempted to hold onto what little they had. Gangs grew out of the need to protect territory to which the inhabitants had no clear title.

The *kalenda* bands institutionalized gang warfare at Carnival. For 40 years, until they were suppressed in the 1880s, bands of stick fighters roamed the streets of Trinidad's cities, especially during Carnival. Every band had its chantwell, or

mans that could put a stick fighter into a state of mind where he would not feel the blows of his opponents. The simple lyrics expressed this magical state of mind and body:

> Rain can't wet me,
> When I have my poui (fighting stick) in my
>   hand.
> Rain can't wet me,
> I advancing on the foe like a roaring lion!

Even in this basic chant, the blended elements of Trinidad and Africa are seen in the singer's invocation of a thoroughly African beast, the lion.

Calypso and Carnival were the centerpieces of this synthesized culture, and Trinidadians guarded them against any attack. In 1859 an American named William Moore had the gall to state pub-

lead singer. When two bands met, their chantwells traded insults in song, anticipating the actual battle. Calypso was stigmatized by its association with violence and the cavalier life-style of those on the margins of society who did not have steady enough employment to be considered working-class. This stigma remained with Carnival until well into this century.

The songs of the chantwells were not mere entertainment but powerful and magical talis-

Left to right, up-beat drummer at Carnival; discarded oil drums were among the first steel pans; and horns add a soca beat to a Carnival band.

licly that calypso, then called cariso, was merely a Trinidadian version of British and American ballads. In the streets outside Moore's hotel, Surisima the Carib, an excellent calypso singer, ridiculed Moore, singing, "Moore, the monkey from America," while a crowd answered, "Tell me wha' you know about we cariso!"

In bringing Moore's business to the streets, Surisima fulfilled an important social function, ridiculing behavior offensive to society. Calypso in one sense is a poor man's newspaper, one-part *New York Times* and one-part *National Enquirer*, extremely important to have in the 19th century when literacy was less widespread. Calypso is a cultural record of events as seen from the perspective of the people, and as a result, the whole course of Trinidad's social and political development can be traced through its calypso songs.

Censoring the newspaper: By the mid-19th century, Trinidad had been a British colony for more than 50 years, but its culture was anything but British. Its language, for example, was not English but Creole, a French-African mixture. The British were convinced of the need to Anglicize the natives for political stability, and Trinidadians, of course, resolved to resist. The struggle lasted more than 40 years.

First, calypso and Carnival came under attack from the press, the police, the church and the courts. The attacks focused on the obscenity and violence associated with them. For years, these

produced a rhythmic percussion like that of drums, but without their carrying power. The skilled art of these instruments has a long history in Africa, Venezuela and the Caribbean.

The purge of the drummers cleared the way for the middle and upper classes to participate in both calypso and Carnival. Businessmen sponsored calypso and Carnival competitions to ensure that bourgeois standards of taste would not be violated. White and mixed race calypsonians appeared in larger numbers than ever before.

Known as jacketmen because they wore jackets as a sign of true status, they were nonetheless ostracized for their ventures into the social milieu of the poor blacks. They fought with sticks (individually, not in gangs), sang calypsos and chased

aspects of calypso and Carnival had been denounced, but now the full power of the state was brought to bear. In 1884 drumming and *kalenda* bands were outlawed, despite the successful efforts of Carnival revelers to police themselves. Troops were called out to enforce the ban. In the 1890s, various masquerade characters were outlawed. Using police and army troops, the government was able to break the back of resistance.

Although masquerade bands continued to be led by calypsonians, the ban on drumming altered the sound of the music itself. Within a few years, tamboo bamboo bands replaced the outlawed drums. Tamboo bamboo consisted of tuned lengths of cured bamboo that when stamped on the ground

women in poor neighborhoods; college students, seeking thrills, hired calypsonians for parties. All this activity tended to increase calypso's acceptance by broadening its audience, but, of course, a price had to be paid. Bourgeois taste became much more important.

Soon the Venezuelan string bands, like those associated with parang, began to accompany the singing of the middle and upper classes. These string bands were eventually replaced by jazz bands in the 1920s. However, poor blacks continued to accompany their calypsos with tamboo bamboo until the steel drums replaced them in the 1930s and '40s.

In this period of rapid change, one event stands

out as a symbol of the transformation of Trinidadian culture. In 1899 the first completely English calypso appeared sung by Norman Le Blanc, a white calypsonian:

Jerningham, the Governor,
He so fas' listening to you.
He so rude listening to you,
To break the laws of the Borough Council.

Following the tradition of the poor man's newspaper, Le Blanc's song reported on the action of the British Governor, Sir Hubert Jerningham, who disbanded the Port of Spain Borough Council in a dispute between the Council and the Governor. Jerningham's unpopular and heavy-handed response offended most Trinidadians, who saw it as further evidence of British arrogance.

marks a milestone in the cultural history of Trinidad. After 100 years of British rule, the English language was finally understood widely enough to be used in a popular song. The Anglicization of Trinidad's culture was succeeding and, from 1899 on, Creole was increasingly replaced by English in calypso, marking the decline of French culture in Trinidad.

Anglophilia: In the early 20th century, the country experienced a wave of Anglophilia inspired by the death of Queen Victoria (widely believed to have abolished slavery). Britain encouraged this feeling as a means to support its involvement in the Boer War and World War I, and the names of many calypsonians of that time – the Duke of Albany and Richard Coeur de Lion, for example

Typically, the calypso does not explain all of the circumstances surrounding Jerningham's action. Instead, the song presupposes certain knowledge and is aimed at people already familiar with the issue. The implicit, almost cryptic quality of the lyrics is common in many African-American traditions, from soul to reggae. A pithy, four-line stanza characterizes the single-tone style of calypso, a style rooted in the verbal duels and acerbic comments of the *kalenda* and masquerade bands and work gangs of the 19th century.

The fact that the song was sung in English

Left, the Police band plays. **Above**, shimmering steel.

– reflect the process of change.

A new style of calypso was also emerging. Known as the double-tone or oratorical style, it featured eight-line stanzas which gave calypsonians more room to present ideas in an explicit, step-by-step fashion, leaving much less to the listeners' interpretation. Chieftain Douglas' "Mourn, Trinidadians, Mourn" is a good example.

Mourn, Trinidadians, mourn
For Queen Victoria who is dead and gone.
Mourn, Trinidadians, mourn
For Queen Victoria who is dead and gone.
It was she who abolished slavery,
And set our forefathers free.
So sing R.I.P.

May she rest in peace eternally.
Mourn, Trinidadians, mourn.

The oratorical style was preferred by jacketmen such as Atilla the Hun, Lord Executor and Chieftain Douglas, men who tried to elevate calypso by avoiding gossip and scandal in favor of more dignified subjects. These men fought long and hard to change the tastes of the common people, who still preferred the older single-tone style with its implicit meanings and spicy flavor.

In a *picong* battle staged early in this century, Lord Executor explained the requirements for success in oratorical calypso to his opponent, Atilla the Hun.

I admire your ambition, you'd like to sing,
But you will never be a kaiso king.

We are ruled with an iron hand.
Class legislation is the order of the land.
We are ruled with an iron hand.
Britain boasts of democracy,
Brotherly love and fraternity,
But British colonists have been ruled in
    perpetual misery.

Jones was nearly indicted for sedition.

By the end of the 1920s, it was clear that the oratorical style would not replace the single-tone style any more than Venezuelan-style string bands would replace tamboo bamboo in street parades. But the style was being converted into a voice for incipient nationalism and opposition to colonial rule. Poor blacks and even the middle class chafed under British dominance and calypsos expressed

To reach such a height without a blemish or
    spot,
You must study Shakespeare, Byron, Milton
    and Scott.
But, I'm afraid I'm casting pearls before swine,
For you'll never inculcate such thoughts divine.
You really got a good intention, but poor
    education.

By the 1920s, Trinidad's taste for things British had begun to go sour. Britain had fought wars for freedom, but the fruits of democracy eluded Trinidadians. In 1920, Patrick Jones, formerly a singer of pro-British songs, sang the following controversial lyrics:

Class legislation is the order of the land.

this discontent. As a result, police spies began to sit in the audiences of calypso performances.

Despite surveillance and repression, the Anglicization of Trinidadian culture was not a complete success. Instead, Trinidad absorbed some British elements, adding to it a mixture that already contained a number of other ingredients. By the 1920s, calypso had proven that it could adapt and continue, capturing a wider audience by expressing the feelings of a majority. Furthermore, some were just beginning to realize how to cash in on calypso's popularity. The commercialization of calypso laid the foundation for its golden years.

Commercial calypso: Between the 1920s and World War II, calypso enjoyed its heyday; gaining both independence from Carnival and international recognition. Businessmen had long perceived the mass appeal and potential financial value of Trinidad's indigenous culture – especially calypso and Carnival, which is in part why they were not completely destroyed in the late 19th century. By sponsoring various competitions, the business community was able to reform and influence calypso and Carnival.

Calypsonians themselves began to set up their own tents independent of masquerade bands, and for the first time charge admission. According to Atilla the Hun, King Fanto was the first calypsonian to do so, but others soon followed. By 1929, syndicates or cooperatives of calypsonians were setting up tents and competing for audiences.

The American band leader Paul Whiteman scored a hit with the calypso "Sly Mongoose" early in the 1920s. In 1929, calypsonian Houdini became the first calypsonian to emigrate to the United States to perform. And by 1934, when Atilla the Hun and Lion left to record for Decca, the prestigious American record label, Trinidadians were beginning to realize the potential of the international market. A crowd of thousands jammed the docks to see them off, and it was obvious that calypso was something Trinidad could be proud of.

In the United States, calypso became the rage. Rudy Vallee and Bing Crosby attended Atilla and Lion's recording session, and Vallee included Lion's "Ugly Woman" in a coast-to-coast NBC

Frequently, the musicians secured the sponsorship of businessmen in return for advertising. The Toddy Syndicate, for example, took its name from a chocolate malt drink. Their jingle in praise of it seemed to herald the transition from folk songs to professional entertainment.

As fewer and fewer Carnival bands could afford the services of the best calypsonians, mass media – radio and records – spread calypso's message at home and abroad, opening up new markets for musicians but changing the nature of their art.

Left, homage to musical history in San Fernando. **Above**, a calypso performance, *circa* 1940.

broadcast. The show was picked up in parts of Trinidad, and thousands crowded around radios and public loudspeakers to hear it.

If you want to be happy and live a king's life,
Never make a pretty woman your wife.
If you want to be happy and live a king's life,
Never make a pretty woman your wife.
All you've got to do is just what I say,
And you'll always be happy and gay.
From a logical point of view,
Always marry a woman uglier than you,

An ugly woman gives you your meals on time,
And will always try to console your mind.
At night when you lie on your cosy bed,

She will coax, caress you and scratch your
  head.
And she will never shame her husband at all,
By exhibiting herself with Peter and Paul.
So from a logical point of view,
Always marry a woman uglier than you.

Upon their return, Atilla and Lion received a hero's welcome. Crowds filled the streets and speeches were made in their praise. Distributors couldn't keep the stores stocked with the records Atilla and Lion recorded abroad. Atilla composed the following to commemorate the tour:

A prophet hath no honor in his own land.
The truth of the proverb I now understand.
When you sing kaiso in Trinidad,
You are a vagabond and everything that's bad.

those current in popular music from the United States, tamboo bamboo bands were out, but string and wind bands, rooted in Trinidad's Spanish tradition, were in, as were jazz bands featuring trumpets, clarinets and saxophones. Also popular were ensembles derived from minstrel bands, consisting of piano, bass, woodwinds and violin.

The folk tradition of calypso was also moving in several different directions, developing new forms of instrumental music, since so many of the calypsonians had become professional entertainers. Radio and the record industry distributed jazz and other American popular music in Trinidad as well as calypso, and the calypso folk tradition accommodated itself to the influence of mass media. Masquerade bands parading through the

In your native land, you are a hooligan.
In New York, you are an artiste and a
  gentleman,
For instance, take the Lion and me
Having dinner with Rudy Vallee.

Lords, Kings, Lions and Dictators: The first wave of professional calypsonians became known as the Old Brigade, and included singers such as Growling Tiger, Lord Beginner, Atilla the Hun, King Radio, the Roaring Lion, Lord Pretender and the Mighty Dictator.

King Radio's "Matilda" was a hit in the United States, but the influence of the recording industry was a mixed blessing. Since it required that the emsembles accompanying the songs resemble

streets at Carnival began to use jazz instruments such as the trumpet, clarinet and trombone which had already proven themselves to have the carrying power necessary for marching bands in the streets of New Orleans. So the Trinidadian folk tradition absorbed elements of the Afro-American jazz and marching band tradition in the United States as well.

Though most Trinidadians could not afford these instruments, and tamboo bamboo bands and Venezuelan string and wind ensembles continued to provide music for calypso and masquerade bands in the countryside, these ensembles could not satisfy the tastes of the growing urban working-class. In the urban areas, tamboo bamboo bands were replaced by percussion bands which transformed the flotsam of industrial society – brake linings, trash cans, paint cans and biscuit tins – into musical instruments. These cast-off metal products had more carrying power than the tamboo bamboo.

Tin pan alley: The development of the new percussion bands was a collective process in which many participated without necessarily knowing where their innovations would lead. Bertie Marshall describes the scene outside a slaughter house during the butchers' lunch break: "They [the butchers] used to get into the old train carriages opposite the abbatoir and beat out a rhythm from old brake drums which they got from Kehela's scrapyard. They also used their knives,

When drums were not available, substitutes were improvised from tin kettles, salt boxes and almost anything else. When drums were banned in 1884, tamboo bamboo bands replaced them. The ancestors of all these percussion bands are the ensembles of drums, bells and rattles that dominate West African music, but what is interesting is that the percussion bands of the 1930s satisfied the African preference for percussion by using the materials available in an industrial environment.

At first, the metal objects in these new bands produced only rhythm, and bugles were used to provide a melodic line. But by chance musicians discovered that the metal tins they had been beating on could produce more than one tone if the surfaces struck were shaped in certain ways.

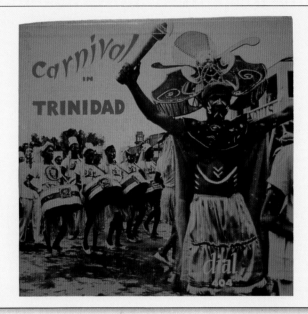

pieces of steel which all butchers carried, and oil tins into which they put their ends of meat…"

By the late 1930s, the new percussion ensembles were popular with masquerade bands at Carnival. In 1937 newspapers reported on the "terrific din set up by the clanking pieces of tin" in these bands. But in fact this was not an entirely new development, for percussion of one kind or another had been part of Carnival since the emancipation of the slaves.

Nineteenth-century *kalenda* bands marched to the beating of drums and the blowing of horns.

Left and **above**, the music of Trinidad and Tobago flooded America after World War II.

They began a process of experimentation, heating and pounding out the metal containers to produce several notes. A few claim to have been the first to discover the possibility of producing several notes from a metal tin and the conflicting claims probably indicate that a folk process was in operation, with many moving in the same direction at the same time.

Gradually, musicians began to use oil drums because their larger surfaces could accommodate more notes than paint cans and biscuit tins. From this process of experimentation, the steel drum was born. It was during the golden years of calypso that the steel bands started on the rocky road to international acclaim. Since steel bands were musically and socially the direct descendants of *kalenda* bands, at first they were perceived as lower class gangs and not musical ensembles. It is, perhaps, the great effort to overcome the stigma of its social origins which has caused many steel bands to develop a broad musical repertoire.

Steel band struggle: Although calypso flourished in the '30s and '40s, opposition to it had far from disappeared. The Theatre and Dance Halls Ordinance of 1934 gave the English officers within the police the power to censor song texts, and the Colonial Secretary had the right to ban any record. Furthermore, calypsonians had to obtain licenses to sing in tents. In 1937, King Radio expressed the calypsonian's reaction to this repression.

and commercial value made calypso difficult to suppress, and so the colonial government fought a holding action, muzzling calypsonians to keep them in line. A.A. Cipriani and other nationalist leaders rose to their defense, and the battle raged back and forth. But the calypsonians' achievements became harder and harder to deny, especially after World War II brought the Yankee soldiers to Trinidad in large numbers.

The Yankee dollar: World War II affected Trinidad deeply although no fighting took place there, and most Trinidadians who enlisted never saw combat. The War ushered in a new era – one characterized by the influence of the Yankee dollar. The colonial government signed a 99-year lease granting the US government land for a

They want to licen' me foot,
They no want me to walk.
They want to licen' me mouth
They no want me to talk

Calypso was still under attack, but it held its own by expressing the experience of a colonized nation. The period between 1920 and World War II had seen disillusionment with British concepts of democracy, the growth of militant trade unionism in response to the Great Depression, and the growth of a Trinidadian middle class anxious to lead the country to independence.

As always, calypso accurately reflected the feelings of the people and the British could not ignore its ridicule of their failures. Its mass appeal

major naval base at Chaguaramas, in northwestern Trinidad. The US Airforce and Army also built bases, and work there provided jobs paying 10 or 20 times the 40 cents an hour previously earned by the average laborer. The influx of thousands of soldiers fueled the economy and in particular the entertainment industry.

The number of calypsonians grew as nightclubs opened to entertain the troops: in the words of Chieftain Douglas, "all the little ducks are bathing." Steel bands suddenly found themselves in demand to entertain soldiers at the bases, and wartime shortages of imported goods, including musical instruments, increased their popularity. The more foreigners at the bases expressed their enthusiasm for calypso and steel band, the harder it was for the detractors of Trinidad's indigenous culture to be heard. This wartime boost was important, especially for the calypsonian, as during the war the record industry experienced a slump worldwide and in Trinidad, all Carnival and street processions were banned.

Soon a boom mentality set in, and for a while everyone was happy. It did not take long, however, before the presence of so many soldiers with money to spend caused an increase in prostitution and promiscuity. Trinidadians of all social classes were shocked by the sudden increase in light-skinned, fatherless children, and Trinidadian men felt their wives and daughters had betrayed them.

Invader's 1943 "Rum and Coca Cola" summed the difficulties faced by Trinidadians in another respect. The song became one of the greatest calypso hits of all time, but Invader had to fight to receive any financial rewards. Americans on the bases had heard the tune and taken it back to the States, where the calypso craze of the '30s was not forgotten. The Andrews Sisters then released a cover version which sold more than four million copies around the world, paying Invader nothing since he had no copyright.

Invader sued and almost lost, but Lion and Atilla had fortunately included the lyrics in a copyrighted booklet of calypso lyrics before the Andrews Sisters released their version. In the end, Invader prevailed, narrowly avoiding the plight of many calypsonians: fame and poverty.

it all up:

Since the Yankees come to Trinidad,
They have the young girls going mad.
The girls say they treat them nice,
And they give them a better price.

They buy rum and Coca Cola.
Go down Point Cumana.
Both mother and daughter
Working for the Yankee dollar.

But "Rum and Coca Cola" came to symbolize

Left, an American book taught calypso dance steps. Above, vacationers enjoy their version of island life.

The Young Brigade: By 1945 a new challenge faced the Old Brigade. During the war, calypso's foreign audience had grown but, although these fans loved the music, lyrics referring to local Trinidadian events were irrelevant to them. To increase calypso's share of the international market, calypsonians and their musicians needed to change their lyrics, gain greater technical facility with Western musical instruments, and incorporate more elements of American jazz and popular music. American GIs and Trinidad's middle and upper class, who supported calypso in nightclubs and tents, wanted entertainment, not political satire and news reports.

A new generation of singers rose to meet the

demand, de-emphasizing *picong*, satire and politics in favor of sex and fantasy, describing events not linked to a particular time or place. Killer's "Green Fowl," which concerns itself with a priapic rooster, is a good example of the prevailing style.

These more commercially oriented calypsonians called themselves the Young Brigade and, although the style was new, in many ways they continued calypso traditions, adopting names symbolizing power: Lord Kitchener, Mighty Killer, Mighty Spoiler, Mighty Dictator and Lord Wonder. Lord Melody was one of a few exceptions, and his name may reflect the importance of expanded melodic techniques in the new style.

The Young Brigade announced their intentions:
Everybody knows or have been told

That the young bound to conquer the old.
So tell them we are not afraid.
We're going to mash up the Old Brigade.

To defend themselves from the challengers, the Old Brigade began to monopolize the tents, refusing to allow the Young Brigade to sing. But these measures were soon circumvented, as the Young Brigade opened their own tent, and, having gained a forum, soon became the people's choice. In 1945 Lion released "Mary Ann," which showed his acceptance of the new concern with love and sex. "Mary Ann" has since become a calypso classic.

Calypso's audience broadened, and the music became more of a national art, something with which all classes and ethnic groups identified. It was a creative, experimental period, and musical styles proliferated, as calypsonians incorporated elements of many ethnic styles. Killer sang "Grinding Massala," using Indian rhythms and speech patterns, and Kitchener's "Double Ten" celebrated the founding of Sun Yat Sen's republican China with Chinese rhythms.

Like Trinidad itself, these songs represent a synthesis of elements drawn from Africa, Europe and Asia. A new national consciousness had begun to emerge, and the indigenous culture of Trinidad gained new respect.

National recognition: There was such joy after the Allies' victory in Europe that the creativity of the Trinidadian people could hardly be restrained. And as a part of the 1946 Carnival, a special concert was organized to showcase steel drums. In the first solo concert of steel drum music, Winston Spree Simon demonstrated the versatility of pans, which now had up to 14 notes apiece. He selected a program which included all kinds of music: a hymn, "I am a Warrior"; Schubert's "Ave Maria"; Kitchener's "Tie Tongue Mopsy"; and "God Save the King." Legend has it that at the sound of the last, the Governor sprang to attention, popping all the buttons on his coat.

That the Governor and other dignitaries attended at all was a sign of new respect and a major advance for steel band. The concert proved that pans could play even classical music, but skeptics were not completely silenced by the applause Simon received. An aura of violence was still associated with steel band, and this had to be removed before they could gain final acceptance. As in the clean-up of 19th-century Carnival and calypso, the government took the lead.

In 1948, the Trinidad and Tobago Youth Council asked the government to establish a committee to identify the causes of violence among the steel bands. This committee, chaired by Canon Farquhar, made several landmark recommendations, including the creation of the Trinidad and Tobago Steelbandmen's Association to provide a mechanism for resolving conflicts and promoting steel band music. The Association was successful and soon radio stations began to broadcast programs of steel band music.

Changing attitudes toward steel band and calypso were part of a general shift in support of indigenous culture. The British Government had come to realize that the colony would not be so forever and that it would be best to prepare Trinidadians to rule themselves. It had become increasingly clear to middle-class Trinidadians that they could not hope to lead the common people to independence if they didn't respect their culture.

Acclaim: In 1948 Beryl McBurnie opened the Little Carib Theatre to promote indigenous music and dance. There were other dance groups at the time, but they presented ballet and other European forms. The very first performance by McBurnie's company was attended by prominent people in government, in church, academia and the press. The movers and shakers in Trinidadian society had finally decided that the limbo, bongo, bel air and other local dances were art, along with calypso and steel band.

Within a few years, Dr Eric Williams, who later led Trinidad to independence, was praising

and its versions of "The Bells of St Mary" and Chopin's "Nocturne in E-Flat" were well received. Still, some were amazed that illiterate musicians could perform these compositions. Significantly, Casablanca's members were of African, East Indian and Venezuelan descent – a cross-section of the Trinidadian nation, struggling for identity through pan.

Soon steel bands were being asked to perform abroad. In 1951 the Trinidad and Tobago All Steel Percussion Orchestra, comprising the best musicians from all bands, represented Trinidad at the Festival of Britain. At first, skepticism and sarcasm greeted "the tin can boys from Trinidad" but British audiences went wild when they heard the music. The success of this tour opened the door

McBurnie, saying that "the Little Carib Theatre teaches our people that their hands are capable to build a temple and nothing can hide its nobility." Things had changed since the days when, as one observer noticed, "(all) one had to do... (was) to walk the streets with a pan stick in his pocket and a beebop cap on his head to be recognized as a curse to our society."

In 1950, the first national steel band competition was held in Trinidad, and in the same year, the "Concerto in Pan" was held at the prestigious Trinidad Turf Club. Casablanca performed last

Left, basic rhythms. **Above**, horns add a modern beat.

for steel band at home. They now became indispensable at national festivals, dances, parties, weddings and even church services.

Calypso campaign: During the 1950s, the bands grew larger and larger, as more pans were added for sound and melodic possibility. Eventually, steel bands rivaled the costumes of the masqueraders as a Carnival attraction. Pan became a national obsession. Bands were formed in the best schools, and people of every race and class joined in a celebration of their common culture. The tremendous popularity of steel bands during the '50s created the opportunity for calypsonians to compose specifically for pans.

In 1950, Atilla the Hun, one of the Old Brigade

who never gave up political calypso, was elected to the Trinidad Legislative Council. In true calypso fashion, Atilla ran his campaign from the calypso tents and, apparently, his songs were more eloquent than the speeches of his opponent. Once elected, Atilla attacked the 1934 Ordinance which required calypsonians to secure licenses to sing and forced them to submit their songs to the censors. Never before had the voice of the calypsonian been heard in legislative debate. In the same year, the colonial government created a new post, Director of Dance in the Ministry of Education, specifically for Beryl McBurnie. This was the first time performers had been elected or appointed officials in government.

Calypso tents were now packed with mainly

Sparrow sings: The most successful Trinidadian musician of the 1950s was a newcomer to the Young Brigade, the Mighty Sparrow. The record industry was working hard to supply enough records to meet the international demand, and the pressure was on calypsonians to develop greater marketability. Sparrow, with his music talent and business acumen, responded to the challenge more successfully than most.

In the mid-1950s, long-playing records began to compete with 45s, and recording artists needed to produce an LP regularly to remain popular. Calypsonians could no longer rely on the stock of about 50 melodies that had served so well up to that point. Sparrow produced a new album every year and has continued to do so since 1957. The

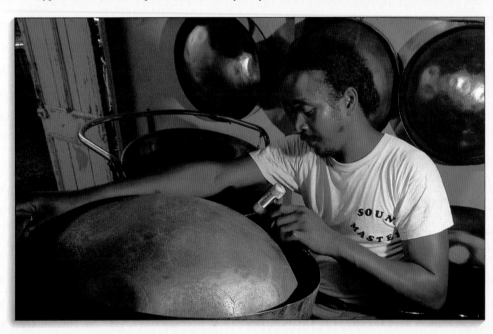

white audiences: Trinidadians, tourists and G.I.s, continuing a trend begun in the mid-1940s. In the United States and England, many nightclubs now featured calypso, and Kitchener, of the Young Brigade, lived and performed in England, though he sent a steady stream of records back home.

Kitchener was one of several calypsonians who migrated to England or the United States to pursue their careers, a trend begun in the 1920s and '30s reflecting both the international appeal of calypso and the limitations of its Trinidadian market. The Mighty Terror sang at the Young Brigade's tent until 1953, when he left for England to sing in the nightclubs, and in 1957, was crowned Calypso King of Britain.

singles released by other artists were no match for Sparrow's LPs, which he produced at his own record company while at the same time maintaining his own calypso tent outside Port of Spain.

In 1956, Sparrow's "Jean and Dinah" won the first calypso king competition sponsored by the Carnival Development Committee (CDC), a government agency which still sponsors competitions for calypsonians, steel bands and masqueraders. Established after Eric Williams' People's National Movement won the 1956 elections and formed a government, the CDC's support of Trinidadian culture meant official recognition by government.

But even professional calypsonians with international reputations continued to produce songs on local topics, encouraged by the progress Trinidad was making toward independence. Although these did not sell well abroad, at home they still carried weight. And in 1958, Striker won the Road March with "Don't Blame the PNM."

Fame, no fortune: In 1962, Trinidad finally gained its independence under a government led by Williams, whose People's National Movement has so far enjoyed 24 years in power. Calypsonians helped elect the new government with songs such as the following by the Mighty Wrangler:

Who built the schools in George Street for us?
Nobody but the Doctor (Williams).
And the North Coast road going Las Cuevas?
Nobody but the Doctor.

for them. And the government did continue to send calypso and steel bands abroad to represent the country, and to organize competitions like Best Village, and Panorama, a competition for steel bands.

But once-a-year competitions and engagements at occasional international festivals are not enough to sustain performers. Too many talented calypsonians and panmen returned home to obscurity, after a moment of fame on a foreign stage, without the ongoing support necessary to sustain interest: something which could be as simple as playing the music on the government-controlled radio. Even today, Trinidadian radio inundates listeners with calypso and steel band during the Carnival season, but for the rest of the year they comprise

And the Housing Scheme we have in Morvant?
Nobody but the Doctor.
And who do you think the bridge we call the Flyover?
Nobody but the Doctor.

Like most Trinidadians, calypsonians had high hopes for the new government, believing it would reverse years of underdevelopment and colonialism. Specifically, calypsonians and panmen hoped that Williams' new government would actively promote indigenous music and dance, in keeping with Williams' stated appreciation and respect

Left, pounding out a pan. **Above**, a carnival band bring music to life.

less than a fourth of the programming.

Scrunting and sex: In the 1960s disillusionment set in as Trinidadians realized that, despite independence, pan and calypso were still scrunting – struggling for survival. And dissatisfaction with the results of the cultural policies of the Williams government paralleled disappointment with economic and social conditions.

For example, dark-skinned black people could not secure employment as tellers in banks, despite the fact that their Prime Minister was a black himself! It seemed that institutionalized discrimination was being tolerated, even condoned. Several calypsos addressed to the Williams government voiced this discontent with the status quo.

Although the Young Brigade concentrated on lighter themes, political calypsos never really died out in Trinidad. They resurfaced in the mid-'50s, as independence neared, and with the discontent of the '60s, there was again incentive to speak out. But still relationships between men and women and especially the sexuality at Carnival were the most popular themes.

By the mid-1960s, the CDC's calypso competition had fallen into a predictable pattern. The calypsonian sang a serious song of social commentary and a lighter, catchy tune good for wining (moving your hips) through the streets. Some calypsonians began to complain, and the Mighty Chalkdust put his complaints into a song.

If you want to win the crown,

time. In 1975, Maestro expressed the feelings of many locals:

Masqueraders bawling
I hear them complaining.
Steel bands playing too slow.
They say they want tempo.
Playing too much classic.
Too much Yankee music.
Straying from the beat,
And they leaving we in heat.

To recapture their proper place in Carnival, steel bands needed to amplify their sound and ride on flatbed trucks to move through the streets alongside the mas' players. They also needed to expand their repertoire to include more rhythmic music, and in the late '80s there were indications

Sing about wine, women, and song.
Sing about your neighbor's wife.
Sing about your own sex life.

Panorama: Steel bands went into decline for a variety of reasons during the 1970s. They lost touch with the masquerade bands, no longer concentrating on providing music for them, and became totally absorbed in the CDC's Panorama competition, becoming so large and so expensive that they priced themselves out of the masquerade market.

They also began to play more and more classical music, perhaps in an effort to legitimate themselves. In any case, classical music does not go over well in the streets of Trinidad at Carnival

that many bands were moving in these directions.

From the late '60s on, while pan has been having its problems, calypso has moved in a very different direction. Absorbing the impact of the Civil Rights and Black Power movements from the United States, it has responded to the deteriorating economic conditions of the working-class. Out of the social ferment of 1970 and the Black Power movement came a new generation of calypsonians: Mighty Chalkdust, Black Stalin, Explainer and Valentino, who once again concentrated on political calypso. In the '60s, calypsonians like Sparrow, Kitchener and Terror sang a range of material which included political calypsos as but one aspect of their repertoire.

108

A schoolteacher speaks: The most important of these new calypsonians is the Mighty Chalkdust, who dominated the '70s as far as political calypso is concerned and continues to be influential. A schoolteacher, Chalkie's lyrics are always well-constructed as, according to Chalkdust, the calypsonian is "...not only an articulator of the population, he is also a fount of public opinion. He expresses the mood of the people, the beliefs of the people. He is a mouthpiece of the people."

Chalkdust's first album, released on the 10th-anniversary of independence, included "We're Ten Years Old" and "Our Cultural Heritage" wherein he encourages the use of indigenous food and music, and wonders why the Port of Spain Hilton serves American, not Trinidadian, food.

case to the people through a calypso which pointed out that other Ministry employees worked part-time in journalism, the military, the theater and other occupations. The Ministry dropped its case.

In 1989, Chalkdust won his fourth National Calypso Monarch title with, arguably, the most bitingly humorous political critique of his long career. "Driver Wanted" casts the leadership of the NAR coalition government in the role of the driver of a fine new Maxi-Taxi – the mid-size vans that transport thousands of commuters each day. Fitted with every conceivable accessory, the swerving, bouncing and erratically braking vehicle frightens everyone from school children to civil servants along the road.

Calypso Rose: The women's movement of the

The album also includes "Ah 'Fraid Karl," a reference to the Attorney-General, Karl Hudson-Phillips, who could charge dissidents with sedition and had, in fact, jailed government opponents under the State of Emergency declared after the Black Power rebellion of 1970.

Chalkdust was never indicted, but various attempts were made to muzzle him. In 1969, the Ministry of Education tried to prevent him from singing because, as a Ministry employee, he needed its permission before accepting outside employment. In true calypso fashion, Chalkdust took his

'70s also had a major effect on calypso. Until then, calypso had been a male bastion but, when women claimed their right to sing, the Calypso King Competition was renamed the Monarch Competition, reflecting the fact that it now included women. In 1978, the competition was won by a woman for the first time. Calypso Rose had already won the Road March title in 1977, and then captured it again in 1978. Since Rose's success, the ranks of female calypsonians continue to grow with performers like Singing Francine, Twiggy and others.

Soca fever: While politics gave lyrical focus to calypso, another force, the international pop music industry, was about to change its sound. As pro-

<u>Left</u>, the Mighty Sparrow at Panorama 1986.
<u>Above</u>, floor show, Carnival 1986.

fessional entertainers, calypsonians have always had to accommodate changes in the music industry. And in the late 1970s, a new style of calypso emerged which shook calypso to its foundations.

Called soca, the new style is much more than a simple blend of soul music and calypso, as its name seems to suggest. The new style incorporates technological advances that changed the nature of the pop music industry in the United States as well. By the mid-1970s, the US music industry was producing dance music heavily dependent on synthesizers and advanced production techniques.

The disco craze was only one manifestation of the changes going on. As electronic gadgetry grew in sophistication, musicians depended more

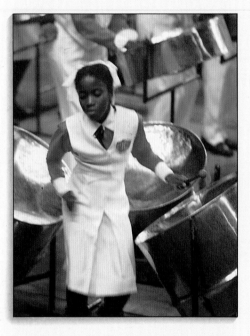

and more heavily on arrangers and producers to create the final product. Faced with the need to expand their share of the pop music market, calypsonians began to incorporate the new technology into their recordings. The result was soca.

Soca features furious tempos, funky bass lines, hot horn sections with plenty of riffs, independent rhythms on bass drum and snare, and assorted percussion to fill out the sound. Soca is an electronic big band assembled in the studio to create sounds nearly impossible to duplicate on stage.

The first to master the new style were Maestro and Lord Short (now Ras Shorty I). Although he was a creator of the new style, Maestro seemed to have mixed feelings about its effect on calypso.

I did not intend to lose control,
To promote my calypso through soul,
But it seems it is the only way
To survive in this business today.

In any case, soca shows no signs of yielding ground. The rage of the '80s in Trinidad, every calypsonian must pay homage to the style or face failure in the marketplace. The demand for soca has placed new burdens on the calypsonian, who must travel to New York or other recording centers because Trinidad lacks adequate facilities to manufacture the new sound. In "Soca Fever," Sparrow almost makes catching the disease a patriotic duty:

You say you could wave the flag.
You say you could wine.
You used to boast and brag.
You could do the grind.
But this is a new era.

People getting soca fever.
If you want to make it sister,
wine faster, grind faster.

Don't drop the tempo.
Don't stop the tempo.
Keep up the tempo.

Soca includes songs on all topics: sex, politics, religion and more. Penguin's "Freedom Road" celebrates the government's decision to declare August 1 a national holiday, Emancipation Day, in honor of the day the slaves were freed. Blue Boy's "Soca Baptist" landed him in hot water with the Spiritual Baptists, who felt they were being mocked. Sparrow's "Vanessa" reveals that the poor man's newspaper is still in circulation. In it he takes Vanessa Williams, the first black Miss America, to task for appearing nude in a magazine, but Sparrow softens his criticism at the end of the song:

Sexy Vanessa, I hope you understand
I love your pictures and I'm still your greatest
*   fan.*
I'm upset with you, and jealous I'll admit.
Not for what you do
But because it's not me you do it with.

Today, calypso lives in soca. Soca is not the end of calypso, as some have feared, but another creative avenue for the mind of the calypsonian. Through it, calypsonians continue to express themselves on the range of issues that concern them – unemployment, inflation, politics, scandal, or sex.

Left, never too young to soca. Right, not just a male province.

Each year, two days before Ash Wednesday, the citizens of Trinidad and Tobago pay homage to the gods of antiquity and their ancestors, follow their muses and the promptings of the flesh, and celebrate life in an explosive and beautiful two-day bacchanal. The climax to a year-long build up of energy, creativity and ingenuity, Carnival is the ultimate expression of the spirit of Trinidad and Tobago. A kaleidoscopic display of musical and artistic creativity, of high-spirited camaraderie and hedonistic beauty, it opens the floodgates to unbridled self-expression, a spectacle of color, movement, music, sensuality and the lavish joy in life which is a hallmark of Trinidad and Tobago.

In many ways the epitome of the country and certainly the primary attraction for most visitors, Carnival meshes all fibers of Trinidadian life – the histories of Europe, Africa, Asia and oppression, calypso and steel band, imaginative and applied artistry – into a dazzling parade. Every year, race, color and idea bind together without prejudice, united in the potent force of a truly universal festival.

A national party: Carnival in Trinidad and Tobago, or more specifically in Port of Spain, is different and better than any other major pre-Lenten celebration. An integral part of both the black and the white communities for over 200 years, today Carnival knows no boundaries, as children and grandmothers, rich and poor, Indian, black, white and Creole merge in bands and at fêtes in a warm-hearted, exuberant national party.

Even a stranger is drawn in, if willing to soca and wine with the Trinis, and there is nothing that makes a Trinidadian prouder or more hospitable than a foreigner eager to immerse himself in Carnival. It's a feast for the eyes that can be thoroughly enjoyed as a spectator sport, but for an unforgettable cultural experience you must "play mas" – masquerade – with the locals.

Carnival is a highly organized festivity: you don't just take to the streets in last year's costume – except perhaps during Jour Ouvert, popularly known as "joovay." There are about 15 or 20 clubs whose sole purpose is to plan, execute and display Carnival costumes.

Called by the names of their main designers – Peter Minshall, Raoul Garib, Hart, Carvalho and Stephen Lee Heung are a few of the better-known – these clubs are open to all for a price, but contain a foundation of loyal members who every year wear the costumes of their band, marching together through the streets. Each band has a King and Queen representing that year's theme – Callaloo, Wonders of Buccoo Reef, Rat Race, Bright Africa and Ye Saga of Merrie England are a few – and each band of 500 to 2,000 people is divided into smaller groups dressed as variations on the theme.

The best way to join a band is to know a local who'll help you buy one of his band's costumes, which generally cost about US$100. If you don't know anyone in a band, check with your hotel or TIDCO (tourist office): they often reserve costumes in certain bands.

Wrongly condemned as an excuse for public drunkenness and sensuality, Carnival is, in fact, an exhibition and competition of the best in music and in design. Its influence is felt in the country throughout the coming year.

Months in the making: Preparation for Carnival commences on Ash Wednesday, right after Shrove Tuesday, the last day of the preceding year's Carnival. Even as band leaders relax from the physical and mental exhaustion of the months before, they engage in a post mortem of the recent past. What's done is done, but of vital importance is the theme for next year. Should they play on a historical, fantastical, social, natural, traditional, or cultural theme?

Subject decided, research begins. Historical and ethnic themes require authenticity, and every idea needs multiple inspiration. Libraries and encyclopedias provide impetus, and pictorials are consulted for period and regional costumes. Some leaders explore the structures of the society to be portrayed, and elements of their customs and lifestyle are selected after careful consideration.

There are brainstorming meetings, supplemented by liberal supplies of food and drink, and quiet moments of introspection and imagination, yielding fantastic ideas for the drawing board. The designers then start to produce the enticing drawings displayed as advertisement and blueprint later on. Starting in January, the drawings are hung outside the clubhouses of each band, to be ogled and discussed by potential masqueraders.

Preceding pages: a Carnival band; a Queen of Kiddies' Carnival; a bacchanal; mobile music; two youthful Kings; Dionysus. **Left**, the face of Carnival.

Raw materials must be decided upon, trips are made abroad for bulk purchases of brilliant lamés, velvets, satins, imitation fabrics of animal prints, plastic materials, beads, feathers and the multifarious components of elaborate costume making. Several band organizers and designers choose to use local materials like wood, seeds, leaves, straw, shells and locally manufactured cottons, wire, foam, steel, fiberglass and the other articles of construction.

Years ago, before the advent of mechanical devices now commonplace – plastic molding machines and the numerous ready-made articles of decoration – there was the laborious task of making clay molds for papier mâché forms. Today this has given way to mass production of

pulled, or motorized. Devices such as small wheels and ball bearings placed to take the peripheral weight are used to facilitate easy carriage.

Numerous man-hours are dedicated to the production of these masterpieces. The end result is fussed over, admired and considered a birth experience by those who labored. During the first appearance on stage during the week preceding Carnival, when the costumes are judged in their categories, thousands crowd the Savannah to get a preview of the splendor of the mas'.

As the Kings and Queens prepare to cross the open stage in front of the grandstands crammed with party-goers, members of rival bands – aficionados not content to sit in the stands and await the presentations and the direct supporters of the

lightweight forms for head pieces and props, as well as molded parts for the bases of large costumes. The costume-making commences many months before Carnival, and each step requires ingenuity and meticulousness, as the final result can be a complete failure if there is a lack of engineering and construction skill to make ideas practical reality.

For the large and often cumbersome costumes of the Kings, Queens, and principal characters in the bands, a great deal of experience is necessary to construct a costume light, mobile and effective from a theatrical standpoint. Some could indeed be called floats, except they are carried by one individual and are not permitted to be pushed,

contestants – crowd the holding bay where all the real-life drama takes place. Excitement mounts as they line up and speculation as to the finalists and eventual winners runs rampant. Light-hearted banter is exchanged, some comments building confidence while others even in jest make for uncertainty.

The determination to win and the excitement of living the fantasy inspires each character to take to the stage with zest and flourish. The sight of these magnificent structures animated by their human motivators glittering under the lights as their movements synchronize with the calypso or soca is overwhelming.

On the night of Dimanche Gras, the Sunday

before the actual days of Carnival, the finals are held and the King and Queen of Carnival chosen amidst fanfare and boisterous applause. The new monarchs will lead their respective bands with great pride and prestige.

Saturnalia and slaves: Carnival traces its origin into ancient times, to the Phoenician celebrations of Dionysus, god of wine, vegetation, new growth and survival, and to the Roman Saturnalias honoring the god of birth and renewal. The Latin *carne levare*, to take away flesh, is said to be the root of the word carnival, which is an orgy of the senses preceding the Lenten period in Christianity when the things of the flesh are prohibited.

During the Roman conquest of Europe, these pagan rituals underwent several changes in order

Haiti. The slaves brought the Christian custom of celebrating Christmas on into Ash Wednesday, with a mixture of African rites and traditions.

At first the slaves' festivals were modest, and although there was fragmentation among the slaves according to the variety of African "nations," the commonality of their belief systems, secret societies and rites of passage allowed for shared celebration of ancestral dramas.

The slaves' fervor in music and dancing made up for the rusticity and makeshift quality of their disguises, and they ventured outside their areas grouped in bands accompanied by *batonniers* – stick men, ritual protectors and champions of their bands. In 18th- and 19th-century Trinidad and Tobago, Carnival masquerade became a means

to survive, and ended by being the exclusive province of the aristocracy. In this way the pantheistic customs survived the rigid decrees of the Middle Ages, when all celebrations that could be termed Bacchanalian or Saturnalian were licentious abominations akin to devilry. By 1783, when Trinidad and Tobago experienced an influx of French settlers, Carnival was well established among the French as an aristocratic celebration.

With the French settlers came slaves acquired in other Caribbean islands, especially the French-speaking lands of Martinique, Guadeloupe and

Left, carnival children. Right, time-out from the "Sombrero" band.

for the slaves to relieve frustration with their lot, as within the confines of Carnival they could mimic and buffoon the styles and habits of their masters.

Meantime, the grand balls of masquing (dressing up) and revelry continued on a more sumptuous scale in the plantation houses. By the early 19th century the elite had taken their masquing into the streets in their own fashion, traveling in carriages from estate party to estate party.

After Emancipation, the days of Carnival became days of protest as ex-slave revelers threatened the ruling class and their towns in a number of ways. The lit torches of the Canboulay procession (from the French *cannes brulées*, burning

canes) endangered the wooden buildings of Port of Spain as much as the lascivious playacting compromised the morality of the aristocracy, and the government feared the violence of the *batonniers* who accompanied every band. Attempts were made to outlaw Carnival but the French aristocracy, also at odds with the now-British government, intervened to protect their own right to revelry.

In the years since, each new group of immigrants has added to the festival, and old traditions – that of *jamet*, or the "underworld" carnival, of throwing powder and streamers, of Canboulay and *kalenda* – have faded. The nightly parties at friends' homes have given way to enormous public fêtes, and the steel band and calypso competitions are as much a focus of attention as the masquing. Carnival is now a thoroughly modern event, but one with a deep underpinning of history and ritual.

Fêtes and finals: Carnival officially begins at about 4am Monday morning, and the Sunday night before, Dimanche Gras, is one of great anticipation and revelry. Fêtes are held everywhere in Port of Spain: in private homes, hotels, bars, clubs and restaurants.

Most parties are huge, with hundreds of people dancing en masse. Though Jour Ouvert is the official start to Carnival, it is by no means the beginning of the fun. Excitement has been building for days as various calypso and steel band competitions are held nightly for the preceding couple of weeks, particularly at the Spektakula Forum. The new calypsos for that year have been introduced at shows and on the radio, and by Carnival all are thoroughly familiar, and music lovers have chosen their personal favorites for "Road March."

Starting the Friday before Carnival, there are nightly finals for King and Queen titles, steel bands and calypsonians at the Queen's Park Savannah grandstands. Huge fêtes with live and taped music are held at the big hotels and are open to all for a small entrance fee. They're as full of locals as they are of foreign guests. The pounding music begins around 5pm each night and plays without let-up until 3am in the morning both Friday and Saturday nights, and with the exuberant fun of Kiddie's Carnival on Saturday, by Sunday evening the mood is already one of joyful exhaustion.

But there's something about rum punch, beer

and the rhythmic soca that lends a second wind, and by midnight Sunday the city is ready to explode. As the great countdown begins, players gather in costume at special band headquarters.

Joovay jump-up: Around 4am, strong coffee and tea, coconut sweet bread, sandwiches and other goodies counteract the liquor heads and provide sustenance for the next few hours. The cocks crow to herald the break of the day – Jour Ouvert – but thousands won't hear for the din of music and the shouts of laughter as players spill out into the streets, thronging behind their favorite steel band, or more traditional brass bands and drums accompanied by folk instruments.

The costumes of *joovay* are at once less elaborate and more satirical than the colorful masquer-

ades of Monday and Tuesday. For joovay morning, revelers don homemade costumes satirizing the political and social scene, or illustrating grotesque historical figures who have been a part of Carnival since its beginnings. The music makers are more rhythmical and more primitive than the amplified, electrified groups who lead mainstream Carnival, beating tin cans, brake pans and glass bottles with spoons and knives. Human rivers move slowly through the crepuscular light, jumping, gyrating and shuffling along in varying states of consciousness, all driven by the relentless drumming.

Traditionally called "Ole Mas," short for Old Masquerade, in this parade anything goes, as

<u>Left</u>, playing Ole Mas'. <u>Right</u>, a West Indian Hiawatha.

costumes are personal statements ranging from the horrendous and bizarre to the lewd and jocular. There are grown men in oversized diapers sucking on a baby's bottle full of rum, male politicians with a penchant for their aunt's underwear, caricatures of prominent figures and, most popular, those who have smeared their bodies with mud and axle grease from head to toe. These last delight in hugging onlookers, especially those dressed in white.

Today the traditional costumes of sweepers, tailors, doctors, pierrot grenades and *pai banan* (banana straw) characters rarely appear in the city. These familiar figures of days gone by used to rouse sleeping families with their falsetto speeches as they rushed into open yards offering their services for a small fee. The traditional players have given way to organized bands similar to the fancy dress bands, with well-thought-out themes and more colorful costumes than players of yore. The masqueraders and observers dance through the streets until morning, when it's time to get ready for the first Road March "jump up." Do try to get some sleep between 7am and 11am, because the Road March is seven or eight hours of feverish dancing and singing.

Jams and judges: Around 10 or 11am the larger bands begin to converge in costume at their clubhouses to prepare for the street parade – the heart of modern Carnival. There are four judging stands throughout the city, including Independence Square and the main and final one at the Savannah, and each of the bands must pass by each judging area. Routes have been set long in advance to prevent, as far as possible, traffic jams, but the main streets are packed from noon until dusk with parading bands. The bands are simply enormous parties led and inspired by the ear-splitting calypsos coming from accompanying flatbed trucks full of musicians and huge speakers.

When bands cross paths there are calypso battles, with each group of musicians trying to drown the other out with its favorite tune. Eventually one or two songs win out and one is chosen Road March, People's Choice. Until then a variety of songs inspires the revelers to dance for hours on end in the blistering sun.

Though Port of Spain is the center of Carnival activity and the locus for all the big competitions, San Fernando, Scarborough and other smaller towns have their own parades and fêtes, often preferred by veterans who can no longer stomach the incessant music and crowds of Port of Spain.

Right, all that glisters is Carnival.

To the casual onlooker at a Trinidadian Hosay (or Hussein) festival, it may seem incredible that what is being celebrated is a procession of deep mourning observed by Shiite Muslims in places such as Iran, Iraq, Lebanon and India. To those Muslims of the Eastern hemisphere, Hosay in Trinidad would seem a travesty of what in essence should reflect the grief, pain and martyrdom of Hussein and his brother Hassan, grandsons of the prophet Mohammed, during the famous Jihad (Holy War) at Kerbela in long-ago Persia. But in the one hundred years since Indian Muslims first arrived on these islands, there has been much intermingling of the European, African and Indian cultures.

Hosay: What the hundreds of onlookers in the present-day procession see, then, is the effect of a century of indigenization. Since 1884, when the Hussein Festival was first observed in Trinidad, there has been a painstaking attempt to keep the tradition alive, and until about 40 years ago, Hosay retained its aura of mourning, with austere rituals brought over intact from the subcontinent.

Now the holy men who used to walk on beds of fire (some Hindus and Africans among them) no longer perform their daring feats, and gone also are the old women who sang the *maseehahs*, wailing dirges, behind the *tadjahs* (Ta'ziyeh), the elaborate and beautiful replicas of Hussein's tomb. But fire-eating is still seen on occasion, as is *banaithi*, the dance where whirling sticks of fire make eerie patterns against the night sky.

The massacre of Hussein and his party was said to have taken place on Ashura, the 10th day of the Muharram month, in AD 680. The modern celebration takes place around the month of Muharram, and could occur twice within the Roman year, with different areas observing each occasion. The most popular processions are between February and March in towns such as St James, Curepe, Tunapuna, Couva and Cedros.

After 40 days of fasting, abstinence and prayers, devotees begin the festival with Flag Night. Flags of various sizes and colors are carried through the streets to symbolise the beginning of the battle of Kerbela, and are then ceremoniously placed on a mud and wattle dais amidst burning incense.

Preceding pages: Phagwa procession. **Left,** Hosay 1904; and **right,** Hosay today, with tassa drummers.

The following night, two small tadjahs, minareted tombs made of bamboo with brightly-colored tissue, tinfoil, crepe paper, mirrors and coconut leis, are carried on the heads of the dancers through the streets, accompanied by drums. At midnight there is symbolic contact, with dancers gently touching tadjahs with their heads and against each other.

The highlight, however, is on the third night, when the large tadjahs are produced to gasps of delight. These incredible works of art have borrowed from the Carnival tradition over the years,

with a lavish flair blending Eastern designs with local innovations. Six or so feet tall, and covered with glitter and color, the tadjahs emerge from different yards to pass through streets bearing great significance for the descendants of those who brought the tradition. In the area of St James, for example, in close proximity are Lucknow, Hyderabad and Delhi streets, named after main centers of Muslim observance in India.

In addition to the tadjahs, the two moons representing Hussein and Hassan are carried by specially trained dancers. These large crescent-shaped structures 6 feet across and 3 feet at their highest point (2 meters by 1) are usually red, to represent the decapitation of Hussein, and green or blue, for the poisoning of Hassan. Sharp blades are inserted between the thickly ruched material, projecting upward for a spiked effect that gives the sign of battle.

The dancers whirl in a stately dance of the brothers' triumph over death as they move with one foot raised onto the ball and the other flat. The moons are placed over one shoulder with the pole end stuck in the *shamotee* at the waist. The dancers appear mesmerized, and they enthrall the crowd. At midnight, there is a ritual kissing of the two moons as the dancers come together with great ceremony and allow the moons to meet as if in brotherly embrace. This brings cheers of delight from the onlookers and perhaps twinges of pain for devotees.

The excitement of the festival is further moti-

They perform in a circle drawn around them in the street, and go through their symbolic battle.

The climax of Hosay comes as the tadjahs and moons are wheeled into the streets the following day for their last procession to the sea. There they are ceremoniously cast after prayers and offerings have been made.

Phagwa: Spring is not known as a season in Trinidad and Tobago, but the vernal equinox doesn't go unnoticed among people whose traditions are based in lands far away. The Hindu festival of Phagwa celebrates this event as it does in India each year, heralding the Hindu New Year with gay abandonment.

Around the full moon in March, elaborate rituals celebrate the triumph of light over darkness

vated by the pulsating drums of the *tassa* players. These drummers are quite famous and attract great crowds who follow behind them dancing. Among the drummers are some of African descent, drawn to tassa as they are to the African tamboo bamboo and steel drum. The younger generation of this Carnival-oriented society see this later part of the procession as a time to jump up and make merry. The West African attitude of jovial celebration at funeral rites surely influences their actions.

Another attraction is the dancing of the *ghadka*. A stick fight/dance between two men, each holding in one hand a stick about 3 feet (1 meter) long and a small leather pouch as a shield in the other.

and good over evil. As with other religious festivals in Trinidad, a Carnival spirit has gradually pervaded the festivities as a wider population becomes involved. Phagwa is not confined to Hindus, but includes anyone wishing to participate.

Bonfires are lit to symbolize the destruction of Holika, the evil sister of King Hiranya Kashipu, and before the actual day of Phagwa, there are chowtal singing competitions. Chowtal is a mixture of the religious and the secular, and the competitions display the skills of singers who perform both devotional songs and local compositions. The latter being influenced by calypso, borrowing from its extemporaneous artistry. Special instruments such as the *dholak* (a small skin drum), *kartals, mageeras* and *janjs* (cymbals) accompany the Hindi singing and dancing.

One of the more popular rituals is the spraying of the *abeer* powder, a red vegetable dye made into a bright fuchsia liquid and sprayed over observer and devotee alike. It creates a messy but colorful scene as clothes take on a tie-dyed effect and skin and hair are drenched. Recently other colors have been introduced as the festival becomes more secular, including the innovations of other ethnic and religious groups.

Dancing is a central part of Phagwa, and varies in style, tending toward the suggestive dances of Carnival but with a good admixture of East Indian movements.

There are re-enactments of the legend of Holika

mers and dancing revelers who blend the African, calypso and East Indian rhythms and fashions.

Divali: On one October night Trinidad sparkles with the light of thousands of tiny flames and electric bulbs, strung through trees and across buildings, wherever a light can be affixed. The festival of Deepa Divali (pronounced "Duwali") is a national religious holiday celebrated by hundreds of thousands of Hindus. This they do to honor Lakshmi, goddess of light, beauty, riches and love, she who was the wife of Vishnu and who was born out of the churning of the great ocean. For her they make elaborate advance preparations, offering pujas – sacrifices and prayers – in her name.

Weeks before the actual event, men cut long

during the day as bands similar to those of Carnival participate in competitions set up at several locations throughout the island. All manner of oriental costumes, many of them white, are worn with crowns, garlands, jewelry and flowers, and various characters from the epic drama are portrayed. The plays are more or less light-hearted, as befitting a celebration of rebirth.

A recent innovation has been the use of trucks as floats on which pretty girls are paraded as queens in fine vestments accompanied by drum-

bamboo poles to build structures in village parks, school and *mandir* (temple) grounds, and their own yards. On these structures are placed tiny clay pots called *deyas*, filled with coconut oil and a cotton wick. The *deyas* are also placed along the walls of verandahs and fences, on the ground and all possible vantage points.

On the evening of Divali the *deyas* are lit and tended during the night. They illuminate the way for the visitation of Lakshmi and must not be allowed to go out before the appointed hour. Modern embellishments have also made their mark on this festival as, more and more, electricity is used to augment the lights of the *deyas*. Strings of colored bulbs are used in the manner of

Left, Phagwa celebrants covered with abeer powder. Above: Phagwa dancers, left; and right, *deyas* lit for Divali.

Christmas lights, and, needless to say, this phenomenon brings thousands of non-Hindus out to visit the various well-illuminated public places.

Prior to the night of lights there are shows and pageants where Divali Queens are chosen amidst oriental dancing and singing. Special song competitions highlight local composers and feature star Indian musicians. It is a joyous occasion, and everyone tries to emulate the qualities of Lakshmi, spreading peace and goodwill.

Greetings and gifts are exchanged, with food being the traditional gift, and there is the usual abundance provided in private homes, shared liberally with non-Indian neighbors and friends and the less fortunate in the vicinity. A special sacrificial meal of *parsad*, a doughy concoction

none of the diverse ethnic groups (except the near extinct Caribs) in Trinidad and Tobago are indigenous to the country. But this changed in the late 1990s and became a specifically asian event.

March 30 is Spiritual Baptist Liberation Day, but to avoid adding another official non-working day to the calendar, Republic Day (September 24) was dropped. African religions are rarely acknowledged, so the day is celebrated with verve and jubilation. Religious rituals at the National Stadium in Port of Spain include bell ringing and enthusiastic hand clapping.

The Tobago Heritage Festival is held during the second week of July, it attempts to keep Tobago's indigenous traditions alive, such as folk tales and superstitions, courtship codes, old time

of flour, sugar, milk and raisins, provides an offering to the gods.

The import of Divali, the triumph of good over evil, has meaning on a national scale and so public prayer services are held for thousands, with the celebrants including clergy from other denominations who come together with their Hindu brothers and sisters to celebrate a shared ideal.

Indian Arrival Day: Traditional Arrival Day was re-named Indian Arrival Day, it is observed on May 30 and replaced the Roman Catholic holiday of Whit Monday. Arrival Day was initially inspired by the 150th anniversary of the coming of East Indian indentured labourers to Trinidad. The concept was broadened to include all races, since

weddings, the saraka feast and wakes. This is Tobago's version of Trinidad's Best Village event (*see* page 138). The Festival attracts many visitors.

Eid-ul-Fitr: The new moon of Ramadan marks the observance of Eid-ul-Fitr, the Muslim New Year, occurring around the month of June. It is a national holiday, but cannot be predicted exactly, as the actual day depends on the sighting of the new moon by a holy Imam. Official announcement comes after this sighting, and what follows is an obligatory day of feasting to break the month-long daylight fast. The usual visit to the *masjids* (mosques) for prayers and thanksgiving is followed by almsgiving to the poor in the form of money and items of food and clothing.

Observers prepare sumptuous dinners and large gatherings of all ethnic groups are invited to celebrate the occasion with Muslim friends. The traditional dish of *sawine* is a requisite on the menu. A rich, tantalizing concoction of fine vermicelli boiled in milk, it contains raisins, sugar and chopped almonds.Throughout the country there is an air of spiritual renewal as Muslims and non-Muslims alike honor and respect Allah, wishing each other *Assalam O Alaikum.*

Emancipation Day: For those of African descent – almost half of Trinidad and Tobago's population – the newly designated Emancipation Day on August 1 is of special significance.

The day commences with an all-night vigil and includes church services, street processions past

ain, and on September 24, 1976, became a Republic. The fact that both these events were achieved in a peaceful and civilized manner is enough to warrant enthusiastic revelry and thanksgiving. Republic Day on September 24 has been replaced by Shouter Baptist Liberation Day celebrated on the Sunday closest to the 24th.

Throughout the country the various villages and towns celebrate with sporting events, dances, concerts, exhibitions and seaside activities. Among the highlights is the military parade at the Queen's Park Savannah on the morning of August 31.

The emphasis here is on pomp, tradition and ceremony, without the ominous overtones of military might. The Regiment, Coast Guard, Police and Fire Services lead a host of voluntary

historic landmarks, addresses by dignitaries and an evening of shows with a torchlight procession to the National Stadium.

The event marks the achievements of the sons and daughters of slavery as well as reflecting on sobering thoughts of man's inhumanity to man, and honors the multiple contributions of the black people to Trinidad and Tobago's rich culture.

Independence and Republic Days: In August and September, Trinidad and Tobago also celebrate two patriotic milestones. On August 31, 1962, the country gained its independence from Great Brit-

organizations in an impressive parade observed by thousands.

The Police and Regiment Bands arrange popular calypsos into military marches and, at the end of the parade everyone traditionally follows the band through the streets to the Barracks, like children behind the legendary Pied Piper of Hamelin, only this time in Carnival style.

That evening, the National Awards Ceremony is held, when local awards like Chaconia, Hummingbird, and the highest Trinity Cross are bestowed on recipients who have made outstanding contributions to the nation.

Before the secular observances take place, however, official and unofficial church services are

Left, a Best Village dance performance. **Above**, traditional dances on the beach.

arranged. A great achievement in this multi-ethnic, multi-religious country is the meeting of the various denominations as a mark of national unity.

During the first week of September, the annual Folk Fair brings a big taste of rural life and customs to Port of Spain. Over a hundred booths are established to display and sell handcrafted items, locally made works of art and clothing, and traditional cuisine, sweetmeats and beverages. Traditional music and dance performances encourage the air of festivity. One week later, around September 15, the Family Fair opens for a 10-day run. The emphasis is on family participation in art and food displays, lectures and nightly shows. On the Sunday nearest the 24th, a parade of historical floats climaxes the weeks of celebration.

Best Village: The Prime Minister's Best Village Trophy Competition began in 1963 as a small handicrafts fair, and has since expanded to five categories involving numerous towns and villages and hundreds of participants.

An effort to encourage and record the folk arts and local pride, Best Village is a month-long series of small contests culminating in a feast of music, dance, drama and song. Under the guidance of elders, young people create shows on various themes pertaining to life in the village, using traditional dances, music, storytelling, and song.

It is in this setting that the African-French *bele* and *pique* are seen alongside the Hispanic *parang* and the African-derived *bongo* and *saraka* dances.

Stick fighters are in full cry as they dance the *kalenda*, while others choose to excite their audiences with spectacular dances like the *limbo*.

Rich folk music is sung by choirs including grandparents, grandchildren and everyone in between. Whole families participate in some villages. Around 32 villages reach the finals, presenting their shows at the grandstand of the Queen's Park Savannah, where at other times Carnival Kings and Queens display their arts.

In addition to the theatrical presentations, in the fall there are also craft shows, concerts, and a beauty pageant called "La Reine Rivée," patois for "The Queen Arrives," with costumes approaching the elaborateness of Carnival.

The limbo: Along with steel drum music, visitors to the Caribbean associate the limbo with the sexy abandon of a tropical island. But the limbo as we know it today – exhibitionistic, glittery, sensual – is not the limbo of a bygone era, when men (and women) symbolically passed below the bar of the underworld to rise toward light and deliverance, representing the path the soul of the deceased takes in its journey to the next world.

The limbo was a way of assisting, encouraging and guiding the soul into the world of the ancestors. With much singing, clapping, drumming and ribald taunts, each dancer shimmied under the length of wood, held by two supporters who allowed the dancers to go no lower than hip level.

Now, of course, expert limbo dancers can easily clear 6 inches (15 cm) with a soda pop bottle as the standard measure, and the limbo is more a display of athletic prowess than an acknowledgement of another world.

Easter sports events: The Tobago Easter Goat and Crab Races are amongst the more bizarre traditions in Trinidad and Tobago. During the long Easter weekend, Tobago is flooded with vacationers from abroad and from the bigger island, and when people aren't on the beaches, they go to the races.

The crab races are a riot of fun as the owners spur their crustaceans on to the finish line. But crabs are wont to be wayward, and gamblers take their losses seriously as the crabs make their usual sideways movements. The goat races, featuring large sanaan goats, are not so popular. Those who do come are assured of a full crowd of spectators, especially children, who delight in the butting antics of some furious and rebellious goats.

Left, a participant in the last Discovery Day celebration, now replaced by Emancipation Day. **Right**, the Independence Day parade.

Its native Indian inhabitants called it Ieri, "land of the hummingbird," and even today Trinidad and Tobago is home to about 15 different species of these brilliant fluttering creatures, amongst them over 420 species of birds, 617 species of butterfly, and a wealth of flora and fauna matched only by the South American continent itself. Unlike other Caribbean islands, which are volcanic in origin, as recently as 11,000 years ago Trinidad and Tobago were a part of the coast of Venezuela. Thus despite their small size, the two islands are graced with a diversity of environment which includes four mountain ranges, four major rivers, mangrove swamps, tropical savannahs, numerous streams and small rivers, and a marine environment influenced by Venezuela's Orinoco River as well as the Atlantic and Caribbean.

The rich rain forest: The Northern Range of Trinidad is only minutes away from downtown Port of Spain, yet is almost primeval in its unspoiled richness of life. In the dry season, December to March, the cultivated valleys and slopes glow with the deep orange blossoms of the tall mountain immortelle tree, *erythrina micropteryx*, introduced to the islands over 150 years ago as shade for cocoa and coffee trees.

At the end of the dry season, around the beginning of April, the yellow poui tree blooms spectacularly, its leaves dropping to present the yellow flowers in solitary splendor. It is a popular belief that the rains arrive with the third burst of blooms.

In the early months of the year, when forest trees are in flower, honeycreepers and hummingbirds, as well as other nectar feeders, are visible in profusion. This is nesting time for many of these birds. With the coming of the rains in April and May and thus the seeding of the numerous grasses, finches and other seed-eaters bring forth their young while there is an abundance of food.

In August the hundreds of butterflies that have lain dormant during the dry season emerge to paint the islands in vibrant colors. In short, there is no bad time for nature-watching in Trinidad and Tobago and every season offers its particular beauties and wonders.

Victorian nature retreat: There is perhaps no bet-

ter place to begin than at the Asa Wright Nature Centre and Lodge, in the Northern Range's Arima Valley 1,200 feet (370 meters) above sea level. The winding, mountainous drive from Port of Spain to Asa Wright climbs through a tropical rain forest comprised of several tiers of lush vegetation.

The uppermost tier is that of the spreading branches of trees growing up to 150 feet (50 meters). Orchids, bromeliads called "wild pines," and liana vines grow in profusion on their trunks and limbs and even telephone wires. Various

species of ferns, heliconias and philodendrons are common below, and huge stands of bamboo and small mossy waterfalls line the road.

Along the way are glimpses of sliding-roofed sheds used for drying coffee on the big estates; Asa Wright was originally a private cocoa, coffee and citrus plantation, and is surrounded by working estates.

The center still retains the aura of a civilized country retreat. At the end of a bumpy driveway is the "Great House," constructed in 1906–08 as a Victorian estate house and perched over a forest valley alive with birds and butterflies.

Since the turn of the century the 197-acre (80-hectare) estate has changed hands a couple of

Preceding pages: seining at Castara; an elusive parrot. **Left**, oilbirds roosting in a Northern Range cave. **Right**, a mountain immortelle in the Northern Range is garlanded with epiphytes.

times, ending up in 1947, in the possession of Dr Newcome Wright and his Icelandic-born wife Asa, who came to Trinidad from England.

In 1950, Dr William Beebe, a famous explorer and naturalist, established the Tropical Research Station of the New York Zoological Society in the Arima Valley close to the Wright's property. Dr Beebe and many of the research staff at Simla, as it was called after a sister station in India, befriended the Wrights, and it was not long before the Wrights were host to visiting naturalists and bird-watchers who wished to take advantage of the rich flora and fauna of the valley.

Among these early visitors was Donald Eckelberry, an American bird artist and naturalist who came to paint the species of the Arima

Little devils of eternal darkness: One of the most renowned species to be observed at Asa Wright is the *steatornis caripensis*, or nocturnal oilbird. In hiking distance of the world's most accessible colony of these birds, Asa Wright offers a rare opportunity to see them in their strange natural habitat.

Guacharos – "he who cries," to the Spanish-speaking people of South America – oilbirds are known in French patois as diablotin, or "little devils," and Jon Lindblad, the famous nature photographer, described them as "the bird of eternal darkness." The medium-brown oilbird can be as much as 15 inches (38 cm) long with a wing span of 3 feet (1 meter) and lives deep in caves, leaving only at night to forage for food in

Valley. It was Eckelberry who, after the death of Mr Wright, persuaded Asa to sell the property in order that a non-profit trust might be established to preserve that part of the Valley in perpetuity as a conservation, study and recreation area.

And thus in October 1967 the Asa Wright Nature Centre, the first of its kind in the Caribbean, was established. Following the closing of Simla in 1970, the Society donated its property – 230 acres (93 hectares) and several small buildings – to the Asa Wright Centre as a gift. Today researchers and students of natural history are housed at Simla, while amateur naturalists can stay in the colonial comfort of the Great House and enjoy nature hikes guided by experts.

the forest. The only known nocturnal fruit-eating bird, oilbirds prefer the fruit of the palm, laurel and incense trees, which they pull off in flight.

The young birds become very fat on this diet, and at about 70 days are approximately 2 lbs (1 kg): one and a half times the weight of the adult bird. The Amerindians and other inhabitants of Caribe chose this time – mid June – to collect the fat young nestlings, which they then boiled and rendered for their oil, which never went rancid. They ate the flesh and used the oil for lamps and torches – hence the name.

In Trinidad there are eight known nesting colonies of oilbirds: some in the limestone caves of the Northern Range, and some on Huevos, an offshore island. The colony at Asa Wright has increased from 22 birds in 1967 to 170 in 1980, but since then there has been some migration to a more remote cave. In December 1985, during the annual Christmas bird count, only 48 birds were recorded at the cave near the Centre. However, since limits were placed on the number of visitors to the interior of the cave, the population has stabilized at about 100 birds in 1989. A cave about 10 miles east of the Arima Valley, at Cumaca, also supports a large oilbird colony.

High level birds: For a chance to see such birds as the yellow-legged thrush, the nightingale thrush and the blue-capped tanager, which only appear at elevations above 2,000 feet (650 meters), the intrepid must make an all-day trip to the heights of

species including red-bellied macaws and orange-winged parrots which feed on the fruit of the Moriche palms growing abundantly at the fringes of the grasslands. The drooping fronds of that palm also provide a home for the uncommon fork-tailed palm swift and, during the rainy season, the rare white-tailed golden-throated hummingbird may be found nesting in the shrubbery of the savannah.

The area is interesting for its plant life as well. Sundew, or *drossera capilaris*, a kind of Venus-flytrap, covers the surface of the grasslands, waiting for insects upon which to feed. These plants have little competition here because a layer of impervious clay just beneath the surface keeps the soil very dry in the dry season and water-logged

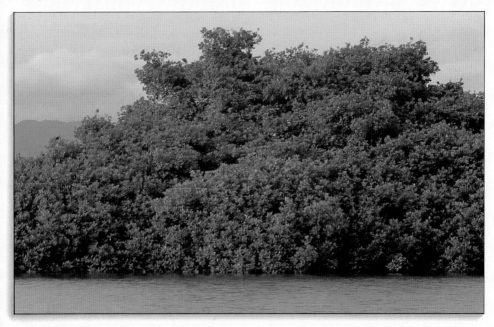

Aripo, slightly south and east of Asa Wright. With luck, you might also see a poui or piping guan, the only bird endemic to Trinidad and Tobago but very rarely seen even here.

A less strenuous trip is one to the Aripo Savannah and the Arima Forest, which may provide sightings of up to 70 species. A short stop at the Government Cattle farm on the road to the savannah can yield a glimpse of the savannah hawk, the southern lapwing and flocks of jacanas. In the savannah are many colorful and easily spotted

Left, the tangled roots of mangrove trees in Nariva Swamp. **Above**, Scarlet ibises roosting at dusk, Caroni.

when the rains come. Because its soil is therefore very poor in nutrients, many of the plants found there must capture insects for food.

Flying sunset: Another fertile area for bird-watching is the Caroni Swamp, where the white, red and black mangrove trees sink their spidery support roots into the brackish water. The entire swamp comprises over 12,000 acres (4,800 hectares) of mangrove forests, tidal lagoons and marshlands which are subject to daily tidal fluctuations. It is in the Caroni Swamp that the beautiful scarlet ibis, one of Trinidad and Tobago's national birds, makes its home.

In flocks that number up to 100, the scarlet birds Trinidadians call flamingos fly in from all directions and perch on the top branches of the mangrove islands. During the rainy season as many as 12,000 birds will arrive in the twilight hours, but in the earlier part of the year, there are fewer, as most migrate to the mainland to nest.

While you are waiting to see the birds you might want to drop a line, as the swamp waters are thick with fish, including tarpon, grouper, snook, salmon and mangrove snapper, and 100-lbs (45-kg) groupers are not a rarity. The blue crabs used in crab and *callaloo*, a popular souplike dish, and in curried crab and dumplings, traditional in Tobago, are also caught in the mangrove swamps of both islands. During their egg-laying season, hundreds of crabs leave the mangroves and "run" to the sea to release their eggs.

Tobago's tropical pheasant: For most of T&T's wildlife, life hasn't changed for thousands of years. So with the cocrico, or rufous-vented chachalaca, a turkey or pheasant-like bird indigenous to Tobago, and one of the Republic's national birds.

Hurricane Flora struck Tobago in September of 1963, inflicting severe damage on the elevated forests. With their original habitat destroyed, many birds and beasts, including the cocrico, had to seek food in the lowlands close to the human areas of habitation.

Aware of the birds' predicament, Eleanor Alefounder, the owner of the 400-acre (160-hectare) Grafton Estate on Tobago's north shore,

along with a number of other residents, began to feed the birds regularly. By 1970, the cocricos at the Grafton feeding tables were so tame that they could be fed from the hand. In a short while, racquet-tailed blue-crowned motmots began to swoop from their perches to take bits of cheese from between the fingers of visitors as well.

The verandah of the Grafton Great House became a popular rendezvous for visitors to Tobago, who joined the birds at teatime. Nowhere else could cocricos, motmots, red-crowned woodpeckers, blue-gray tanagers and many more species be seen and photographed at such short range and such leisure. Since the death of Mrs Alefounder the house has fallen into disrepair and the bird feedings have become less of a tradition, but it is still possible to see a goodly number hovering around the estate.

Sea birds and sanctuaries: In 1968, Charles Turpin, proprietor of Charlotteville Estate in northeast Tobago, presented a group of islands known as the Melvilles to the Government of Trinidad and Tobago for the establishment of a wildlife sanctuary. The largest of these islands, which are situated about a half mile off the northeast coast of Tobago, is the 72-acre (30-hectare) St Giles Island. Thick masses of cacti, low shrubs and deciduous trees cover the steep slopes which rise from the water to a height of 350 feet (107 meters).

Owing largely to their inaccessibility to man and other beasts, these islands are able to support one of the most important seabird breeding grounds in the southern West Indies. Noddy terns, brown boobies, the beautiful red-billed white tropic birds, red-footed boobies, magnificent frigate birds and other species feed and nest on the rocky shores.

Little Tobago, or Bird of Paradise Island, is another fertile place for bird watchers, situated about one mile off the northeast coast of Tobago near the village of Speyside. In 1909, Sir William Ingram, a former owner of the island, became concerned about the threat posed to Birds of Paradise in their native New Guinea by trade in their plumes. So he arranged to have 48 greater Birds of Paradise captured in the Aru Islands off the coast of New Guinea and released on Little Tobago. The birds, along with their new home, were presented to the Government in 1928 as a sanctuary by Sir William's heirs.

Hurricane Flora ravished this smaller island as well, and since then there has been a constant decline in the number of Birds of Paradise. Nevertheless, Little Tobago offers the naturalist and nature photographer an opportunity to see at least 58 other species, including brown boobies, brown noddies, sooty and bridled terns, laughing gulls, Audubon shearwaters and red-billed tropic birds.

From March to July, sooty terns and brown noddies nest in considerable numbers on the 2-acre (1-hectare) rock called Soldado. Six miles (10 km) west of the extreme western point of Trinidad, only 7 miles (11 km) from Venezuela, Soldado was declared a sanctuary in 1934. Brown pelicans, royal terns, sandwich terns and brown boobies are also to be found there, attracted by the abundant fish around the island. Boats may be hired for fishing around Soldado, take care not to pass the rock into Venezuela's territorial waters.

A gilded cage: In rural areas it is not uncommon to see, during open season, caged birds hanging from the eaves of houses. Songbirds especially

are often shot by farmers who consider them pests, and consequently are confined to forested areas and rarely seen.

Relatively more common are brocket deer, white-collared peccary or quenk, tattoo or nine-banded armadillo, manicou or oppossum, and two members of the rodent family – the agouti, and the lappe or paca.

Aficionados maintain packs of well-trained beagle hounds to hunt with, but mongrels can be taught the job as well. Though protected by law, manicou, tamandua, ocelot and other mammals are much sought-after by gourmets and are sold for as much as twice the price of the best tender-loin. From October to March these are all in season and can be hunted with a permit. Hiking in

are enticed into cages with decoys and "laglue" or "laglee," a honey-like substance made from the sap of the breadfruit tree. As a result, there has been a steady decline in the songbird population, and the Twa-twa, or large-billed seed finch; the Chickichong, or lesser seed finch; and the Tobago picoplat, or variable seedeater, are in great peril.

Elusive forest dwellers: The forests of Trinidad and Tobago also abound in mammals, the most beautiful of which is arguably the ocelot, *felis pardalis*. Although fully protected by law, ocelots

Trinidad and Tobago has a rich and colorful birdlife including: the cocroni at <u>far left</u>; and the motmot, <u>above left</u>.

the Forest Reserves is another good way to see wild animals.

Below the water: The swamps and rivers and streams of Trinidad and Tobago support over 70 species of fish. Perhaps the most familiar is *Lebistes reticulatus*, or the guppy. Locals called the prolific wild guppy "millions"; they appear everywhere, even in roadside drains and provide the welcome service of eating mosquitoes. Selective breeding has also produced the beautiful delta-tailed varieties so popular for aquariums.

Many streams and rivers are replete with the South American plated catfish, *hoplosternum littorale*, dubbed cascadura or cascadoo. Considered a delicacy despite its external covering of bony plates, legend has it that anyone who eats of the cascadoo must return to Trinidad to rest his bones.

Another common freshwater fish is the *tilapia mossambica*, a species of the cichlid family which was imported from Africa with a view to farming the fish in ponds and rice paddies. While experiments were being conducted in the Government fish farms at Valsayn, several slippery specimens escaped into the nearby St Joseph river and found their way to Caroni Swamp.

Now, 25 years later, *tilapia* is so plentiful in the shallower parts of the swamp that it has become a popular sport to catch 1 to 1½-lbs (up to 3 kg) fish with bare hands. Unfortunately, however, the *tilapia* has destroyed the feeding grounds of the

These rivers teem with life and, through the swamps, affect the life in the ocean as well.

But the river that most greatly affects Trinidad's marine life is the Orinoco in Venezuela. Its fresh, turbid floodwaters prevent any major corn growth on Trinidad's coast. Tobago, on the other hand, is relatively free from the Orinoco's influence and its marine fauna are more like that of an oceanic island.

Reef life: The turquoise waters of Buccoo Reef lie just off the southwestern corner of Tobago. A shadow fringing reef made up primarily of stag and elkhorn coral, Buccoo swarms with electric-colored French angels, grunts, trigger, butterfly, surgeon and parrot fish, all of which are accustomed enough to the snorkeler to remain uncon-

thousands of migratory ducks which used to visit Trinidad every year.

But the swamp still provides much food for man and beast. Tree oysters sold on the street as oyster cocktails grow on the roots of the red mangrove, just below high water mark. Embedded in the muddy bottom one can find Trinidad's indigenous mussels, which, steamed in garlic sauce, make their way onto the menus of local restaurants. And although manatee are not common, a boat trip up the Ortoire or into Nariva Swamp may provide sightings of these charmingly ugly sea mammals.

Rarer still are the otters which live in the Paria and Madamas rivers on Trinidad's north coast.

cerned with his investigations. The Buccoo Reef ecosystem is complex and includes not only the reef crest and flats where the tourist boats anchor, but also the Nylon Pool, an area where the white sand of broken coral fragments has settled into an offshore sandbar, creating a swimming-pool-like area. The mangrove-fringed Bon Accord Lagoon which is home to the vohites or cone shells so prized by collectors serves as the nursery for many of the reef-dwelling fish.

During World War II, Buccoo Reef and the Nylon Pool first gained popularity as sister attractions after Dillon and Cecil Anthony, two Buccoo village residents, located the more beautiful areas and identified the channels which led to the reef crest. But over the years the popularity of the area has resulted in serious destruction of the coral heads. Boats, anchors, walking on the coral head and the removal of the corals, conch, lobsters and fish by visitors and boatmen have all contributed to the reef's demise.

Under the Marine Preservation Act, Buccoo was declared a protected area, but unfortunately this legislation is not enforced. The destruction continues and has resulted in a reef which is a poor cousin to the less spoiled environments of some other Caribbean tourist islands.

A deep area of the reef called the Marine Gardens is still undamaged and supports a variety of coral formations. It is alive with star, fire, brain, staghorn, elkhorn, and soft corals, as well as sea

and red snapper present in lesser numbers. Crevalle and bluefish, or ancho, are plentiful during their breeding season, as is albacore.

Professional fishing expeditions will supply comfortable motorboats, rods and reels, and knowledgeable guides at a price. The impecunious might try to persuade a local fisherman to take them out some early morning, for a fraction of the cost. Tobagonian fisherman, though, tend to use small outboard motorboats and heavy handlines with massive hooks, but they can read the waters as if their lives depended on it.

On Turtle Beach: Perhaps the most mysterious marine phenomenon is the nesting ritual of the leatherback turtle. These are the largest – up to 7 feet long (about 2 meters) and weighing up to

fans, sea ferns and sea whips. This area and the less popular reefs of Tobago's northeast coast can provide a memorable experience for the scuba diver, protected as they are from the heavier waves of visitors. Professional Association of Diving Instructors (PADI) certified instructors are available to conduct tours, and can be found through the major hotels.

Tobago also provides variety in abundance for the fisherman. Spanish mackerel, locally carite, is the most abundant fish food, with king mackerel

Left, a rock beauty underwater. **Above**, a leatherback turtle lays eggs, unperturbed by observers.

1,200 lbs (3,000 kg) – of the five species of sea turtle (of seven in the world) which nest on the beaches of Trinidad and Tobago. The green, the loggerhead, the hawksbill, and the olive ridley turtle – smallest at around 3 feet (1 meter) – all visit the beaches at Matura on the east coast of Trinidad; Toco, Tacarib and Las Cuevas on the north coast; and on Tobago at Courland (or Turtle), Grafton, Bloody, Speyside and Charlotteville bays. There the females climb up on the beach to lay anywhere from 100 to 150 eggs at a time. They dig relatively deep holes, lay the eggs within, and cover them with sand. They then return to the sea to continue their annual far-flung migrations, sometimes swimming as far as Australia. The turtles seem unconcerned with the humans who observe them at their labors.

Legislation protects turtles during their nesting season from March to July, but from September to February when the turtles are at sea, the season is open and turtle steak is a delicacy and local favorite. Each year since 1965 the Trinidad and Tobago Field Naturalists' Club has organized regular night trips to see the turtles nesting. Inquire at your hotel reception about how to join one of these trips.

Local flora: It would be virtually impossible to list all the species of plants and trees the visiting naturalist is likely to see on a tour of the two islands, and even the simple beach-loving tourist is certain to notice tens upon tens of tropical

plants. But certain ones crop up over and over again, whether for their ubiquity or their beauty, and the following is a list of some of those species with a brief, un-scientific description of each, designed to make it easy to name those trees and shrubs the visitors notice.

Coconut palms: The groves of tall, graceful palms with smooth trunks and fronds emanating in a circle from the top which line the beaches of Trinidad and Tobago are money-producing coconut palms.

Royal palms: They look similar to the more common coconuts, but their trunks are white and tend to be straight, and often have a few feet of green trunk below the frond ball at the top.

Banana palms: The banana tree is not really a palm but rather the largest member of the herb family. Low, squat plants about 6 feet (2 meters) high, banana trees are also planted in groves, though not usually along the beach. They look like miniature palm trees, with trunks peeling thick pieces of bark, and wide, flat fronds whose edges look as though they'd been ripped, unevenly, by hand. There are numerous groves on the Arnos Vale Road towards Les Coteaux and the road that passes the Turtle Beach Hotel, both in Tobago.

Traveler's palm: A gray trunk holds long stems standing straight up and ending in regular fronds. It grows two-dimensionally, and looks like a wonderfully huge fan.

Almond: On resort beaches you will notice low trees with dark green, rubbery round leaves, often trained into umbrella shapes. These are almond trees, though not the kind that produces the delectable nut – their fruit just looks like almonds. The flat leaves turn red before they fall, and the branches grow horizontally from the trunk.

Banyan: The banyan is hard to mistake; its enormous trunk looks like hundreds of woody vines growing down from the upper branches.

Breadfruit: This evergreen tree has glossy dark leaves with deep lobes, and its round fruits are yellowish and covered with small, pointy puckers. The breadnut tree can be distinguished by its fruit which is similar but covered with sharp points, like a medieval mace.

Cocoa: With their deep red pods and ovoid leaves in various stages of green, these low trees have a bush look. They, too, grow in groves, and are often shaded by the rusty-blossomed immortelle. There are numerous groves in the Northern Range, and one small one on the path to the King's Bay waterfall in Tobago.

Flamboyant: This umbrella-shaped tree is crowned all over with bright red flowers from February through August, or longer. It can be distinguished from the immortelle because it retains its leaves when in flower.

Mango: Tall and glossy, it has slender, waxy dark green leaves. The fruits are purply-brown and round and are ripe from March to October. The leaves smell like turpentine when broken.

Papaya: At the top of a palm-like trunk is a cluster of large, green melons, from which extend deeply lobed leaves at the end of long stems. Looks a little like a windmill.

Left, a crab blends into the coral polyps. Right, a diver encounters a scorpion fish.

Like Trinidad and Tobago's rhythmic soca music, island food and drink are a sensual blend of many continents and countries. A mouth-watering melange of African, East Indian, Amerindian, Chinese, Middle Eastern and European flavors combines in recipes that have survived conquest, slavery and indentureship, offering a staggering variety of the most exotic foods in the Caribbean.

The *joie de vivre* that the people of these two islands demand as a birthright is as concentrated in their culinary culture as it is in their Carnival. Good eating is an important part of what Trinidadians and Tobagonians enjoy about living in a part of the world where food is plentiful and fresh, though sometimes expensive. And islanders like to cook and love to eat, so they do both in abundance. The streets of Port of Spain are crowded with food vendors, bars, snack shops and open markets, and every little hamlet has at least a roti stand. T&Ters are quick to have a "cookup" the minute friends drop by, and any social event, like playing All Fours – a card game – or watching a video, is a respectable pretense for a meal. At parties, a full dinner is more the rule than hors d'oeuvres. The style of food you find in private homes depends to a good degree on the ethnic background of your hosts, but a certain blurring of culinary borders has occurred so that Trinidadian cuisine might be said to be made up of unique variations on other people's themes.

Some local names: The names of local specialties reflect their mixed and exotic sources, encouraging even the jaded to experiment. Who wouldn't be curious about *callaloo coocoo, pelau, roti, buljol, accra* and "oil down" or *sans coche*, a recent import from the smaller islands of the Caribbean? And there are unfamiliar and delicious fruit punches – soursop, shaddock, barbadine – and rum drinks to cool off the heat.

Creole food, which with Indian is most prevalent, is an amalgamation of dishes with an African past that incorporates contributions from French settlers who brought slaves here two centuries ago. *Pelau, callaloo* and *coocoo* are all Creole dishes whose likenesses can be found in other Caribbean islands. The country's former Spanish colonists have also left their enduring influence. *Pastelles* and *arepas*, spiced corn patties filled with meat or chicken, for example, are purely

Spanish, although they taste less of olive oil than their Latin American counterparts.

Curries, roti and other exotically spiced dishes brought here by indentured East Indian laborers in the 19th century add to the already singular potpourri. Indian foods, like those of other cultures commingling in Trinidad and Tobago, sometimes takes completely new forms, so that many no longer bear resemblance to their originals.

The Chinese, who also came under indentureship, brought a crisper, fresher version of their cuisine than that usually found in the Chinatowns of the world. *Chow mein* in Trinidad, for instance, is quickly stir fried, without the cornstarch that gives it the gooey consistency familiar to North Americans and others. Like some Indian dishes, many Chinese foods have been "creolized." Their fried rice borrows spices and flavor from *pelau*, a rice and peas dish, and many Chinese meat and poultry dishes look suspiciously as if they've been "browned down," the Creole process of cooking in a caramelized sugar.

The Syrians, Lebanese and Portuguese have also contributed to the Trinidad and Tobago menu though to a lesser degree, since their arrival here is more recent. Middle Easterners spread the use of vermicelli, and influenced the popular potato salad, augmenting it with beets, carrots and peas.

The Rafters on Warner Street is a small restaurant with a typically Trinidadian atmosphere and menu. It used to be an old rum shop and the exterior and interior have been left virtually unchanged. For Creole cuisine there is Veni Mange on Lucknow Street.

The best place for Indian food is Monsoon in Tragavete Road. The authentic, hot curries and ample buffet are worth the expense. For good Chinese food and a romantic view, Tiki Village is situated on the roof at the Kapok Hotel. Shay Shay Tien, Singho in Long Circular Mall and China Palace on Maraval Road also offer authentic Chinese cuisine.

Roti on the run: One of the most delicious and popular foods to be found anywhere and everywhere is the roti. A complete meal, roti consists of a delicate Indian flat bread filled with curried beef, chicken, goat, shrimp or vegetables. Curried potatoes and chick peas are added and the bread is folded over everything to create a portable crepe. The bread, called *dhalpourri,* is made of two flat thin layers of dough seasoned with ground split

Left, roadside menu in Port of Spain.

peas in between. In many shops the *dhalpourri* is still baked on iron rolling stones heated over coal pots. There are also other breads used with the curried meats, like *paratha*, *aloopourri* and *dosti*, more common in the homemade varieties.

Rotis are sold from roadside stands, bars and restaurants, and are practically the cheapest food you can buy. They are ideal for lunch, or as an informal dinner. Specialty roti shops still do the briskest business of all food sellers, although American-style fast-food restaurants have mushroomed in recent years. In places like St James along the Western Main Road, and Back Chain Street in San Juan you'll find what might be called "roti rows." Downtown Port of Spain is checkered with small, reliable restaurants open for lunch,

related to the Portuguese dish *bacalao*; *coocoo*, a dumpling of cornmeal and okra; *callaloo*, pureed okra and spinach; and *pelau*, rice and peas spiced with cinnamon, allspice and any number of secret ingredients such as coconut milk or red wine, depending on the cook.

Rumshop society: An aspect of city life that is sadly disappearing is the once vibrant rumshop, a liquor bar where working-class men used to gather after work for simple socializing and drinking at a cheap rate. Outside the rumshop on the pavement, vendors sold black pudding, a sort of blood pudding, and souse or pig's trotters. Akra and float, a salt-fish cake and pancake, and thick slices of fried shark in hops bread were also available. Inside, men (women never entered) sat at tables

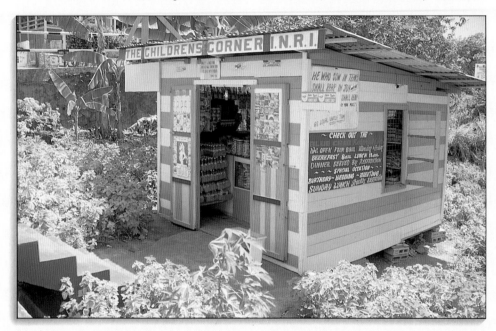

each with its own loyal following of gourmets.

A day at the beach should include fried shark and hops, called *bake 'n' shark,* usual fare at beachside bars and restaurants. The deep fried roll and thick fish steak are doused with the ever handy hot pepper sauce, and downed with a number of Carib beers. These hot sauces are usually mustard- or oil-based, and may contain papaya (or pawpaw), lime, onions and plenty of the hot, yellow variety of pepper that grows all over the islands.

The hungry visitor must be an adventurous traveler to discover the out-of-the-way (and unassuming) places serving serious local food; *buljol,* salted codfish, onions, tomatoes and hot pepper,

under ornate ceilings, or lounged, against equally ornate bars and drank their rum and talked. The potent effect of the spirit added considerably to the heat of the argument about every subject under the sun, voices raised so loudly they could be heard way down the street.

Outside, and side by side with the vendors, would be small Salvation Army bands and groups of Baptist preachers with lighted candles and ringing bells, conducting services.

There used to be a rumshop at the corner of Park and Tragarete Road, the walls of which were painted green, so the corner became known as Green Corner. It was a terminal for taxis commuting to and from the districts on the western outskirts of the city known as Carenage and Point Cumana, which were close to the US Naval Bases at Chaguaramas, during World War II. With foreign servicemen patronizing the shop, Green Corner grew notorious.

Today, only a few rumshops still remain, but wherever they are found, they provide the same atmosphere of friendship and lively conversation. Brooklyn Bar at Roberts Street, Woodbrook, still exists. So, too, do Broadway Bar on South Quay, the Empire at the corner of Prince and Henry Street, and the only all-night rumshop, Canton Bar, at the corner of St Vincent and Duke, all of which retain the old character and atmosphere of traditional rumshops.

Trinidad produces over 4 million gallons (15

Street sweets: During Carnival, food shacks spring up all around the Savannah, and even during the rest of the year street vendors offer a broad choice in one of the safest cities in the Caribbean to buy roadside food.

Doubles, saucy, curried chick peas spread between two (thus the term "doubles") lightly flavored breads called *barahs,* is another Indian-influenced street food widely eaten as a lunch on the run. Indian vendors also carry *aloo pies, katchowrie, sahina* and *poolouri,* all seasoned breads eaten with mango or tamarind sauces and, invariably, a touch of pepper sauce.

To cool the hot sauce, a nearby vendor will gladly offer coconut water, spilling from the fruit he has just opened with his machete. All around

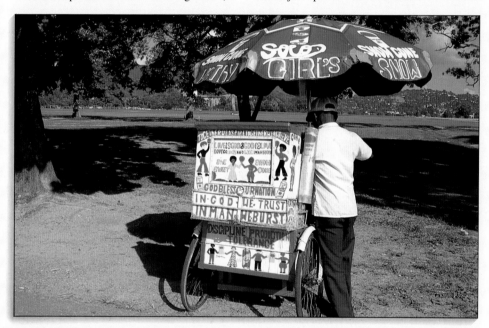

million liters) of rum a year, but grudgingly exports only what the people can't drink themselves, so that Trinidadian brands are less familiar, though no less excellent, than Barbadian and Jamaican brands. Old Oak and Vat 19 are the bestsellers in a country where rum drinking is a national pastime, approached with more gusto than eating. During the Easter, Christmas and Carnival seasons, and much of the time in between, since there are 13 national holidays, and at least seven more religious holidays celebrated annually, drinking becomes a national avocation.

Left, a Tobago food shack. **Above,** selling snow-cones and solo around the Savannah.

the Savannah in Port of Spain, and by the roadside in more rural areas, the coconut trucks dispense fresh coconuts from the full backs of their flatbed trucks. By merely shaking the fruit the seller knows if it is ready or not and, when he finds a ripe one, a few deft, frightening strokes on his blade reveal the milk. It's also an opportunity to savor the jelly that remains after the milk has been drained, which, after hardening, provides the nut that is grated as flavor or main ingredient in numerous dishes.

Pastry vendors are also common, their little glass boxes filled with coconut and currant rolls, sweet cassava breads called *pone,* beer pies and even vegetable patties. Some vendors get fancier, including the less ethnic fare like sponge cake and fruit tarts. In recent years, many vendors have begun selling the Rastafarian-inspired "Ital" or vegetarian patty. Other forms of Ital food, some of which are delicious, have gradually found acceptance among the public.

Wherever sugar is produced, sweet tooths are rampant, and in Trinidad and Tobago confectionaries are to be found everywhere. The islanders use coconut in a variety of these sweets – mixing it with sugar and baking it into a sugar cake, or grating it into chips to be blended with molasses for *tooloom*, a sweet that was favored by slaves. The *tamarind ball* is a wicked idea invented to confuse the tongue. In this candy-like dumpling, sugar and salt collide with the tangy flavor of the

and preserved in varying degrees of sweet and sour. Tropical plums and cherries are also preserved and sold widely by vendors.

Oysters are another roadside victual, feeding the islanders' belief in their aphrodisiac qualities. The oysters are very small in Trinidad, where they grow on mangrove roots in swamps. They are also more succulent than sea oysters. And while health codes now prevent vendors from selling the mollusks in their shell, oyster cocktails have become as popular as the oyster plate that once allowed the aficionado to suck them out. The oysters are dressed in a sauce of hot pepper, tomato ketchup and vinegar.

There are a number of other foods and drinks islanders claim have aphrodisiac powers. These

tamarind fruit. Indian-inspired sweets include *kurma*, a sweet dough dropped in oil and fried until crisp, which is the candy of choice on the islands. Other Indian sweets like *jilebi, ladoo, maleeda*, and *sawaine* can only be found in the market stalls on Sunday morning.

Sea moss and sorrel: As you would expect, fruit is everywhere on these two lush islands. An endless variety of mangoes competes for shelf space with more exotic offerings like pomsitae, guava, sapodilla – the gum of whose bark is used to make chicle – soursop, kymet and sugar apple, in addition to vast quantities of banana and citrus fruit. Mango is curried and used as a side dish, grated and seasoned into chutney as a condiment,

include *sea moss*, a kelp drink; *babande*, made from a tree bark; bush rum or *mountain dew*; and *pachro*, sea urchin. Consumption of these and more obscure concoctions never seems to diminish. We offer no guarantees, but do encourage the adventurous to experiment and report back their findings.

The list of non-alcoholic drinks is long. Most popular are *sorrel*, a tangy, ruby-colored drink made from the petals of the sorrel flower; *ginger beer*, the spicy predecessor of ginger ale; *mauby*, a slightly bitter extract from the bark of the mauby tree; and *peanut punch*, a peanut butter-flavored thick shake. Of course, even non-alcoholic drinks are likely to be spiked with a drop of rum, and the world-famous Angostura Bitters, whose secret herbal ingredients are under lock and key in the company's offices in Trinidad.

Bitters is an important component of *punch-à-crème*, a spiked eggnog that can lay out the light-headed when really potent. Bitters is also used heavily in a potent mixture of Guinness stout, milk and nutmeg called "the Bomb" and said to promote virility.

The ultimate drink on an island that produces some of the finest rums in the world is the rum punch. In Trinidad and Tobago, this fruity drink finds a flavor more subtle and seductive than that found on the other islands. The best rum punches, needless to say, are more likely to be found at a private home than at the bars. Everyone's uncle or aunt adds some secret ingredients that makes his

A meal at home: As so much on-the-run eating is done during the week, weekends are a time for substantial family meals. Sunday dinner might consist of rice, meat, fish or poultry, and some kind of stewed peas or *callaloo*. Or it could be curried crab, gingered *bok choy* stir fried with pork or codfish, and roasted eggplant with garlic. Or *coocoo* and fish steamed with coconut milk in a thin gravy. Ground provisions – root vegetables – also find their way onto most tables. So, quite frequently, do a rich macaroni pie and a Lebanese-inspired potato salad.

Preparation for Sunday dinner sometimes begins Saturday evening, but really gets going with an early Sunday trip to the open market. A Sunday morning market scene begins before full dawn, as

or her rum punch special – anything from whole spices to fruit slices might appear in homemade punch. The bottled variety put out by Angostura and offered in most restaurants is certainly an able substitute until you can wangle a private invitation.

T&Ters consume beer like it's going out of style, blaming their thirst on the heat. The sun and fresh trade winds seem to neutralize alcohol content, particularly during Carnival, making it easy to down four or five in a couple of hours. The local beer, Carib, competes vigorously with the other universal favorites, Heineken and Millers.

<u>Left</u>, colorful culinary delights await. <u>Above</u>, pumpkin pelau.

knowledgeable housewives seize the opportunity for first pick at the offerings. The largest market by far is in Port of Spain, which attracts both wholesalers and retail shoppers. But most medium-sized towns boast their own markets. Back at home, the entire family is conscripted for odd tasks like shelling pigeon peas, cleaning *callaloo* leaves and okra, or peeling the ground provisions. And by late Sunday morning, the entire country is a scented room of seasoned selections.

Callaloo is a mixture of the leaves of the dasheen plant, similar to spinach and called *taro* by the Latins, pureed with chopped okra and flavored with either crab or salted pork. Both the dasheen and okra were brought here by African slaves and were a big part of the slave diet. The *callaloo* can be cooked with a hot pepper for that little extra kick. Generally it is poured over rice, and served with meat or poultry. Gourmets, however, serve it as a soup, an appetizer for the meal to come. *Callaloo* is such an important part of Trinidad and Tobago that band leader Peter Minshall once made it the theme of his Carnival celebration.

Coocoo is a blend of cornflour and okra, steamed with coconut milk into a cake that hardens after it cools, akin to grits or the Italian *polenta*. The okra moisturizes the *coocoo*, although it must still be eaten with lots of gravy to be swallowed smoothly.

If you don't happen to know any Trinidadians to invite you for a home-cooked meal, the Port of

broth. Red snapper, shark, grouper, bonito, carite, yellow tuna and salmon also fill the fishermen's nets. There are also good shrimp, chip-chip (a tiny, clam-like crustacean), lobster and oysters. And a beach party is probably the most likely place to find "bush meat," the several varieties of game that more adventurous islanders enjoy. Some people's eyes glaze over when they speak of *manicou stew*, made with fried iguana or possum. Others love the tender meat of the *tatoo*, a species of armadillo, or *quenk*, a wild boar.

More common meats and poultry are likely to be browned down, which has the added effect of making the food a tad sweet. There's also a habit of slipping bits of vegetables into the browned down meat or poulty. And some stew beans in the

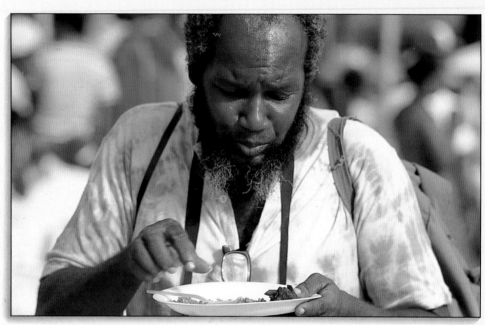

Spain Hilton puts on a Creole spread by the pool once a week which is surprisingly good and close to homemade.

Bush meat and seafood: Seafood, not surprisingly, is plentiful and widely consumed. Be on the lookout for beach parties – open to the public – in Tobago, where beachcombers can quickly "season down" something from the day's catch for a peppery fish broth. The *cascadura*, an oily river fish, has gained almost mythical proportions, allegedly responsible for luring Trinidadians and Tobagonians back home no matter where they roam. Kingfish usually dominates the day's ocean catch. A meaty fish similar to swordfish, it's often fried, curried a lot, and a favorite in fish

pot, but more often that's done separately, and frequently flavored with pumpkin.

Pelau is used either as a side dish or a main course. Variations of this dish are infinite, but always the intent is to produce a sweetly spicy mix of rice, pigeon peas and vegetables. Everyone adds this or that little something else for a particular taste – a whole green pepper, coconut milk, or a bit of wine.

The proof of the pudding is in the eating. Fortunately, there's ample chance to taste these foods wherever T&Ters reside in the world.

Above, eating curry crab. **Right**, chopping Cocos Bay coconuts to sell in town.

PLACES

Trinidad and Tobago are like one of those married couples one sometimes meets who are different enough from one another as to be almost incompatible, but who in successfully joining so many opposing qualities create a union unusually dynamic and all-encompassing. Within this small country are the cosmopolitan enticements of one of the most fascinating and sophisticated cities in the Caribbean and the serenity of a pastoral tropical island; the exuberant bacchanalia of Carnival and the quiet of deserted beaches; the wildlife of a mainland jungle and the beauties of a Caribbean coral reef; East Indians and Africans, Europeans and Asians; a tumultuous past and a wealthy and literate present; the elegance of international hotels and the intimacy of seaside bungalows.

In short, there are the worldliness, ethnicity and industry of Trinidad and the friendliness, languor, natural beauty and beaches of Tobago.

The travel section that follows has been divided into three chapters: Port of Spain, Trinidad and Tobago. The most rewarding visit would include a bit of each. Many visitors come to Port of Spain first, so our tour begins there, with a short history of Port of Spain and how the city grew, as well as an introduction to major sites and excitements. The capital offers a bustling, colorful cross-section of the history, culture and population of the whole country.

Next, a series of short trips, starting from Port of Spain, provide a more in-depth look at a nation unique in its geography and combination of cultural influences. Indian towns of sugarcane farmers and Creole fishing villages, mangrove swamps and mountain savannahs, the heavy industries and the balmy beaches offer everything a visitor could want.

Tobago is a perfect foil for the complications of Trinidad. It is more typically Caribbean, or at least more what vacationers have come to expect: endless sun, clear blue sea and sparkling sands. Many Trinidadians holiday there after the exhaustion of Carnival. In Tobago you can do nothing or a little bit of something, but you can't help but relax.

Finally, one of the country's primary natural resources and attractions is its people. Outgoing and sincerely friendly, Trinidadians are notoriously talkative, and their eagerness to make friends turns a sightseeing trip into a cultural introduction. And once you've been introduced, don't be surpised if you fall in love.

Preceding pages: music is an integral part of this island life; vibrant native, flamboyant tree; temple view. **Left,** Trini transportation.

SITE OF
FORT GEORGE
1804

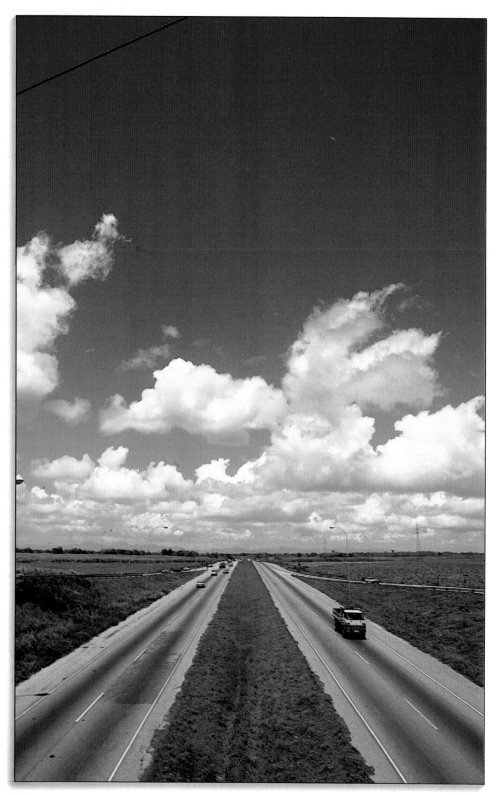

WELCOME TO PORT OF SPAIN

In Port of Spain gingerbread houses and modern 10-story office buildings standing shoulder-to-shoulder with ramshackle curbside stalls and decaying clapboard storefronts tell the story of years of colonial existence recently overlaid with independence and new-found wealth. All the strands of Trinidad and Tobago's multicolored fabric are tangled in a knot in her capital city, providing constant interest, confusion and conflicting images.

This is a good city to walk in, with a compact downtown area, crowded sidewalk life and pleasant parks and gardens. In the heat of the day the Emperor Valley Zoo and Botanical Gardens are a nice place to stroll, and any time there is a roti stand nearby for a cheap, portable snack. Most of the architectural, cultural and shopping attractions are within a couple of miles' radius of one another, and the more energetic might well enjoy walking in the hot, quiet streets of the closer residential suburbs, or (during the day) in the noisy, crowded and lively lanes of Laventille.

Calypso and steel band are a primary attraction of the city, and plenty of small clubs, hotel shows and practice yards provide forums where long-time favorites perform next to newer talents. Around Carnival, of course, Port of Spain is a veritable supermarket of music, with calypso tents, pan yards and huge organized calypso and steel band "play-offs" offering musical events every night for weeks.

Spectators take in only half the pleasure of calypso if they are unfamiliar with the economic and social conditions of the country, because calypso lyrics run a constant, wry commentary on current events and preoccupations. Getting to know Port of Spain and her people during the day will enhance your appreciation of the night's entertainments.

Hotel accommodations run the gamut from the international luxury of the Hilton Hotel, perched on a hill overlooking the Savannah, to private guesthouses in the suburbs. In every locale, warm-hearted Trinis make everyone feel right at home.

Preceding pages: Port of Spain and the Gulf of Paria from Fort George. **Left**, Trinidad's highway system.

1 City Hall
2 P.O.S. General Hospital
3 President's House
4 Prime Minister's Residence
5 Public Library
6 Red House
7 Tourist Board
8 Treasury Building
9 Trinidad House
10 Whitehall
11 Botanical Gardens
12 Central Market
13 Columbus Square
14 Emperor Valley Zoo
15 Fort Chacon
16 Fort George
17 Fort Picton

18 Fort San Andres
19 Lord Harris Square
20 Memorial Park
21 Museum and Art Gallery
22 Queen's Hall
23 Queen's Park Oval
24 Queen's Park Savannah
25 Queen's Royal College
26 Rock Gardens
27 Jean Pierre Sports Complex
28 Woodford Square
29 Hilton Hotel
30 Holiday Inn
31 Kapok Hotel
32 Normandie Hotel
33 Pelican Inn
34 Queen's Park Hotel

Port of Spain

800 m/ 0,5 miles

PORT OF SPAIN

Port of Spain sprawls eastward from the Gulf of Paria, and has for two centuries been spreading itself freely, today nestling in every curve of the Northern Range which rises immediately behind it. In the rainy season the verdant foliage of these hills, stretching from east to west straight across the island, crowns the city with an emerald coronet that shows off the brilliant red of the flamboyant flower and the gold of the yellow poui tree. In the dry season, as the sun dazzles against galvanized roofs and concrete buildings, Port of Spain is as brown and as crisp as toast, its hills at times alive with brushfires that ignite and explode the bamboo and turn the undergrowth into black soot.

Nature, however, is on the side of the city. The rainy season lasts much longer than the dry and it takes only a few showers to effect a miraculous change from brown to green, so that Port of Spain is almost always green, its many parks, squares, gardens and open places living testimony of a tropical land on which nature has been pleased to bestow her bounty.

The lush and decaying confusion of the surrounding hills has a subtle correspondence in the nature of the city. The streets of Port of Spain are well laid out, but there the orderliness ends. The city is in many respects an unruly place, a characteristic deriving from its peculiar history. Port of Spain became the capital almost by accident, a fact that gave it a sort of frontier beginning, as people of different races and cultures flocked to the city willy-nilly, seeking new horizons.

In 1757, Puerto de los Hispañoles was a mere fishing village of mud huts and a few wooden thatched roof houses, surrounded by hills and swamps. Its residents then were mainly Amerindian and Spanish half breeds, most of whom earned their livelihood by fishing and occasional trade with the Venezuelan mainland. It was hardly an appropriate choice for a governor's residence, particularly a Spanish governor representing the grandee of his country. Since the 16th century the capital had been **St Joseph**, 12 miles (19 km) inland. St Joseph, surrounded by cocoa and sugar estates, was often affected by various tropical diseases and in the mid-18th century by a serious shortage of workers. But as Trinidad had neither gold nor silver, she was of little interest to the authorities in Spain, and they permitted her capital to fall into disrepair. The situation was such that when in 1757 a new Governor, Don Pedro de la Moneda, arrived, he found that his house was uninhabitable and there was no money for repairs.

It was then that he decided to leave St Joseph and set up residence elsewhere. Being a seaport, Port of Spain had a definite advantage. The decision to remove the Governor's residence did not find favor with the Cabildo (Town Council), but Governor de la Moneda ignored them and rented a small house somewhere in the vicinity of present-day Piccadilly Street. The Cabildo eventually followed him to Port of Spain, which then had only two streets, **Nelson** and **Duncan**, surrounded by mangrove swamps, hills and high woods.

Around 1780 the arrival of the French in the colony started an agrarian revolution giving rise to commerce and trade, which in turn made expansion of the city inevitable and urgent. The surrounding mangrove swamps were filled in and land reclaimed from the sea. High woods were cut down to make room for more streets.

In addition, just before the British took over, the last Spanish governor, Don José Maria Chacon (after whom Trinidad and Tobago's national flower, the Chaconia, is named) had taken an unusual measure to facilitate the city's expansion.

The Rio Santa Ana then ran from the hills north of the city through the area now known as St Ann's, and straight through the center of Port of Spain, its course being through what is now Woodford Square, down Chacon Street and Independence Square to the sea.

During the rainy season, the growing population suffered the effects of regular flooding, so in 1787 Chacon solved the problem by diverting the river to run along the foot of the Laventille Hills and thence to the sea. The area of the old river bed was filled in, enabling the city to grow as it has.

With the river harnessed, Port of Spain continued its development, and in a few years the city had grown to eleven streets, seven running from south to north – Duncan, Nelson, George, Charlotte, Henry, Frederick

An old plan of Port of Spain and its suburbs.

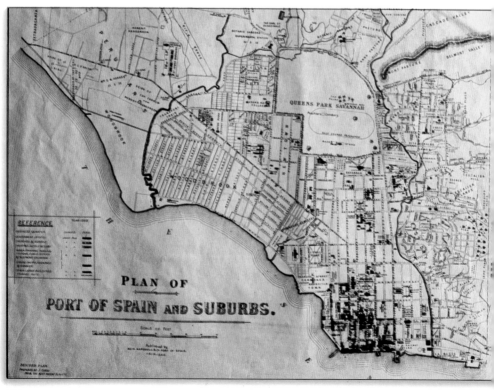

PLAN OF
PORT OF SPAIN and SUBURBS.

and Chacon; and four from east to west – King, Queen, Prince and Duke. Around the same time, with the demands of a burgeoning population, the city began to spread towards the valleys and slopes of what are now the suburbs of Belmont, Laventille, St Ann's, St James and Maraval.

The extent of Port of Spain's spread across the hills of the Northern Range is obvious today, particularly when darkness falls. Then the city is illuminated by twinkling lights from houses on the hills stretching from Laventille in the east, across Belmont, St Ann's, Maraval, St James and even beyond the boundaries of Port of Spain to the western districts of Carenage and Diego Martin. Many of these present-day hill residents are immigrants who came from neighboring Caribbean islands and started as squatters much as earlier inhabitants began. To a large extent, though, crudely constructed wooden huts have been replaced by more solid concrete buildings, and to the west of the city many hill dwellers are wealthy citizens who have built themselves mansions with a view.

It is a breathtaking view of a city at once international, modern, provincial and seedy, both an old colonial town and the capital of one of the most progressive republics in the Caribbean.

Today Port of Spain is a city of modern skyscrapers, old-fashioned gingerbread houses, Gothic cathedrals, Hindu temples and Muslim mosques, all existing happily side by side. It is a city of modern apartments, department stores, fashion boutiques, oriental bazaars, cinemas, nightspots, Indian, Creole, Chinese and Italian restaurants. It is a city of informal malls and sidewalk stalls blaring calypso, soca and dub music from their stands. It is a city of vendors, weaving between traffic selling peanuts and cashew nuts, of carts peddling coconut water, chicken and chips, Chinese fried rice and Indian roti. It is a city of men with long Rasta locks encased in brightly colored woolen caps, burning incense on the sidewalks and selling homemade jewelry. It is also a city of stray dogs and vagrants.

The latest population figures show that half of the country's population of 1.2 million live in what is known as the east-west corridor, which stretches straight across the foothills of the Northern Range from

eft, **trollers in** **Woodford** **quare.** **ight,** **view** **own Duke** **treet toward** **aventille** **hapel.**

Chaguaramas in the west eastward to Arima. A great percentage of this half is centered in Port of Spain itself and its surrounding districts of Diego Martin, Morvant, Barataria and San Juan.

The formal boundaries of the city extend from Wrightson Road near the port, east along South Quay to the southern extremity of Laventille, across the northern end of Belmont, along Belmont Circular Road, then westward along Long Circular Road, St Clair and the Maraval River, down George Cabral Street in St James and to Mucurapo Road in the west, which leads directly back to Wrightson Road.

The majority who live in Port of Spain are to be found in the suburbs, as the inner city is more and more becoming a business and administrative center. The population focus of Port of Spain has shifted to suburbs such as Laventille, Belmont, Woodbrook, New Town, St Clair, St James, Cascade, St Ann's and Ellerslie Park. Downtown Port of Spain is usually crowded during the day, with office workers, shoppers, limers and traffic.

In cosmopolitan Port of Spain residents are also accustomed to a wide choice of up-to-date goods, particularly automobiles, appliances and clothing. Port of Spain is a fashion-conscious city and the oil boom of the 1970s and early '80s allowed indulgence in this regard.

Weekend shopping trips to Miami, Curaçao and Caracas were commonplace then, as were holidays to New York, Toronto and London. There developed what was known as the "suitcase trade," with individuals buying at cheap prices abroad and selling at highly inflated prices in Port of Spain. The subsequent devaluations of the TT dollar affected this pattern but did not lessen the eye for fashion in the boutiques stocked with clothes by local designers.

A great inspiration to style is the Port of Spain pastime of "liming"; standing and shooting the breeze on street corners, outside cinemas, bars and department stores, appreciating the minutiae of daily life. Attractive girls must virtually run the gauntlet every time they pass a lime, and POS women easily pass muster.

More than anywhere else in the islands, Port of Spain shows evidence of the great and unusual variety of races, religions and

Fort Picton panorama.

cultures that make up the country. In a lunch hour lime downtown, one can easily see a panorama of race: people from west, central and eastern Europe, from Africa and India, Asia and the Middle East. Intermarriage has brought variations on the theme, and this blending of races is endemic to Port of Spain, more so than any other part of Trinidad and Tobago. A serendipitous side effect is some of the loveliest women and handsomest men in the Caribbean.

For a panorama that challenges the beauty of the population, the nearby hills of the Northern Range offer an excellent vantage point from which to get a sense of the sweep and size of the city. Four forts define the original boundaries of Port of Spain, and two, Fort George and Fort Picton, afford particularly good views.

Fort George is situated in the hills overlooking St James, northwest of the city. To visit Fort George, take Tragarete Road onto the Western Main Road, and at the Cocorite Junction take the right turn to reach Fort George Road. The winding, hilly road climbs uphill steadily for about 2 miles (3 km).

Fort George was built by Governor Sir Thomas Hislop in 1805, eight years after the island had been conquered by the English. Fears continued that the Spaniards would try to retake the island, and war had just broken out between England and her arch-enemy, France. Hislop knew that the French fleet was in the Caribbean and built the Fort in shooting distance of the Gulf.

The Fort has been well renovated, and one can see the original dungeons, cannon balls and implements used by the soldiers. Above all it has a breathtaking view of Port of Spain and far out to sea. Also at the Fort is a Signal Station designed by Prince Kofi Nti, son of King Kofi Calcali of Ashanti, West Africa.

Fort Picton, in the hills of Laventille, is one of the oldest fortifications in Trinidad. Take the Eastern Main Road to Picton Hill Road up to the Fort. Picton was a member of Sir Ralph Abercromby's victorious expedition in 1797 in which Trinidad passed from Spanish rule to British rule. Abercromby left Picton in charge as governor and the latter built the Fort to protect shipping in the harbor as well as to protect the small settlement of Port of Spain.

The two other forts date back to Spanish

times: **Fort St Andres**, built in 1887 and located on South Quay; and **Fort Chacon**, built in 1770 in Laventille, opposite the Roman Catholic church.

The other classic way to view the city is from the sea, or at least from the seaside, down along the docks of the port. From this vantage, the twin towers of the Financial Complex, the revolving sky restaurant of the Holiday Inn, the slim chimneys of PowerGen Electricity Company and the hood-shaped roofs of the National Stadium stand out from an ocean of red and green roofs of smaller businesses and homes, punctuated by treetops and the mountains of the Northern Range.

Until the mid-1930s, **King's Wharf** had no facilities for docking deep draught ships. Cargo and passengers were off-loaded as they lay at anchor and were brought by launches to the docks. In 1935 work began on a deepwater harbor with an expanded quay frontage created by filling almost 400 acres with the earth excavated from the dredged harbor.

Today the harbor handles an annual average of 1½ million tons of cargo. Several cruise ships dock at the cruise ship complex on their journeys through the Caribbean, and the ferry for Tobago also leaves from here, but overall the port is industrial and not picturesque at all.

Leaving the port, one crosses **Wrightson Road** to Independence Square, the latter stretching from west to east in a straight line. But a word about Wrightson Road, a section of which was known during World War II as the infamous "Gaza Strip."

Numerous and notorious nightclubs were located on Wrightson Road, frequented by US servicemen stationed at various naval and other bases in Trinidad at the time. Part of the evening's entertainment usually included a raid by the vice squad and arrest of striptease dancers. Now the nightclubs are gone and the Gaza Strip is a respectable part of Wrightson Road, scene of commercial and other strictly business activities.

Independence Square was laid out on reclaimed swampland in 1816 by Baron Shack, who planted it with trees imported from Venezuela. Really an avenue of trees with double traffic lanes on either side, it was first known as King Street, later changed to Marine Square, and became Independence in 1962, when Trinidad and Tobago

ended colonial rule. The interior of the square has been landscaped with seats and a stage installed. In 1994 it was re-christened the Brian Lara Promenade, in honor of the record-breaking test cricketer. The promenade is rapidly drawing crowds back to Port of Spain in the evenings. Along the southern side are some of the most important buildings in the country, notably the **Financial Complex** and the TSTT building, its radio antennae proclaiming its function, as well as the offices of the media company, the Caribbean Communications Network (CCN) and banks.

The Financial Complex appears on the newer Trinidad and Tobago currency notes: appropriately as the complex houses the Central Bank of Trinidad and Tobago, and the Ministry of Finance. Designed by a Trinidad architectural firm at a cost of TT$400 million, it opened in March of 1985. Its two 22-story towers are clad in solar insulated glass strong enough to withstand earthquakes and inside the walls are decorated with works of local artists and sculptors. During site excavation the diggers revealed many remains of old Port of Spain, including the old sea wall, ships' anchors, cannon balls and Amerindian pottery.

On the north side of Independence Square are the large **Treasury Building**, which formerly housed the Central Bank, and the head office of **Customs and Excise**, as well as more banks and other business places.

The **Roman Catholic Cathedral of the Immaculate Conception** lies squarely in the center of the eastern end of Independence Square, and is one of two imposing cathedrals erected through the enterprise of a British Governor, Sir Ralph Woodford.

From the time of his arrival in 1813, Governor Woodford began to make improvements in the city, which had been almost completely destroyed in the great fire of 1808. A man of foresight, he recognized that a city was not only a collection of large buildings, streets and commercial and residential houses, but a place that needed open spaces where people could enjoy leisure and physical activity. The heart of Port of Spain, the Queen's Park Savannah, was developed as a result of Woodford's initiative, as were a number of other parks and squares.

Woodford was an Anglican but, for historical reasons dating back to the time of Spanish rule, many state occasions were marked by church services in the Catholic church, at the time a small and unremarkable structure. Woodford considered that Port of Spain should have cathedrals in keeping with the status of a growing town, and so in March 1816 he laid the foundation stone for the Roman Catholic Cathedral of the Immaculate Conception. Designed in the shape of a Latin cross, it is built of blue metal stone from the Laventille quarries.

It took 16 years to build because of a shortage of funds and delays with ships bringing material from abroad, such as the iron framework from England and the Florentine marble used for the high altar and the communion rail. The new cathedral was able to accommodate 1,200 and the first service was held on April 1, 1832. At the time the sea came up to its eastern wall.

In 1984, the Cathedral underwent extensive renovations and 16 stained-glass windows from Ireland were added, as well as 14 Stations of the Cross made of Italian marble. Part of the renovation also included adornment of the inner pillars with heraldic shields depicting the archdiocesan and national coat of arms, as well as the coat of arms of the city

of Port of Spain, and the various religious orders of nuns and priests who have worked here. At the back of the High Altar, a magnificent stained-glass window depicts the apparition of the Blessed Virgin at Lourdes in France. The other windows depict children of Trinidad and Tobago who represent the various ethnic groups that comprise the population.

Immediately behind the Cathedral is **Columbus Square** with a statue of Christopher Columbus. Beyond this square is **Piccadilly Street**, where Port of Spain began, and where today stands the imposing **Riverside Plaza**, with its government ministries and departments. Back towards the more easterly end of Independence Square there are the Chinese and Indian restaurants which cater to the thousands of people who work in the city.

In recent years, the route taxis which most people in Trinidad use for transportation have moved away from Independence Square proper to adjoining streets, like Charlotte, Chacon, Abercromby and Hart as well as South Quay and City Gate. Taxis bound for east, central and south Trinidad operate from the bus terminal on South Quay. Two stands for the more expensive hired taxis favored by business tourists still remain.

Route taxi drivers spend so many hours of the day on the road that they have made their cars as comfortable as possible. Many are air-conditioned or cooled by fans, sprayed with perfumed air fresheners, decorated with ornaments, lucky charms and religious objects, and of course all have stereo music. A trip in a route taxi introduces the visitor to the Trinidadian's love of argument, whether about politics, religion or sport – arguments that can often become heated and rowdy. Some taxi drivers have particular quirks, such as the famous one plying the route between Belmont and Port of Spain, who would never stop to pick up anyone, man or woman, considered by him to be "ugly."

At the foot of **Frederick Street**, the main shopping boulevard in Port of Spain, is a life-size statue of Captain Arthur Andrew Cipriani, the country's first national hero, mayor of the city for many years, and a member of the Legislative Council, a forerunner of today's Parliament. Cipriani campaigned as early as 1914 for unity in the West Indies, self-government, an end to child labor on the sugarcane fields and compulsory education. He died in Port of Spain in 1945 and is buried at Lapeyrouse cemetery.

The intersection of Frederick and Independence Square is a good point to start northwards on a tour of the city, keeping one's sight fixed on the Northern Range as a reference point. Frederick Street has fewer department stores than it once did, with malls like Colsort having taken over. All the traditional names have disappeared, with the exception of the **Y. de Lima** jewellery store, whose entrance is now on Queen Street.

At the corner of Frederick and Queen streets, the first cross street as one moves north is a large conglomeration of small, fragile wooden huts known as the **People's Mall**. Here vendors sell clothing, costume jewelry, foodstuffs and leather goods, among other items. The site was originally a large variety store destroyed by fire some years ago, and individual vendors who previously sold in suitcases and box carts on the sidewalk around the city were relocated to this spot and built these huts, some as high as two stories, for themselves.

Roman Catholic Cathedral of the Immaculate Conception.

There are more stores all the way up Frederick Street until one comes to **Woodford Square**. More than any other British Governor, Sir Ralph Woodford left his mark on Port of Spain. He laid out the large square in the heart of the city named Brunswick Square, rechristened Woodford after his death. Woodford planted the park with many trees which continue to provide beauty and shade today. Its center is adorned by a fetchingly painted water fountain, a gift to the city from local merchant George Turnbull.

A focal point of life in Port of Spain, Woodford Square provides a thoroughfare between the east and west sections of the city, as well as a meeting place and forum for all sorts of people. There is day and night activity in the square: Baptist preachers with lighted candles ring bells, would-be politicians get up on their soap-boxes, and at almost any hour of the day small groups can be found vigorously arguing religion, politics and sports.

The Square has been the scene of much political acitivity and in 1956, at the birth of the national independence movement, it was unofficially renamed the University of Woodford Square because of the lectures delivered there by politicians of the era (*see page 54*).

In 1808, after the great fire wiped out much of Port of Spain, tents pitched in the Square accommodated the homeless. Later that year, following a slave uprising on one of the sugarcane estates, the rebellion leaders were hanged in the Square, their bodies exhibited as a warning to others.

In 1903, Woodford Square was the scene of a mammoth protest meeting against new water rates, following which the crowd surrounded the Red House, seat of Government, and burnt it down in a riot in which 17 people were killed.

In the 1970s, it was again a political focal point, this time of a Black Power uprising, when the Square was referred to as the People's Parliament. The largest funeral ever seen in the city took place in the Square in 1970 to memorialize a member of the Black Power group shot by police.

On the south side of Woodford Square is the **Trinity Cathedral**, main church of the Anglican faith. The original Trinity church was destroyed in the great fire of 1808 and

Bananas being shipped out of the Port of Spain harbor.

rebuilding of the present one began in 1816, in the middle of Woodford Square.

But the residents of the city protested the construction of a church in their Square and won the support of Woodford, who stopped construction. He then laid the cornerstone at the present site. The roof of Trinity is copied from Westminster Hall, London, and is supported by hammer beams of mahogany carved in England and shipped to Port of Spain in sections and fitted here. There are six stained-glass windows and a full-sized marble figure of Sir Ralph Woodford.

Looking west from Trinity Cathedral is the **Red House**, the seat of Parliament. It got its colorful name in 1897 when the building was given a coat of red paint in preparation for the diamond jubilee of Queen Victoria and the public referred to it thereafter as the Red House. The original Red House was burned down during the water riots of 1903. Rebuilding began in 1904 and the new House opened in 1907. It came under attack again in 1990, this time from a rebel Muslim group, the Jamaat-al-Muslimeen, attempting to unseat the then Prime Minister A.N.R. Robinson, who is now President of the Re-

public (*see Forged from the Love of Liberty page 58*). An eternal flame, on the Abercromby Street side of the Red House, reminds all passers-by of the infamous event of local history. West of the Red House, along Sackville Street, is the Police Headquarters, across the road from the old headquarters, which the Muslimeen rebels fire-bombed during their insurrection.

The **Town Hall** or **City Hall** at the corner of Frederick and Knox streets is the administrative heart of the city. The present building was opened in 1961, replacing the original town hall destroyed by fire in 1940s. The front is decorated with a mural entitled "Conquerabia," the Amerindian name for Port of Spain. The mayor, aldermen, and the councillors of Port of Spain have their offices in this building, and there is also a large auditorium for lectures, plays and other functions.

Next to the Town Hall is the **Trinidad Public Library**, and behind that the small church of St John the Baptist, built in 1854 by George Sherman Cowan, a missionary sent to Trinidad from England by the Lady Mico Charity to provide education for the children of former slaves.

The Woodford Square fountain.

Cowan arrived in 1840 shortly after Emancipation and a memorial of his work is this small church with its flat triangular-shaped facade of natural stone and two small turrets. One of its walls is the last remaining relic of the old Spanish Cabildo building, forerunner of today's City Council. An outstanding feature of the building is a beautiful stained-glass window, a replica of Holman Hunt's "The Light of the World."

Opposite the Library and St John's Church, standing on the entire block between Pembroke Street and Abercromby Street, is the new **Hall of Justice**, opened in December 1985. To select its design a competition was held among local architects, but none of the submissions achieved the desired effect of a modern building that blended with the Victorian architecture of the Red House and Trinity Cathedral.

In the end a design by the firm of Anthony Lewis Associates (who also designed the Financial Complex) came closest to the concept and, working in collaboration with a British firm of architects, they created the existing building.

Northward along Pembroke Street are several very old buildings of various architectural styles standing side by side with modern buildings. Further up the street is the country's first secondary school, St Joseph's Convent, which celebrated its 150th anniversary in 1986. The school is run by St Joseph de Cluny nuns who came to Trinidad from France in 1835. The original French nuns were succeeded by Irish sisters and control has now passed to Trinidadians. Today, the convent is one of the leading girls' schools.

Opposite the convent is **St Mary's College**, a leading boys' school established in 1863 by the Holy Ghost Fathers of Ireland. The school numbers several prominent figures among its alumni, including the first president of the Republic, Mr Ellis Clarke.

Pembroke Street ends at Keate Street, where a right turn brings you to the corner of Frederick and Keate, the site of the **National Museum and Art Gallery**. The National Museum and Art Gallery was built as a Science and Art Museum in 1892 to commemorate the jubilee of Queen Victoria and was then called the Victoria Institute. Destroyed by fire in 1920, it was rebuilt in

Shanty shops downtown, Independence Square.

1923. The National Museum houses a disparate collection of Amerindian artifacts, an exhibition of the petroleum industry in Trinidad, lithographs of old Port of Spain by Michel Cazabon and the work of contemporary Trinidad artists. Internationally known Carlisle Chang, Leroy Clarke, Dermot Lousion, Ralph and Vera Baney, Nina Squires and other contemporary artists are also represented here.

To the right of the museum is **Memorial Park** with its cenotaph in memory of Trinidad servicemen who died in World Wars I and II. The Memorial Park is planted with many beautiful flowering trees such as the red flamboyant and the yellow, pink, and purple poui.

But of all the parks, the city's most beautiful is the **Queen's Park Savannah**, across the street at the north end of Memorial Park. The Queen's Park Savannah and its surroundings, which include the **Botanic Gardens** and the **Emperor Valley Zoo**, is in many ways the city's center.

North of early Port of Spain there used to be a sugarcane estate belonging to the Peschier family, known as St Ann's Estate.

In 1817 it was offered for sale to the Government and Governor Woodford made arrangements to acquire 232 acres (94 hectares) for use by the city. A small family cemetery which had been used by the Peschiers was enclosed with a high wall with arrangements for the family to look after it, and even today the walled cemetery in the middle of the Savannah is still in use by the Peschier descendants. At the time of the sale, the Savannah was mainly used as a pasture for cows, but was also a place where the public could stroll and play games among the many beautiful samaan trees that offered shade.

In 1890 attempts were made to convert part of the Savannah into housing lots. This was vigorously protested by city residents, as have been all similar attempts over the years to reduce the size of the park for one reason or another.

The Savannah, Botanic Gardens and Zoo are all within walking distance of each other and can be reached from many avenues. From Port of Spain most route taxis pass around the Savannah or along nearby streets.

Planted with many beautiful trees, the Savannah has a number of notable specimens.

The National Museum and Art Gallery.

One interesting tree is immediately opposite to Chancery Lane on the southern side of the Savannah. The Cannon Ball tree is so called because its fruit is shaped just like a cannon ball. The dominating tree in the Savannah is the samaan, spreading out like a giant umbrella. There are also some beautiful yellow poui trees and flaming flamboyants around the edges of the park. Horse racing no longer takes place in the Savannah and has been relocated out of town. However, the grandstand remains and is used for cultural events.

The grandstand's most popular use is in February, when all the various events and competitions of Carnival culminate in a week-long series of shows on its huge stage. At that time, the Savannah is ringed with makeshift food and beverage stalls and everyone in the city seems to be liming in the park or attending the show.

In summer, the Savannah is the scene of a favorite Trinidadian pastime – kite flying. The sky is then dotted with madbull kites – used for aerial fights – birds, fish, animals and more common kites. The northern end of the Savannah forms a natural declivity which has been converted into a rock garden known as the **Hollows**. Shrubs and flowers and fish ponds offer a pleasant scene.

Across the road from the Hollows is the Botanic Gardens, the oldest in the western hemisphere, having been laid out in 1820. The Botanic Gardens house the official residence of both the President of the Republic of Trinidad and Tobago and the Prime Minister. The former's residence, dating back to 1875, is clearly visible from the walkways in the Gardens and from the street, but the Prime Minister's residence, built in the 1960s, cannot be seen from the street. A good view can be obtained from the back side of the Hilton Hotel.

The Botanic Gardens were laid out by Governor Woodford and David Lockhart, the first curator, who is buried in the small cemetery in the gardens. This cemetery, called "God's Acre," is as old as the Gardens and many former governors are buried there, including the first Governor-General of an independent Trinidad and Tobago, Sir Solomon Hochoy.

The Gardens are laid out across undulating land, and the collection of native and imported trees is most impressive.

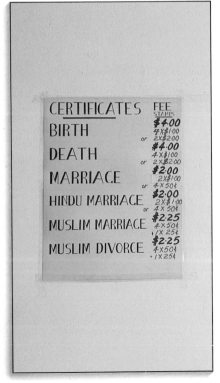

Trinidadians, disregarding the botanical and scientific names of many of these trees, have created their own sobriquets. There is, for example, a tree known as "Raw Beef," because of a reddish sap that flows when the bark is cut. A fence had to be erected around the tree to protect it from over-enthusiastic visitors who wanted to see this strange phenomenon, and continued to cut the bark, seriously damaging the tree.

There is also the "Hat Stand" tree with branches reminiscent of an old-fashioned hat stand. The "Boot Lace" tree is so called because its flowers and fruit hang down from stems that are sometimes as long as 2 or 3 feet (600–900 cm). There are beautiful specimens of palms and a tree called "Napoleon's Hat" because its flowers have three corner points.

In a grove of Palmiste palms, an Australian wallaby, which is not native to Trinidad, lies buried, a small plaque marking the spot. The wallaby was a pet of the Prince of Wales and died while he was a guest at Governor's House, during a visit to Trinidad.

The nearby **Zoo** was established in 1952 and is today the best in the Caribbean. It houses both native and foreign animals, birds, reptiles and fish. There are beautiful wild deer, native to Trinidad, plus a collection of tropical snakes. As far as possible many of the animals and birds live in a setting that closely resembles their natural habitat.

At night, mobile food vendors gather around the periphery of the Savannah, selling various snacks. There is corn on the cob, either roasted over an open charcoal grill or boiled in spicy stock with salted meat, oysters in the shell are cracked open expertly and doused with peppery condiments for the waiting customer. Trucks laden with green coconuts, still on the bunch, do a good business selling delicious coconut water.

The buildings which surround the Savannah are remarkable, their architecture ranging from a Scottish castle to a Moorish house, and offering a fascinating cross-section of cultural influences and prevailing fashions of the 19th century. On one stretch of its western side, known as Maraval Road, seven of these amazing buildings can be seen. They are known as the "**Magnificent Seven**" or the "**Queens of the Bands**." Six were built in 1904 at a time when cocoa was

Taking a break on the Savannah.

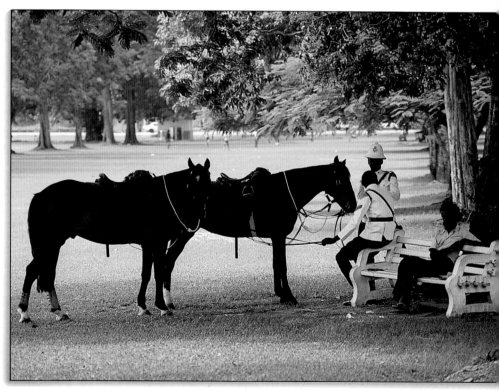

king and there were many wealthy estate owners of Trinidad, who competed with one another for stylish living. The seven are in various states of repair; none is open for public visiting without special arrangements with the owners. For a look at the exteriors, a good starting point is the St Clair Roundabout at the northwestern end of the Savannah.

Standing on the "Pitch," the walkway on the periphery, one looks right at "**Stollmeyer Castle**" also known as "Killarney," built in 1904. A copy of Balmoral Castle in Scotland, it was built by the Scottish architect Robert Giles, for the Stollmeyer family, who were estate owners and whose home it was until the Trinidad and Tobago Government bought it in 1979.

Of imported brick, the house is trimmed with local limestone. An Italian marble gallery surrounds the ground floor. The ceilings on the ground floor are of plaster of Paris, the gesso work of an Italian craftsman, while the woodwork and paneling are of local woods. The floors are of Guyana purpleheart as is the beautiful staircase with its harp-like design on the landing. There is a minstrel gallery with an elegant balustrade of purple-heart overlooking the staircase. A spiral staircase leads to a tower.

The second magnificent building is "**Whitehall,**" Venetian in style, now undergoing major refurbishment. In the early years of this century it was the residence of a wealthy cocoa estate owner, J.L. Agostini, who had Barbados coral brought by sloop to be cut locally.

After Agostini's death, his widow sold the building to Robert Henderson, a wealthy businessman who took up residence there with his family. It was the Hendersons who gave the house the name "Whitehall." At the beginning of World War II, Whitehall was commandeered by the US Armed Forces in Trinidad who occupied it from 1940 to 1944. It was purchased by the Trinidad Government in 1954 and became the Prime Minister's domain for many years following independence until it fell into disrepair. Once the current renovation is complete it will again become the Prime Minister's office.

Next comes **Archbishop's House**, the residence of the Roman Catholic Archbishop of Port of Spain. The architect was an Irishman, but the style has been described as

A samaan tree reflected in the waters of Hollow Pond.

Romanesque, reminiscent of a monastery. The marble and red granite were imported from Ireland and the roof covered with copper sheeting and slates. The interior wood paneling, floors and beautiful Y-shaped staircase are of native hardwood.

Flood Street, named after the Archbishop who built Archbishop's House, separates that house from the next queen, "**Roomor**." Roomor or Ambard House is in the French Baroque colonial style built by Lucien F. Ambard, an estate owner, using marble imported from Italy and tiles from France. Its attractions include Renaissance ironwork in its elongated columns. Of particular interest is its roof of towers, pinnacles, dormers, elaborate galleries and a cupola of unusual proportions. Bought by Timothy Roodal in 1940, it is still the family residence.

"**Mille Fleurs**" is next, the home of one of the city's most distinguished Mayors, Dr Henrique Prada. He was a prominent medical practitioner before he entered politics, serving as mayor of Port of Spain for three consecutive terms from 1914 to 1917. The House is distinguished by its considerable fretwork. It was bought by the government

and for years was the office of the National Security Council.

Next is "**Hayes Court**," residence of the Anglican Bishop of Trinidad. A typical grand house, it is a pleasant mixture of French and English architectural style.

The last of the Magnificent Seven is **Queen's Royal College**, a secondary school for boys. This building is in German Renaissance style, built of concrete with facings of blue limestone and colored with reddish tint to contrast with the limestone. A clock was installed in the tower in 1913 and chimes on the quarter hour. This is where Trinidad and Tobago's most famous novelist, V.S. Naipaul, went to school and where he won a scholarship to Oxford. It is also the alma mater of the country's first Prime Minister, Dr Eric Williams, who was himself a distinguished academic, having also won a scholarship to Oxford from QRC.

Apart from the Magnificent Seven, the Savannah has other outstanding buildings dating back to the last century. There is **Knowsley**, now the Ministry of Foreign Affairs, the grounds of which take up an entire block. This building was constructed

Left, Victorian fretwork. Below, "White Hall," the Prime Minister's former residence.

in 1904, and among its outstanding features is a marble gallery on the ground floor, a beautiful staircase of Guyana purpleheart wood and ceilings of plaster of Paris and gesso work by Italian craftsmen. It was built as a home for William Gordon, a prominent city merchant, and purchased by the Trinidad and Tobago Government in 1956.

The oldest building around the Savannah is **All Saints Church**, built in 1846 and one of the oldest Anglican churches in the country. There are two important foreign missions around the Savannah as well; the United States Embassy and the Indian High Commission. Long lines outside the US Embassy on weekday mornings are not to be mistaken for demonstrations. They are merely attempts by locals to get visas to the United States.

To some degree, the Savannah marks the northern end of the city proper and the beginning of the residential areas, called suburbs by locals though most are within walking distance of downtown.

One of the most fascinating is **Belmont**, which has the distinction of being the first suburb of the city. Situated to the northeast of Port of Spain, it rises on the slopes of the Northern Range and used to be a sugarcane estate until converted into a settlement for a number of African tribes.

These Africans, because of the anti-slave trade patrols along Africa's West Coast, had been able to escape being trapped into slavery. Brought to Trinidad, they were given land in various parts of Belmont. Their settlement stretched from Belmont Circular Road, near Observatory Street, to Belmont Valley Road. The names of some of these original inhabitants live on in place names such as Zampty Lane and Maycock Place, after leading members of the community.

Later on, liberated slaves were brought to Trinidad from other islands and they also settled in Belmont. The early community was a well-organized one, complete with priests, chiefs, leaders and close-knit family units enabling the African cultural traditions to survive even today.

In Belmont one finds an African Rada Community, where religious ceremonial sacrifices are held according to African custom, accompanied by drumming, dancing, food and the sacrifice of feathered animals.

Belmont was never laid out in the conventional sense of the word. Houses were built willy-nilly and it was only later that new streets were laid in a plan. The result is that Belmont is a labyrinth of narrow, winding lanes. The records show that it has more lanes than anywhere else in the city, and it also has more people, more churches, more schools and has produced many leading citizens, including the President of the Republic of Trinidad and Tobago, Mr Ellis Clarke, who was born in Myler Street.

Though many of the houses in Belmont today are still old wooden constructions, or a strange mixture of part wood, part concrete, the suburb has witnessed considerable progress over the years. Because originally the house lots were so small, expansion has largely been upwards. Today there are many narrow two and three-story houses and commercial properties solidly built, some looking down on the tiniest of houses next door.

Belmont has an exquisite Gothic church, **St Francis of Assisi** on Belmont Circular Road, and a rumshop with the unusual name of the **Tiger Cat Bar**. The country's first "lunatic asylum" was here, until it was resited in St Ann's and promptly took on the more respectable name of a mental hospital.

Belmont has the distinction of owning the only upside-down hotel in the world: the **Trinidad Hotel**, set in the foothills of the Northern Range. From the lobby one descends to the other floors, as the hotel is built down the side of a hill. One's balcony hangs over extravagantly verdant surroundings, with a view of the Savannah, the mountains and the Gulf of Paria.

Where Belmont's settlement was African in origin, in **St James**, the city's most westerly suburb, the influence was decidedly East Indian. St James too was a sugarcane estate, and the workers there were largely East Indians who arrived in Trinidad as indentured laborers. The streets of St James bear witness to its earliest inhabitants with names such as Delhi, Bombay, Madras, Calcutta, Benares, Ganges and so on.

Much of the city's nightlife has gravitated around St James. The Western Main Road, which passes through the area, is littered with fast food joints, bars, stalls betting shops and music emporia. The activity spills out on to the pavement, particularly at weekends, creating a carnival-like atmosphere. St

Beetham Market.

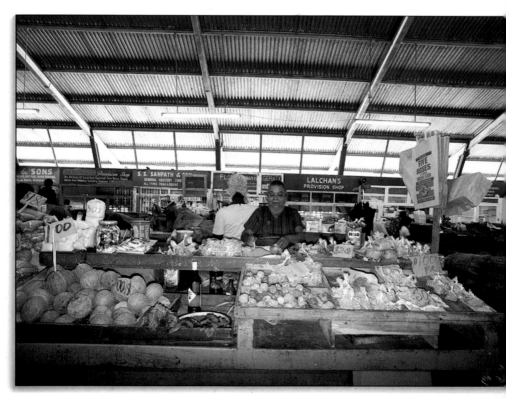

James's most celebrated bar, Smokey and Bunty, is a popular stop off point after a hard days work. The mood changes for the annual Muslim festival of *Hosay*, when tassa drummers replace the loud commercial music.

At the entrance to the suburb is an important building, in fact the oldest government building still in use in Trinidad today. It was built in 1827 by Governor Woodford to provide a barrack for His Majesty's Forces in the Windward and Leeward Islands. Today it is used as the Police Training College, and is known as **St James Barracks**.

Laventille, to the east, is a suburb second only to Belmont in character. The hills are lined roof to roof with houses, some solidly constructed, others makeshift shanties.

The two roads into the area are Duke Street Extension via Piccadilly Street, and Picton Road, a turning off the Eastern Main Road near the Central Market and the Beetham Highway Roundabout. Both roads are winding and narrow and require considerable driving skill, particularly when overtaking, an activity which taxi drivers have exalted to a fine art. The unwary, however, run the risk of crashing off the road and, as has often happened, straight onto the roof of someone's living room or bedroom, as many of the houses are built a foot or two *below* the level of the street, down the hill's incline.

Laventille is a highly depressed area, with much unemployment, and thousands of suspected illegal immigrants from the neighboring islands. There is a resulting lack of running water and sanitation, though there is no shortage of motorcars, television and video sets. Laventille has passed into history in the words of poet and playwright Derek Walcott, who wrote a poem on Laventille hills, and it was at Laventille that a Spanish navigator and astronomer, Don Cosmos Damien Churruca, set up an observatory where, for the first time in the New World, he fixed the meridian. The two huge water tanks in the area became an attraction, after they were painted with the image of a Scarlet Ibis, one of the country's national birds.

Present-day Laventille revolves around its steel band, the famous "**Desperadoes**," whose leader Rudolph Charles was a legend even before he died in 1985. He was carried to his cremation site on a "shariot," a casket made of steel drums. The larger than life

The hills of Laventille.

character of Charles was immortalized in the words of the 1986 Carnival calypso by David Rudder entitled "The Hammer," which won the national calypso contest for the best song and the Carnival Road March – the song that is most popular with the bands.

"The Hammer" eulogized Charles as he lived, always dressed in army fatigues and tall boots, marching across the hills of Laventille with a hammer in his hand, a hammer he used not only for tuning musical notes out of the steel drums, but for keeping wayward Laventillians and "badjohns" in check. The Desperadoes, as their name implies, were once noted for street fights and general rowdiness.

There are many accounts as to exactly where the steel band started in Port of Spain. Some say it was in a yard in East Dry River, when a man called "Fish Eye" experimented on an old oil drum and beat out the tune of "Mary Had a Little Lamb." Others state that the first sounds of the steel band emerged from a yard in Woodbrook, while others argue that it originated in Laventille.

What is not in dispute is that when World War II ended in Europe in 1945, VE Day was marked by an impromptu victorious carnival of celebration on the streets of Port of Spain, accompanied by the music of the steel band for the first time in the history of Carnival. Now every town and neighborhood in the Republic has its own band, and around Carnival, they are all out practicing at night in the pan yards. See the Travel Tips for a list of bands and their practice spaces.

Woodbrook, situated to the west of the city, was settled in 1911. Another sugar estate, it belonged to the Siegert family, creators of Trinidad's famous Angostura Bitters. The streets in Woodbrook bear the names of members of the Siegert family, namely, Petra Ann, Rosalino, Alberto, Luis, Alfredo and Carlos.

For decades Woodbrook was largely residential with comfortable medium-sized dwellings. But since the 1960s, commerce has crept into Woodbrook and several old homes have been converted into business places, resulting in warnings from the City Council, and Town and Country Planning. However, to the credit of the new occupants, efforts have been made to preserve much of the district. Of interest also is that Woodbrook was the traditional suburb of the middle classes and this included all races, including Syrian/Lebanese families who came to Trinidad in the 1930s and 1940s.

Large numbers still live in Woodbrook, but the successful ones and their descendants who are in the professions have moved to the more expensive areas such as St Clair, Ellerslie Park, Federation Park and Fairways in Maraval. Today carnival band leaders set up mas' camps in Woodbrook, including internationally acclaimed carnival band designer Peter Minshall.

The popular suburb of **Federation Park** is a reminder of the period from 1958 to 1962 when Port of Spain was the capital of the short-lived West Indies Federation (*see page 56*). Here the curving roads bear the names of Caribbean islands – Barbados Road, Trinidad Crescent, Jamaica Boulevard, Antigua Drive, Montserrat Avenue – and spacious buildings that could have been ersatz embassies are now gracious private homes.

New Town and **St Clair** are other nearby suburbs. St Clair was laid out in very large lots at the turn of this century and today is still a highly prized neighborhood with many elegant houses and gardens, several occupied by foreign ambassadors. The "Magnificent Seven" were part of the early development of St Clair on the Savannah side, which was most highly sought after by the wealthy planters of the era.

Further north of Port of Spain are the suburbs of **St Ann's** and **Cascade**. The latter started off life as a very large sugarcane estate in 1794 owned by a French royalist from Martinique by the name of de Mallevault. At that time it comprised 1,395 acres (558 hectares) and included the Fondes Amandes Valley.

St Ann's is the official address of both the President and the Prime Minister of Trinidad and Tobago. In St Ann's there are also the high walls of the monastery of the cloistered nuns of the Order of St Dominic. The monastery was founded here in the last century by nuns fleeing political troubles in neighboring Venezuela.

The monastery is entirely self-sufficient, grows its own food, and supplies altar bread for religous ceremonies as well as artistic decorative work for statues and altar vestments. The monastery has its own chapel and the only time the nuns leave the confines of the cloisters is when they die.

Trinidad

8 km/ 5 miles

Saut D'Eau I.
La Vache Bay
Maraca Bay Villag
Corozal Pt.
Santa Cruz

The Dragon's Mouths
Scotland Bay
Tucker Valley
Diego Martin
Morne Coco Rd.
Rd.
Petit Valley
Maraval
Canta

Huevos
Boca de Navios
Monos
Charguaramas
Carenage
St. James
Saddle

Boca Grande
La Tinta Bay
Boca de Huevos
Chaguaramas Bay
Point Gourde
Laventille

Chacachacare
Chaca-chacare Bay
Boca de Monos
Gaspar Grande
Diego Is.
Port of Spain

Patos
El Soccor
Caro

Cacand
Settleme

Barrancones Pt.

G u l f   o f

Waterloo

Mc. Bean

Couva

Cangrejos Pt.

P a r i a

Calif

Lisas Bay
Pt. Lisas

Claxton Bay

Pointe-a-Pierre

Marabe

San Fernando

Ste. Mad

Pitch Pt.
Dunc
La Brea
Rd.
Rd.

Main
St. Mary's
Debe

Southern
Siparia
Point Fortin
Fyzabad
Pena

Pt. Rouge
Cap-de-Ville
Thick
Rd.
Siparia

Rd.
Erin
St. Patrick
Siparia

Granville
Main
San Fernando Rd.
Siparia

Bonasse
Cedros
Palo Seco
Los Bajos
Morne Diab

Los Gallos Pt.
Southern
Buenos Ayres
Sa

Fullarton
Islore Bay
Erin Bay
San Francique

Icacos
Erin Pt.

C o l u m b u s

Chupara
Bay
Filette Pt.
Cuevas
Filette
Blanchisseuse
Las Cuevas

Grand Matelot Pt.
Matelot
Bay
Grande Riviere
Bay
Matelot
Paria
Grande
Riviere
Sans
Souci
Sans Souci
Bay
Toco
Bay
Rd. Toco
Salybia Bay
Galera Pt.

St. David

Cumana Bay
Redhead

Rampanalgas

Brasso Seco
Village

orge
cas
ph
Tunapuna
iversity of the
st Indies
chill
Dinsely
Arouca

La Pastora
Lopinot
Verdant Vale

Hts. of Guanapo

Cumaca

Balandra Bay

Salybia
Saline Bay

Matura

Main

Toco

Rd.

Valencia
Valencia

St. Andrew

Arima

Highway

Waller
Field
Cumuto

Guaico

Eastern

Toco

Main Rd.

Sangre
Grande

Upper
Fishing Pond

Roosevelt
Piarco
Guanapo
Cumuto
Cumuto Tamana
Rd.

Brazil

Cunaripa

Cunapo

Caigual

Upper
Manzanilla

Manzanilla Pt.

Caroni

Las Lomas
Longdenville
Talparo

Nestor

Lower
Manzanilla

ua-
ase Village

Caparo Valley

Todd's Road
Mundo Nuevo
Mamon

Guaico Rd.

Southern

Poole

Atlantic

Ocean

Caparo

Flanagin Town
Brasso
Venado
Naver Dam

Biche
Charuma

Cocos Bay

Manzanilla Mayaro Rd.

Nariva

ysal
ain
Gran Couva
Tabaquite

Southern

Navet

Rd.

Brickfield
Piparo
Unis
Rio
Claro

Ecclesville

Point
Radix
Guataro Pt.
St. Joseph

Victoria
inces Town

Busy Corner

Poole
Naparima
Rio Claro

Mayaro
Rd.

Pierreville

Plaisance

New Grant
Tableland

River

Ortoire

ahambre Rd.
Sixth Company
Third Company
Lengua
Cipero
Ste. Croix

Moruga

Cat's

Hill Rd.

Mayaro

Guayaguayare

ackpore
Preau
Saunders Rd.

Rio Claro Guayaguayare Rd.

Penal Rock Rd.
Basse Terre

Rushville
Guayaguayare
Bay
Gran Cayo Pt.

Galeota Pt.

Moruga
La Lune

Negra Pt.

Channel

Matura Bay

Tacarigua River
Caura Royal Rd.
Caroni River
Caroni Rd.
Southern Main Rd.
Brasso Rd.
Talparo
Tabaquite
Tabaquite Rd.
Terrib
Guayaguayare Rd.
Mayaro Bay

Blanchisseuse
Aripo Rd.
Cumaca Rd.
Tamana
Cunapo
Cunapo

199

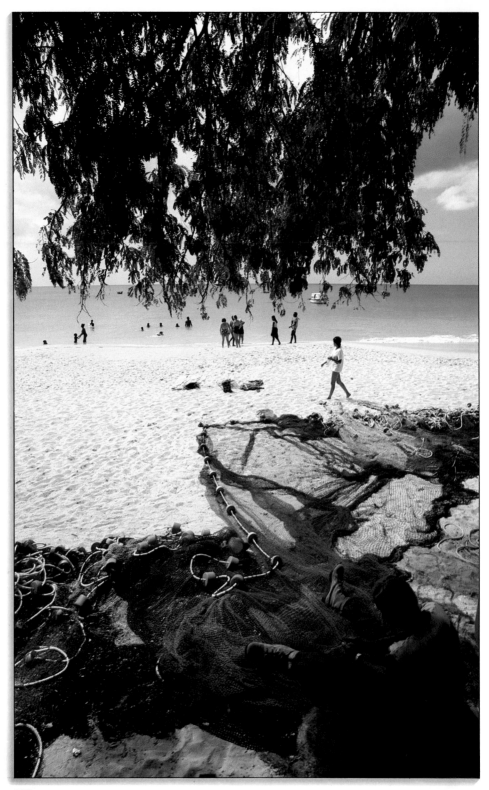

While Port of Spain is the administrative and tourist hub of Trinidad, much of the country's character and wealth emanate from its provincial towns, industries and countryside. It would be difficult to get a true picture of Trinidad without visiting some of the rest of the island: the sharp cliffs of the north coast and flat palm-fringed beaches of the east, the Caroni Swamp and mountain rain forests, the Pitch Lake and oil and sugar industries of the south are all as essential to Trinidad and Tobago as Carnival, calypso and steel band.

You can tour the island by driving yourself or hiring a car with driver, and taxi drivers who serve the major hotels are often glad to sign on for a day's tour, providing an insider's view of the sights. Even the furthest points are only three hours or so from Port of Spain, and a number of tours can be made in a half-day, if necessary. Primary roads are in excellent condition – though often crowded – and even secondary roads tend to be easily negotiable, if a little bumpy.

Since most visitors to Trinidad stay in Port of Spain, this section is organized as a series of day (or two- or three-day) trips starting in Port of Spain. All tours begin from Stollmeyer's Castle, west on the Queen's Park Savannah.

Preceding pages: beach at Plaisance, Trinidad. **Left**, beach at Store Bay, Tobago.

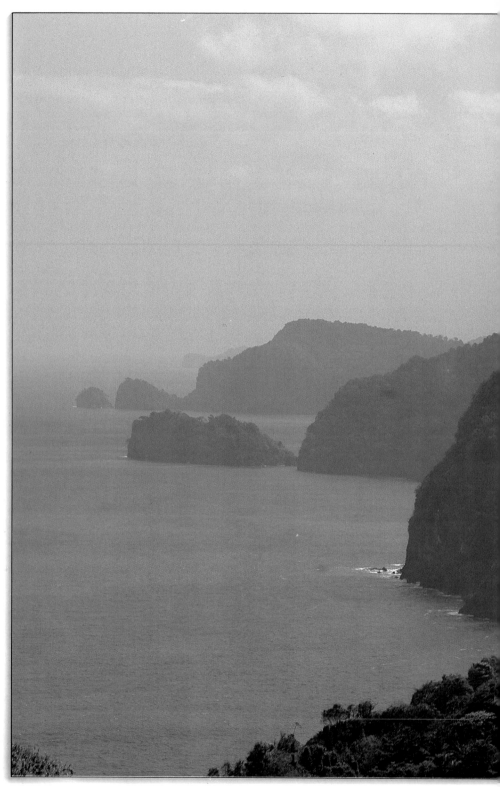

TOURING TRINIDAD

Touring the island its communities and beaches can make a popular day trip.

North Coast and Santa Cruz Valley: The Saddle Road out of Port of Spain passes through some of the more popular suburbs of the city and its coastal continuation, the North Coast Road, provides lovely vistas of valley and sea. On weekends and holidays everyone goes to Maracas or Las Cuevas Bays, so be prepared for some traffic.

Leaving Stollmeyer Castle you will come to a small roundabout by the Ministry of Agriculture, Lands and Food Production, where you should turn left onto Long Circular Road. After the third gas station in Boissière Village turn right onto the Saddle Road. At the left corner is the **Trinidad Country Club**, first the estate of the de Gannes de la Chancellerie family and later the home of the de Boissières, after whom Boissière Village was named.

Made into a club by the Canning family, the Club was used exclusively by whites until about a decade ago. Today membership policy is more liberal, and a visit there is a way to meet and mingle with a variety of residents. It has tennis courts, swimming pool and other facilities and is popular for its Christmas and Carnival dances. Your hotel can arrange for you to attend.

In the residential area of **Maraval** the Saddle Road passes through a highly urbanized area. **St Andrew's** and **La Seiva** were sugar estates, now converted into residential areas – the case with many of Port of Spain's suburbs.

The Chaconia Inn, whose restaurant and club are a weekend haunt for the younger generation, is alongside the road on the right, its walls covered by vines. **Andalucia**, another residential area, is on the left, and immediately after is the Maraval Reservoir, built in 1854. Still in perfect condition, it supplies the area with water from the Maraval River – little more than a stream.

The Roman Catholic church on high ground on the right is characteristic of most churches in Trinidad – a bit of history, an abundance of pride. This one was built in 1931 and dedicated to Our Lady of Lourdes. A grotto behind the church was built by Spanish missionaries of the Augustinian Order who were in Trinidad until 1950. The marble altar was donated in 1872 by J.A. Cipriani, father of Captain Arthur Cipriani, wartime hero and trade unionist. Next to the church is an old tomb and on it is engraved *Et Sacerdot en aetertnum*: You are a priest for eternity.

Haleland Park, a former nutmeg plantation, is another residential area noted for its gracious homes and landscaped gardens. At Catalina Court apartments are signs to the **Moka Golf Course**, the best course on the island. The golf course is on the old Perseverance Estate which was originally owned by William Hardin Burnley, an Anglo-American who took up residence in 1802. Visitors can become temporary members through their hotel.

Further on, the Saddle Road continues into Santa Cruz Valley. On the left, large pillars signal the entrance to the North Coast Road. The vegetation here is abundantly tropical, with balisier palms, the flower of the People's National Movement party; bamboo; samaan – the enormous canopied trees; and every imaginable tropical tree and plant.

Left, a view the East om north of iego Martin. ight, the each at lanchisseuse ay.

In the dry season, March through May, when the immortelles and poui are in bloom, the range is a carpet of red, pink and yellow. Drive up and around curve after curve, but take care: this mountainous trip is best made without the use of alcohol. The flora and fauna of the Northern Range are relics of the Venezuelan jungle, proving that Trinidad is a continental island, dissimilar to the oceanic islands further north in the Caribbean.

There are two official lookout stops on the road, both breathtaking. The first looks down on La Vache Bay, and the second, Maracas.

Maracas is a wide, protected bay, a favorite with weekend picnickers and suntanners. On sunny weekend days, Trinidadians bring hampers of food, floats and games and make a day of it. The length of the beach lends itself to cricket and soccer and pick-up games abound.

Where the sea or shore is marked with a red flag, beware of strong currents. But usually the sea is warm and pleasant with gentle waves.

At the left end of the beach in a cove is the sleepy fishing village of Maracas. Maracas residents are of Spanish-Amerindian descent

and there are still a few who speak a Spanish patois. Seines dry on the beach next to overturned boats and pirogues drift at anchor in the bay. Late afternoon is the best time to buy fish, and carite and kingfish are plentiful in these waters. Ask the villagers for recipes.

In the village is a small chapel dedicated to St Peter, and on his feast, a Sunday toward the end of June, townspeople hold small celebrations.

For those keen on fishing themselves, the fishermen here and at the village of La Filette further on might take you out. Make an evening tide on the Caribbean going out at around 5pm and you'll return before dawn. A night out in the wind in a small boat with only a lantern and the moon for light is not everyone's idea of a good time, so consider well. If you do go, on your return you might see vultures, locally called corbeaux, standing on top of the posts in the cove like sentinels, waiting to catch the first rays of the sun. They prefer fish for food and so can be seen at most ports in Trinidad.

Las Cuevas, about 15 minutes up and down the shore road, is more secluded and usually less crowded than Maracas, though

Farming in the Santa Cruz Valley.

the facilities are similar. The beach restaurant serves fish and wild meat such as lappe, agouti and quenk

"Las Cuevas" is Spanish for caves, and into this long bay flows the Curagate River, creating sandy hollows in the low banks ideal for picnics and outdoor barbecues.

Past Las Cuevas the North Coast Road follows the shoreline past La Chupara Bay and La Filette, ending at the town of Blanchisseuse. Along the way are many small beaches, some quiet, some with heavy surf, and most accessible by footpaths down the rocky cliffs.

Keep an sharp eye out for a large rock offshore which serves as the local equivalent to Los Angeles' "Hollywood" sign: the rock is spray painted with an advertisement for one of this region's chief industriesand reads "HOLLYWEED."

Blanchisseuse is a quiet hamlet with little besides a church and an old bell for announcing masses, funerals, weddings, and the like, a dry goods store, a bar and the school at the top of a hill. There are many families who live year-round in the village, leading, by and large, quiet rural existences, as well as city dwellers who own holiday homes. The coastal road beyond the village is impassable by vehicle, though the town can be approached from the mountains (*see page 213*).

Return the way you came to the pillars marking the entrance to the North Coast Road and make a sharp left over the Saddle, a narrow pass between two slabs of the hill. Santa Cruz is a green valley which used to be an enormous citrus plantation but is now dotted with small settlements. Although it can no longer be described as "the country," it has retained its calm aura.

The San Antonio nursery just off the roadside has an array of both fruiting and flowering plants but, if you buy, check with immigration before attempting to take live species out of the country.

You will come to the church dedicated to the Holy Cross, behind which lies the **La Pastora Estate** and estate house. Owned by Antonio Gomez, a senior judge when Sir Ralph Woodford was governor of Trinidad from 1813 to 1828, it later belonged to Hippolyte Borde, who wrote the first history of Trinidad, covering events on the island from the late 15th to the late 18th centuries.

On a small rise to the right stands the

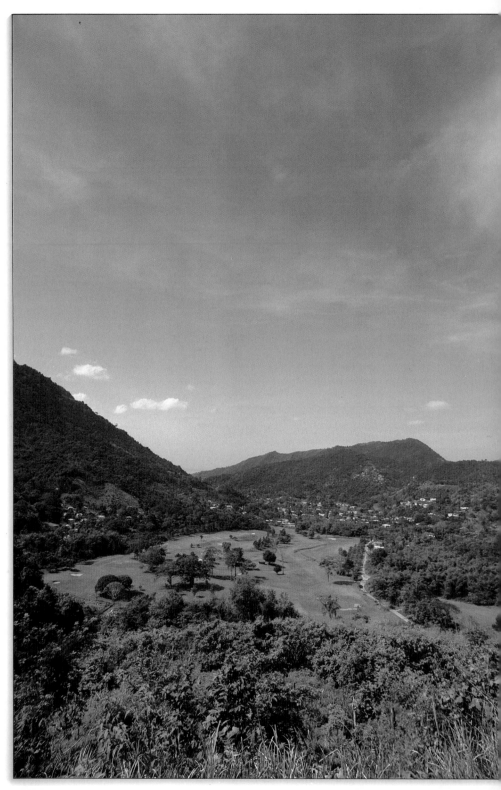

estate house of Dr John Stollmeyer's family, the family who once owned Stollmeyer Castle. They came from America to make their fortune in citrus and cocoa plantations.

The many pools of the **La Canoa River** a little further down are good for swimming, with their clear, cool waters. The village of the valley is called Cantaro, consisting of the hamlets Petial, Gasparillo and La Pastora. The name La Pastora crops up again and again in Trinidad because of Trinidadians' devotion to the Virgin of shepherds, taught to them by Capuchin monks, the first missionaries to this new world.

Branch off from the Saddle, taking the old road on the left to look at Spanish ruins. There is also a monument to the Amerindians here, a statue of an Arawak wearing a loin cloth and painted naturalistic colors. Legend says that wherever a treasure is buried an Indian was killed and buried next to it; hence this monument. However, digging is not suggested. There is also a consecrated chapel and an old cemetery whose tombstones carry part of Trinidad's history.

Backtrack to the Saddle and continue onward. **Croisee**, pronounced "Quasay" by locals, is the heart of activity in **San Juan** (pronounced Sajua). Inhabitants of this area were noted for speaking a French patois, hence the distinctive pronunciation of certain words. Today the community is a mixture of descendants of Africans and East Indians, the patois tongue now almost nonexistent.

In days gone by, San Juan was the first stop for the train; therefore market day is everyday and the town is highly commercialized. You are now on the Eastern Main Road, which will take you, to the right, past Barataria, a suburb of San Juan, onto the Beetham Highway and into downtown Port of Spain with the Laventille hills on your right. The view of Laventille from here is of greenery, water tanks, high tension wires and large clusters of ramshackle homes. This is one of the more depressed areas of Port of Spain but has been home to some of its greatest musicians.

Should you prefer another route to town, at Barataria turn right at the traffic light onto Lady Young Road, named after the wife of the former Governor. Driving over the hill, Morvant, a lower class housing area, is on the left. After several turns and curves is Belmont, then the entrance to the Hilton Hotel on the right, and a few hundred yards down, the Queen's Park Savannah.

Eastern Main Road: The Eastern Main Road leads out of Port of Spain all the way to the Manzanilla coast, and along the way, particularly closer to the city, are a number of points of interest. Mount St Benedict, the Asa Wright Nature Centre, the University of the West Indies and the Aripo Savannah are all along the Eastern Main, as well as other places of interest, and it falls to the traveler to choose how many sites to stop at in one day. The various sites have been grouped into day trips. Some will take an afternoon, while others will take a lot longer, particularly if you choose to linger for picnics or hikes in the woods. An afternoon's tour is the drive to the St Augustine Campus of the University of the West Indies followed by tea at the monastery of Mount St Benedict.

Leave Stollmeyer Castle, taking the Lady Young Road to the Churchill Roosevelt Highway. There are signs of industrialization on the left and parts of the Caroni Swamp on the right. The third traffic light is **Aranguez Junction.**

eft, laraval. elow, a reole amily goes -strolling n Blanchsseuse.

Aranguez was once called the food basket of the country, but now it's just a collection of smallholdings, its farmers suffering the effects of flooding and inadequate market outlets for their produce. Beautifully decorated fruit stalls stand at the junction, and just before rainy season begins in June there are piles and piles of watermelons lining the roadside. The next traffic light leads onto the Uriah Butler Highway, on the left to the **Mount Hope Medical Complex** and on the right to San Fernando. Turn left and go for about a mile if you want to see the very modern medical complex.

Straight ahead, the Churchill Roosevelt leads to the **University of the West Indies campus**. The campus is spread over more than 200 acres (81 hectares), and official tours can be arranged by contacting in advance the Public Relations Department of the University at 663-1359.

The University of the West Indies was first established in 1948 in Mona, Jamaica. In 1960, the Imperial College of Tropical Agriculture at St Augustine, founded in 1923 as an agricultural college for the British Commonwealth, was incorporated as the Faculty of Agriculture of the UWI, heralding the opening of the St Augustine Campus. There is a third campus of the University of Barbados, and extramural offices in several other Eastern Caribbean islands.

In 1963, the first Chancellor, Princess Alice, Countess of Athlone, opened the new buildings for the Faculty of Engineering and, later on, the John F. Kennedy College of Arts and Sciences and the Faculty of Agriculture building. In that same year the library, notable for its collection of West Indian references, was moved to new premises in the JFK complex. Nature lovers might want to look at the slide collection of flora and fauna of Trinidad housed at the library. It was compiled by Professor Julian Kenny in honor of UWI's 25th anniversary.

Faculties at the St Augustine campus include agriculture, engineering, arts and sciences, natural sciences, social sciences, and, strange as it may seem to some, the first year of law and education and the final year of medicine. At the northern end of the campus is the exit to the Eastern Main Road. Turn right and drive to St John's Road, on the left, the well-paved entrance to the monastery.

Butterfly, Asa Wright Nature Centre.

Eight hundred feet above sea level, Mount St Benedict affords an excellent view of the Caroni Plains and the Piarco Savannah.

The white-walled, red-roofed collection of buildings which comprise the monastery were first home to Benedictine monks in 1912, when civil unrest in Brazil forced them to flee temporarily. Later, communication with Brazil became difficult and the monks affiliated themselves with the Belgian Congregation.

Since then, Mount St Benedict has expanded and now includes St Bede's School for teenagers, the seminary where most Roman Catholic priests for the English-speaking Caribbean are trained. There is a guesthouse used for retreats, where visitors can stay overnight or just for tea, awaiting the ringing of the bells for the Angelus. The vista over the plains is well worth the trip, both in bright sunshine or hazy weather, or perhaps at dusk when the variable light provides an entirely different scene.

Beyond the UWI, the Eastern Main Road passes Lopinot, a restored 19th-century agricultural estate, and thence leads into Arima, the turn-off to the Asa Wright Nature Centre high in the Northern Range. Around Arima are a number of other nature sites, including the Cleaver Woods, the Aripo Savannah and the Arena Forest. Any one of these destinations would provide a good day's trip, and ardent bird-watchers might well choose to stay a few nights at Asa Wright.

Take the Eastern Main Road into the Croisee, passing the wide open green spaces of the Aranguez savannah. Between Port of Spain and Arima, the road is highly populated, commercialized and busy, with one housing area succeeding the other in an unbroken chain.

St Joseph, once St Jose de Oruna, then St Josef, and finally its present Anglicized name, was the first capital of Trinidad during Spanish rule. Beyond that, there is little to remark.

At St Joseph the Maracas Royal Road meets the Eastern Main, leading into the Maracas Valley. The Royal Road provides a delightful drive through thick green vegetation past small, privately owned estates.

You can bathe in the **Maracas River**, visit the modest **Maracas waterfalls**, or climb **El Turuche**, at 3,075 feet (932 meters) high, one of the higher peaks in the Northern Range. If you do choose to hike up the mountain, find an experienced guide before setting out, as trails can be precarious and poorly marked. For the falls, follow the Waterfall Road and then walk for 20 minutes through the forest. The falls are 312 feet (100 meters) high.

Back on the Eastern Main Road past Tunapuna and the UWI is the turn-off onto the **Caura Royal Road**, just after the El Dorado Consumer Cooperative.

The Tacarigua River follows the Caura Road for miles, and presents a number of cool, breezy picnic areas. There are a number of dirt nature trails, including a beautiful one linking this valley to Maracas. Check at the Forest Division Recreation Centre 5 miles (8 km) up the Caura Road for advice and directions.

In the 1950s, a dam was partially built in Caura, and a Roman Catholic church had to be torn down to accommodate it. Residents, Amerindian descendants, were resettled in Arouca and Lopinot. The dam couldn't be completed because of sandy soil and a scandal ensued. Village gossip has it that the Catholic priest's resistance to the whole idea doomed the project from its inception.

Mount St Benedict Monastery.

On the Eastern Main Road, continue east to the Tacarigua Orphanage. The sign to **Lopinot** is clearly marked. Charles Josef, Comte de Lopinot, left Haiti (then St Domingue) after a slave uprising in the mid-18th century. He went to Jamaica, heard about land grants in Trinidad, and came here in 1799 with his wife and 100 slaves. These land grants came about because Romme St Laurent, a French Grenadian, visited Trinidad and was so impressed with the richness of the soil and flourishing crops that he advised the King of Spain to grant lands to French settlers.

In 1783 the Royal Cedula of Population was passed, the conditions for grants being that settlers observe allegiance to the King of Spain and be Roman Catholics. Lopinot's first land grant was in Tacarigua. This estate, however, was his second, deep in Arouca where he moved when his sugar crop in Tacarigua failed.

The road to the estate is narrow and winding, climbing gradually through the lush forest. There are a few houses as you enter, then a well-kept savannah, with tables for picnickers. Also a few vendors of lettuce and other greens as you travel on, and a bar near the car park.

Over the ravine is the restored portion of the original house. The few pieces of furniture within were said to belong to Colonel Thomas Picton, the first Governor of Trinidad under the British. In 1803, the Comte de Lopinot completed the residence on the Estate he named La Reconnaisance. He died there in 1819. Both he and his wife are buried on the banks of the river named after him. Although there is nothing spectacular about the site itself, the Comte de Lopinot played an important part in the history of Trinidad as an estate owner and eschater – a sort of tribunal head and judge. There are no Lopinots left in Trinidad today, but the elders of the village have been honored by a photographic exhibition on permanent display at the house.

On leaving the estate, drive back to the Main Road and into **Arouca**. The Spanish-style church on one side of the square is dedicated to San Rafael, and across from it is the building that used to be the Cabildo, or municipal building. Many Aroucans betray their Amerindian heritage by their features.

Jinnah Mosque at St Joseph.

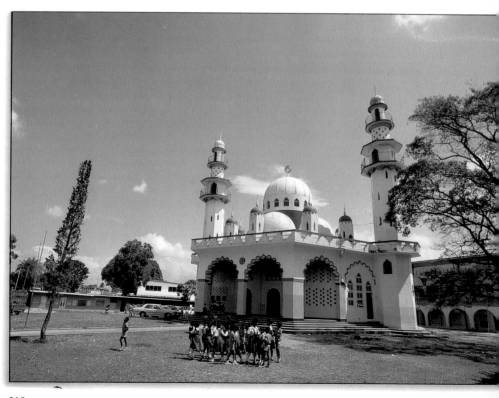

Further on, the town of **D'Abadie** is an area of small crop and livestock farms. At the fir forest, look for Cleaver Trace, which leads to the **Cleaver Woods**.

The **Ajoupa Hut** here is a reproduction of an Amerindian shelter, with clay utensils and copies of other artifacts used by Amerindians. Modified versions of the clay oven are still used in many parts of the Trinidadian countryside. Heated with wood or dry coconut shells, the baking pans are placed on long wooden pallets and thus inserted in the oven. Ovens are housed in small outdoor sheds. The track leads to a small ravine and clean stream, a pleasant short walk.

Arima was once the third largest town in Trinidad, but has now given way in importance to such towns as Chaguanas, nearer the heavy industries down south. Arima began as a large Amerindian settlement and then became popular with French planters. Today the population is a mixture of African and Spanish blood, but those who claim to have descended from the Amerindians still celebrate their heritage during the month of August and crown a "Queen of the Caribs."

Arima has a certain old-world charm, and there is architectural evidence of the French and Spanish presences. The dial at the town center is a familiar traveler's landmark.

Past Arima is **Waller Field**, an old American base now a farming area. The Cumuto Road connects the Eastern Main with the Field, across a broad, lovely savannah.

The **Aripo Savannah** and **Arena Forest** are prime bird-watching spots, with over 50 species to be seen. If you come to the savannah and forest to bird-watch or hike, plan on an all-day trip. If you follow the Cumuto Road over the river and past a small pump house, a dirt trail immediately after leads deep into this natural grassland dotted with palms and other tropical trees.

Another alternative is to hike up the **Aripo Valley** into the mountain forest. Three-high-level species, the blue-capped tanager, the orange-billed nightingale-thrush and the yellow-legged thrush inhabit the upper heights of the range.

Just outside of Arima is the Blanchisseuse Road, leading to the Asa Wright Nature Centre and thence to the shore. The Blanchisseuse Road is near a government estate called Mount Pleasant which once

elow, arming at t Joseph. ight, poui looms litter attle grazing rounds at ripo Heights.

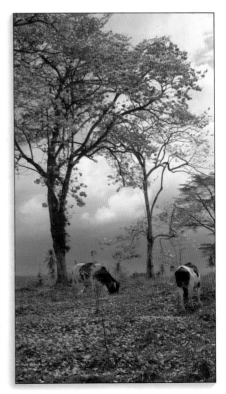

bore cocoa and coffee but is now mostly abandoned. The road winds up through a deserted area, paralleling the Arima River through stands of all sorts of jungle vegetation. Look for nutmeg trees with their brown and red nuts. There are also mahogany, cedar, samaan, poui, immortelle, corote and the odd teak.

The balisier can also be seen, but is noted for having snakes hidden in its palm. Keep in mind while hiking that there are many species of snake in the Range and a number are venomous. In the last century, the English brought the mongoose from India to eat them, but instead the mongoose is near extinct and the snakes are thriving.

Much of this area of the Northern Range was used for cocoa and coffee farming, and you might notice the sliding-roof drying houses across the hills. The panoramic views of rain-forested peaks and valleys, with enormous bamboo plants and exotic wild flowers is a pleasure not found elsewhere in the Caribbean islands.

Asa Wright is an ideal starting point for nature hikes, not least because they will provide expert guides. Go early in the morning and have lunch at the Centre, or else spend the night and take night and dawn bird-watching hikes.

Do not return to Port of Spain through Arima but continue to Blanchisseuse. The forest drive is awe-inspiring, as it climbs up and then descends gently to the sea. Again, the roundship tour to Asa Wright via Arima and back by the North Coast Road is a good day's journey.

Caroni Swamp: The huge flocks of brilliant red scarlet ibises coming home to roost at dusk across the flat deep green vistas of the **Caroni Swamp** is perhaps one of the most unforgettable sights in Trinidad. A visit to the Bird Sanctuary is an afternoon's tour, one best taken on the weekends when traffic on the Uriah Butler Highway is lighter.

You can book a boat in advance by calling Nanan on 646-1305, or set off without a reservation and make arrangements upon arrival. Binoculars, mosquito repellent and a sweater are recommended.

Start as usual from Stollmeyer Castle taking the Lady Young Road to the Churchill Roosevelt past Aranguez where you turn right onto the Butler Highway which con- **Balandra Bay.**

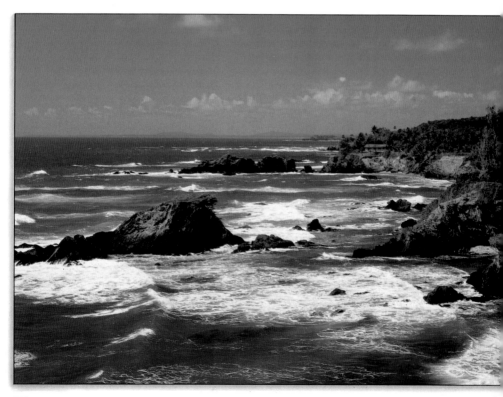

nects Port of Spain with San Fernando and the south. The drive from Port of Spain takes a little over an hour.

The highway was named after Princess Margaret when it first opened in 1955 but was renamed in honor of Uriah "Buzz" Butler, an oilfield worker who led labor uprisings in 1937 (*see History section, page 47*).

The highway takes you through County Caroni. The Caroni River can be seen on both sides of the road, with the swamps to the right. Take the first turn left onto the flyover bridge and turn sharp right into the swamp, where you will see the jetty from which boats depart. It is best to arrive around 4.30pm. Flat-bottomed outboard motorboats ply narrow mangrove waterways where the trees are entangled with branches and undergrowth and thick roots show above the water level. There are 157 species of birds to be found here, spread out over 15,000 acres (6,000 hectares) of protected land.

Tell the boatman that you wish to await the arrival of the egrets and the scarlet ibises or he will only tour you through the waterways. The birds travel in squadron formation, transforming the drab landscape with movement and color, just as the sunset lends its own brilliance to the scene.

It is said that the ibis feeds on the Venezuelan coast and flies to the swamp for the night, a distance of about 40 miles (64 km) across the Dragon's Mouth. No one seems to see them during the day.

At dusk, between 6 and 7pm, you may be in need of refreshment. Where the Butler Highway meets the Churchill Roosevelt, there is a shopping mall called City of Grand Bazaar, which has several restaurants and bars. Or you can turn right into the Churchill Roosevelt Highway and head for **Valsayn**, a built-up area by-passed on the way to the UWI.

It was at Valsayn on the present site of the Government Stock Farm that on February 18, 1787, the Articles of Capitulation were signed by José Maria Chacon, the Spanish Governor of Trinidad, handing over the island to the British. Valsayn is now a middle-class residential area on both sides of the highway. **Valpark Plaza** offers a number of restaurants and a cocktail bar. Afterwards, take the highway back to the Lady Young Road and down into town.

ypical scenes at Salybia Beach near Toco.

Northeast to Toco: The county of St David on the Northeast Coast is Trinidad's closest point to the sister isle of Tobago. Take the Lady Young Road to the Churchill Roosevelt Highway, and pass Valsayn. Near the end of the Highway there is a left turn onto the Eastern Main Road. This takes you straight onto the Valencia Road, through the Valencia Forest and past the Valencia River.

Trinidadians often light a wood fire and cook on the banks of the river. Up the Camaca Road are hiking trails which lead to the Oropouche Caves, housing colonies of the nocturnal oilbird. The **Oropouche River**, which crosses the Camaca Road about 11 or 12 miles (19 km) up, is excellent for fishing and swimming.

Drive straight through fir and pine forest on the Valencia Road to a sign which gives directions to Toco and Sangre Grande. Turn left to Toco. The side roads are traces and trails, the main road curving past estates in Matura on the left. You will go over the Oropouche River, and come to a beach further on where the famous leatherback turtles come to lay their eggs.

The leatherbacks are an oceanic species weighing up to 500 lbs (1,100 kg) which live out at sea but come to the temperate countries to lay their eggs. Between the months of March and June they come to an open or exposed beach where there is heavy surf and coarse sand like Matura or Turtle Beach on Tobago. They lay an average of a hundred eggs each of the four to six times during a ten-day interval that they lay, and seem unperturbed by the interested eyes of naturalists.

Go on to **Balandra Bay**, good for swimming and body surfing. There are many holiday homes in Balandra, some of which can be rented for a weekend. A visit to this part of the island should ideally be not less than a weekend. Check the newspaper columns to see if there is a house for rent and, having arranged for a house, take linen and towels, food and drink. Avoid parking your car under a coconut tree. There is no prize for guessing correctly what would happen.

Although Blanchisseuse is not that far from Matelot, the North Coast Road is not accessible by car. If it were, getting to Matelot would certainly have been easier by avoiding the Churchill Roosevelt Highway and

A sylvan sunset in Toco.

traveling the beautiful terrain of the North Coast. Many Matelot villagers travel the coast by boat, however, and many of them have found marriage partners in Las Cuevas.

After Balandra you are on the **Toco Coast**. This entire coast is more awe-inspiring than the East Coast, with sharp, sheer cliffs and protected bays and coves. Breakfast River with its lovely bay is good for swimming.

From Port of Spain to Breakfast River is about an hour and three quarters, but to the village of Toco it will be a further half hour for it is on the other side of Point Galera. There is a marvelous bay between Toco proper and Point Galera called Salybia. Off the beach are large trees, providing shade for snack vendors.

In Toco you are back on the North Coast in the county of St David. There is a spot between Toco Bay and Sans Souci Bay good for surfing, and at Sans Souci the road takes you inland to high ground to a place known as Monte Video. As you go down again towards the sea cross the Grand Riviere, another beautiful swimming spot. This river flows on both sides of the road and is lined by huge trees. From there go on to Paria and Shark River (also good for swimming) where in days gone by there used to be a tub race. This bay goes on further after Paria than Matelot and is ideal territory for hunters, swimmers, fishermen and artists.

Matelot is a small coastal fishing village on a bay good for swimming. At what appears to be the very end of the road is the Roman Catholic church and presbytery. A left turn just at the church leads through the village to the river. You will have to walk part of the way. Cross the bridge some 30 feet (10 meters) above the river and walk to the playground, and from there to the river's bay. This is a very quiet area and is worth an hour's stay in good weather.

Return as you came, back to Valencia and Waller Field onto the Churchill Roosevelt Highway and straight into Port of Spain.

Down the islands: Because the network of roads in Trinidad is built for getting into Port of Spain, touring the island means using the same route time and again. Break the monotony by going across the sea "down the islands," or "down the main" to the small archipelago that reaches across the Dragon's Mouth toward Venezuela. **Chacachacare**, **Huevos**, **Monos** and the others provide resorts, prisons, beaches and good fishing waters for Port of Spain residents, and can be seen on day trips or weekend jaunts. Monos, Huevos and Chacachacare are the links to the mainland, while **Gasparee** and **Patos** are outside the chain.

In 1791, Don Gaspar Antonio de la Guardia, Procurator Syndic, in charge of state lands in Port of Spain, presented Governor Don José Maria Chacon with a petition that these islands be ceded to the Cabildo of Port of Spain to increase revenue. The petition was passed on to the first commissary of population, Don Pedro Ybarrate, who replied that the King of Spain had no occasion for the islands of Monos, Huevos and Patos and was pleased to cede them to the Cabildo.

Chacachacare had already been given to Gerald Fitzpatrick Carry, an Irishman, for services rendered to the King of Spain, though it had to be returned if the King needed it. He grew cotton and sugar apples there for a while, and later there were whaling stations located on Chaca, as it is fondly called by Trinidadians. Chaca is now a solid part of "down the islands," though Patos has remained outside of Trinidadian ownership.

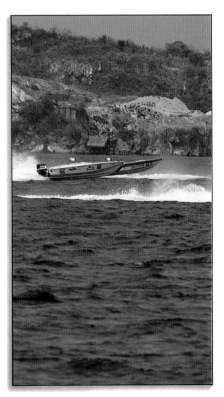

Patos was leased in 1876 to one L. Dennis O'Connor for 30 years, to raise stock and catch fish for salting. Patos soon grew too lonely for Mr O'Connor. The land reverted to Spain, and in 1940 was ceded to Venezuela in connection with establishing boundaries. When you are near Patos you are in Venezuelan territorial waters, so do not visit it as travel between the two countries is not entirely free.

There are several routes to "down the islands." You may take a boat from the Port of Spain harbor and your hotel can assist you in doing so. You can also leave from the **Yacht Club**, privately owned but with facilities for visiting yachts, from the **Yachting Association** or the **Island Owners' Association**.

For the first, call in advance and see what facilities they have to offer. There are members who are prepared to make tours. The Yachting Association will also provide information on what arrangements can be made. At Island Owners', Mr Daniels owns a well supplied shop. You can call him through the Chaguaramas Naval station and arrange to rent a boat.

To go to the Yacht Club, turn sharp left at the Castle on the Serpentine Road and get on to the Western Main Road, driving through St James. Keep on the highway at the end of the highly commercialized area, and go past Cocorite, once the port for the old sea planes.

Straight ahead there will be several roads on your left but keep on the highway with two lanes. There is a fork in the road, the right going to the suburb of Diego Martin and the left, which you will take, going towards West Mall. The highway becomes a single lane and on the right is the entrance to Goodwood Park and on the left Bayshore, two housing areas with expensive homes. Just before the supermarket in Glencoe on your right you will see the entrance to the Yacht Club. For the Yachting Association, drive through **Carenage**, a sizable village and hometown of one of Trinidad's former leading cricketers, Bernard Julien. Julien played professional cricket with Kent County in England and then joined the blacklist of sportsmen when he toured South Africa with a rebel team of West Indian cricketers.

The sea is always on your left. St Peter's church, which holds its festivities in grander **North Coast view.**

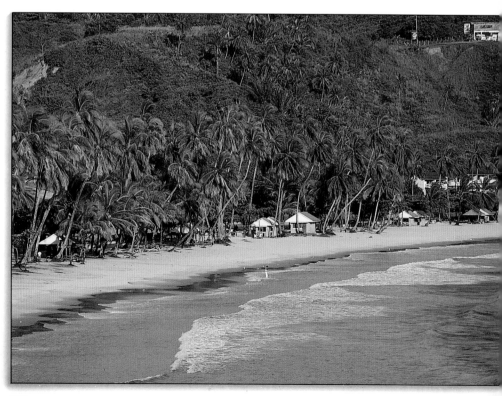

style than that in the tiny village of Maracas, is nearby.

Chaguaramas is a long stretch of beach, very popular with people employed in Port of Spain who use it during their lunch break or in the evening. When Chaguaramas was leased to the US Armed Forces during World War II everyone had to show a pass to enter. This is no longer the case, but you still cannot get past the sentinels of the Trinidad and Tobago Defense Force at what appears to be the very end of the road.

Before you reach there, however, you will come to the Convention Centre with flags of all nations flying. On your left is the helicopter port of the National Security services. Just beyond are the tall masts of yachts in the natural marina. It is a beautiful spot, with blue waters and colorful sails atop the boats. Below them as they reflect in the water are the hills of the bay in the background, the trees under which you may be standing and the even greener Northern Range.

On the far side of the marina is **Hart's Cut**. Fifteen feet (5 meters) wide and 4 feet (1 meter) deep, it cuts across the Isthmus of Chaguaramas. The proposal for the scheme came from a police superintendent named Hart and the cut was opened in 1856. It proved to be a great service to both fishermen and residents for it allowed them to avoid the long, difficult pull around Pointe Gourde.

Your first tour of the islands is to Monos. Cruising and boating along the mainland, you will pass **Staubles Bay**. Today the Trinidad and Tobago Naval Station, it was from Staubles that the Northern Range was shelled by government forces during the Black Power uprising of 1970.

For years Staubles was the point of departure for Island Owners', before then a very fashionable club. You will see many derelict homes which were once holiday resorts and later, during the war, homes of senior officers of the US Armed Forces. The house on the very point belonged to the Canning family, and later the US Armed Forces turned it into a club called the Crow's Nest. Later still, Prime Minister Dr Eric Williams turned it into a resort home for himself and his daughter Erica when she was a young girl.

The open channel of water is the first Boca, or mouth, and the small rock next to

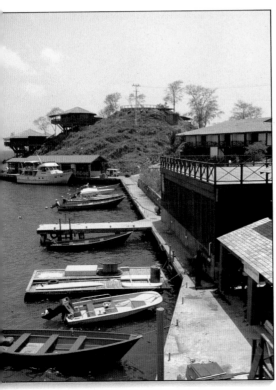

...elow, ...shing ...inghies. ...ight, the ...elaxed ...ttitude of ...down the ...slands."

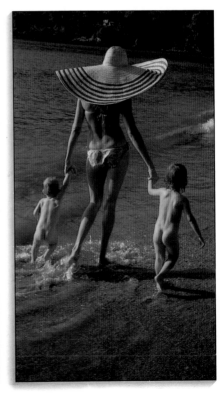

Monos is called "Dent Ma Tetron." There is a special current here called Raymoo (phonetically spelt) which inspired the old Trinidadian caution, "Don't row your boat if Raymoo is running." It is a strong and tricky current, and if you are fishing you will feel Raymoo pulling your line.

All the bays or points on Monos have names. The first one, **Maria Elba**, is owned today by the Gatcliffe family. Tommy Gatcliffe is said to be one of the two people alive who know the secret formula for the world-famous Angostura Bitters. There is a large house sitting on a projecting rock and a good bank for fishing "Jacks" not far off this point. The second point is known as **Gittens**, the third is **Copperhole**, and was originally a whaling station. You can see the copper cauldrons in which the whale blubber was boiled partly submerged in the shallow waters at this point. The bay is called **Turtle's Bay**.

Your boatman will be able to tell you the owners of the homes which face the mainland or the Gulf of Paria. To the back of Monos is a sharp drop of sheer rocks into the sea – a spectacular sight. This channel divides Monos from Huevos, which is owned by the Boos family. This is the second Boca and most beaches here are open to the public. The deep sea fishing "down the islands" is famous. Franklin Delano Roosevelt came here to fish during the war. If you are keen on this sport then you would either have taken along your tackle or the man on the boat may have brought his. There are good grouper banks behind Monos and Huevos.

It is through the huge swells and choppy waters of these Bocas that speedboats are tested every year during the Great Race. This race is held around Emancipation Day on the Saturday before the first Monday in August. All boats leave the Yacht Club, pass through the Bocas, around the North Coast and finish at Store Bay in Tobago.

Scotland Bay on the mainland near Teteron is a good point for a swim. This is a white sandy beach where you can anchor in the shallow waters.

Gasparee: Another tour is to Gasparee, which originally belonged to Don Gaspar de Percin. When the Spaniards capitulated in 1779, there were lengthy litigations as to whom and to which country these islands

The rich fishing waters offshore gave Point Baleine its name.

1. Ile de la Trinité – Baleines.
1. Isla de la Trinidad – Ballenas.

218

belonged. Prior to capitulating, Chacon built additional forts on Gasparee, hoping to defend the island, but the Spanish fleets did not give enough assistance for his plan to work.

Later there were two whaling stations at Point Baleine or Whale Point. Cotton was grown on this island, and there is a fort on Bombshell Hill facing the mainland. There was a well-run guesthouse at Point Baleine where Noel Coward stayed and wrote the novel *Point Valeine*. There is also a Roman Catholic chapel where boats can be seen heading about 7 o'clock on Sunday mornings.

Today the **Gaspar Grande** area of Gasparee contains several holiday homes. On the other side of the island are some underground caves popular with visitors. The entrance is at Point Baleine. You go down steps now and not a rope ladder as children did long ago. There are the usual stalactites, stalagmites and bats. At high tide the caves fill with sea water.

On your return to the mainland you pass a small island inhabited by centipedes. The five smaller islands to the east of Gaspar Grande were originally the Diego Martin islands. They are **Caldeonia**, **Lenegan's**

and **Nelson**. Here the East Indians who arrived as indentured laborers were kept until they were assigned to estates. **Pelican** and **Rock** were quarantine stations. There are also two larger islands: **Creteau**, sometimes known as Begorrat, and **Carrera**, at one time called Long Islands, were first holiday resorts. Creteau is now a stone quarry and Carrera became a prison in 1877. Today prisoners are sent there for hard labor.

Chaca: The adventurous visit **Chacachacare**, the largest island of the link. Chacachacare is supposedly a word resembling the chattering of monkeys, but in Venezuela it is called the island of the deer, and when the Spanish first arrived they called it El Caracol. Whatever, it has been Chaca as far back as most Trinis can recall.

The third Boca separates the islands of Huevos and Chacachacare, and between Chacachacare and the Venezuelan mainland is the Dragon's Mouth. Sailors of the Spanish fleet prayed and offered masses to their favorite virgins and saints to go through the Dragon's Mouth safely. There are months when it is calm like a lake and others when it truly earns its name.

Yachts at anchor in a natural marina.

On the island is a saltwater lagoon and an attempt to extract salt was once made. Chaca is neatly divided into two separate landmasses, with a narrow strip of land joining them. The island slopes towards the inside of the bay, and the west sides of the hills descend sharply to the Caribbean Sea. The bay on the west side has black sand and is called **La Tinta**, meaning ink. Smugglers from the mainland, and there were many, brought their boats from the Venezuelan side into Trinidad territorial waters via the island.

In 1877, the British established a leper colony here, building extraordinary red brick Victorian houses: the doctors' residence, the home for the nuns who cared for the lepers, a hospital and a chapel. The lepers lived all over the island, but the sanatorium is now closed. Swimming and fishing are excellent. A boat larger than a pirogue should be used for a visit to Chaca. Call the Yacht Club and a member may be prepared to rent his boat and provide company for the journey. Choose mid-afternoon, say around 4.30pm.

Leave Chaguaramas, passing Carenage. On your left you will come to Glencoe and Newbury Hill, both residential areas. Bayshore is on the waterfront on your right. The view from Windy Ridge, one of the housing areas, is terrific. On a clear day look all around you from here, down on the sea, across the Northern Range and the city.

At the traffic light, turn left for **Westmoorings**. This was a swamp where it was customary to catch crabs in the moonlight to be used in the local *callaloo* dish until the swamp was filled in the '40s and developed for housing. You will come to St Finbar's Roman Catholic church and St Anthony's school, where you turn right onto the Morne Coco Road for a scenic drive which takes you all the way to the church in Maraval on a hill dedicated to the Virgin of Lourdes. Make a right turn and you are on the Saddle Road. You may wish to stop at Chaconia Inn for a drink.

On another day, you might take the road to your left before the Seventh Day Adventist Community Hospital. The sign reads Mucurapo. This will take you to the foreshore named after Audrey Jeffers, a prominent social worker. It gives another view of Port of Spain from the lay-by where many

The modern equivalent of the donkey cart, near Gran Couva.

cars park in the night – a sort of lovers' lane.

On your right is the **Jean Pierre Complex** for indoor sports. Jean Pierre was captain of the national netball team which in 1979 won the world championship jointly with New Zealand. The competition was held in this very stadium. The highway takes you straight onto Wrightson Road. On another day visit Blue Basin, the River Estate where a small falls and old estate provide an attraction for local children. Just after West Mall take the turning for Diego Martin.

Victoria Gardens is a new housing development on your left. Ridgewood Tower apartments are also on your left. At the sign saying Crystal Stream turn right and bear left again. At Majuba Crossing head for the residential area of Blue Range.

At the junction of Diego Martin Main Road and Petit Valley, turn right, then left and you will come to the River Estate, bought by the government in 1897. A cocoa, coffee and citrus estate, it is now urbanized. The old water wheel has been restored and there is a shed with historical information about the area. The Blue Basin River and Falls are a cool and invigorating stop-off on a hot day.

Chemical factory, Point Lisas.

San Fernando and the south: The southern part of Trinidad – which to Trinidadians seems to be anything below the latitude of Port of Spain – comprises everything from oil and heavy industries to East Indian cane-farming villages to the pitch lake at La Brea.

Though the sights of the south are not always amongst Trinidad's most picturesque, to know the country one must see the lower two-thirds of the island. San Fernando is only about an hour's drive from Port of Spain, and there are many people who commute daily between the two cities.

The southeastern coastline presents another kind of marine beauty from that of the rocky northern coast, as beaches here lie beside flat coconut groves which stretch for miles to the sea. The first tour goes to a part of the deep south including Chaguanas, Couva, San Fernando and Pointe-à-Pierre.

Go to the Butler Highway and take the first flyover as if going to the Swamp, but this time make a left into Charlieville along the Caroni Savannah Road. The Charlieville Road leads into the highly commercialized city of **Chaguanas**. People here are mainly of East Indian descent, children of indentured laborers, many of whom left the declining sugar industry to become professionals. Chaguanas is a growing area, and what was a depressed collection of small villages 10 years ago has mushroomed into a town with nice middle-class homes, now the third most important city in Trinidad.

The town is built around a one-way main road with a market and branches of the big chain stores and commercial banks. The many malls – Mid-Centre, Ramsaran Park, Centre City, Medford Plaza – are an indication of Chaguanas' prosperity.

On Chaguanas Main Road can be found the **Lion House**, former home of V.S. Naipaul, the Trinidad-born novelist now living in London. In the tragicomic *A House for Mr Biswas*, Naipaul described the house as the home of the Biswas family. A two-storied building painted white with stone figures of lions against the pillars of the top floor, this modest dwelling was the crowning achievement of Biswas' life, in a novel that describes with exquisite detail and humor the pathos of a man whose intelligence and sophistication are sufficient only to make him realize his limitations.

From Chaguanas take the Old Southern

Main Road to **Edinburgh Gardens**, another housing area. Edinburgh was the site of a US Armed Forces Airbase during the war and Chaguanas is synomymous in many Trinidadian minds with the Yankee base. The soil here has a degree of clay and is therefore unsuitable for cane, but there are some beef herds and vegetable farms and several potters in the area. It is from here that every year millions of *deyas* (small earthen bowls) are made for use by Hindus to celebrate the Festival of Lights, Divali (*see Festivals, page 133*).

Further along you come to **Brechin Castle**, the beautifully kept main factory area of Caroni Limited, the state-owned sugar company purchased from the British firm of Tate and Lyle in 1977. **Sevilla House**, occupied by senior management of the company, is perched on a hill. The road leading to this former estate house is lined by royal palms and the grounds take the form of an 18-hole golf course used by senior management. Caroni Limited owns another factory at Usine Ste Madeleine near San Fernando.

Couva is a sleepy town compared to Chaguanas. Though the vendors have been provided with a market, it suits them financially to sell their wares on the sidewalks. The old railway station is still the heart of activity here.

Not far away is the Convent of the Holy Faith, a school in the grounds of the house of a former overseer of a plantation. The old house is beautiful, though the school is merely a collection of new buildings spread across large areas of land. Visitors to Couva always look for the popular Chorro's Restaurant, well known for its roti.

Keep on the old road past **California by the sea** where there is a sugar warehouse. California is mainly a sugar housing settlement, where many residents were granted small loans by the Sugar Welfare Association to build houses. It is from Point Lisas Bay next door that Caroni Ltd sends its sugar abroad.

Point Lisas is a massive industrial complex built at the cost of almost TT$3 billion. The steel company, Caribbean Ispat, Arcadian, the PowerGen power station and other heavy industries are all house here. Tours of these areas are available for those having a special interest in industry, or for

A sugar mill in Couva.

potential investors interested in downstream industries.

Just after is **Claxton Bay**, a small village made dirty by the dust from the Cement Factory. Further down is Farrell House, a hotel up on a hill on the right with an excellent view of the Gulf of Paria. The sunset is beautiful from here. Farrell House is a good hotel used mainly by businessmen visiting the oil and industrial sector. Conference facilities are available. You can have an excellent lunch on your stop here or you may decide to stay overnight.

When you leave Claxton Bay, you enter Victoria County. The entrance to the city of **Pointe-à-Pierre** was heavily guarded during the war, close as it was to strategic industries. You will come to the large Pointe-à-Pierre refinery, formerly owned by Texaco but acquired by the Trinidad and Tobago Government in 1984. Almost everything in this area is government-owned, an indication of the massive nationalization and industrialization program embarked on during the oil boom.

This is a beautifully hilly area and the natural scenery provides a stark contrast to the abundant man-made scenery. In driving through you will see the Augustus Long Hospital and Club House. The bungalows and the bachelors' quarters are located on the high ground looking down on the rigs and tanks.

Pointe-à-Pierre's lake is in the hands of the Wild Fowl Trust because of the hundreds of species of birds that alight here, and the special lily which grows in this lake. A small wooden building, like an enlarged version of a bird house, provides literature on the various species. Bird-watchers and nature lovers should contact members of the committee or Molly Gaskin, who heads the Trust, if they wish to visit this nature center. She can be reached at tel: 637-5145.

Pointe-à-Pierre has the sulfurous smell of any refinery area. The **Guaracara Park**, owned by the oil company, is a good sporting center. Formerly the scene of the popular Southern Games, with leading international track and field stars, the ground's use has been expanded to include football games, territorial cricket matches and night cricket under floodlights.

The next town is **Marabella**, urbanized, commercialized and with a daily roadside market. You will by-pass San Fernando by skirting St Joseph Village, a middle-class housing area in San Fernando.

The sugar crop begins in January and ends in June, so in these months buffalo-drawn carts traverse the southern outskirts of San Fernando. The sign on the right saying Siparia is the one you will take.

Enter the **Phillipines Estate**, once owned by Sir Norman Lamont, a Scotsman who was gored by a bull on his own plantation. Part of the estate has been developed into Bryan's Gate, a residential area.

The Phillipines Estate was left to the government for agricultural development, but they turned it down. Then it was offered to the Imperial College of Tropical Agriculture and they too turned it down. Thirdly it was to go to a distant relative of Sir Norman's soldiering in Africa. He had no interest in an estate in Trinidad and instructed it to be sold. And so it landed in the hands of property developers. The old estate residence surrounded by samaan trees is now used as site offices.

Pass by **Penal**, mainly an East Indian town with its power plant serving the entire

Making earthenware pottery in Chaguanas.

southwestern peninsula. At Siparia there is a well-known statue of La Divina Pastora at the main Catholic church called the Black Virgin of Siparia.

This devotion to Mary, the divine Shepherdess, was brought from the sheep-rearing community of Andalucia in southern Spain. The Capuchin monks were the first missionaries to come from Spain to convert the Amerindians, and they instilled their traditional devotion to La Divina Pastora. In 1759, the last mission was formed in Siparia. According to legend the statue was brought by the Capuchins from Venezuela when fleeing an Amerindian revolt.

The statue is rather small, of brown complexion with pink cheeks and black hair. She is dressed in blue voile, her hair adorned with artificial lilies. Around her neck are many necklaces, offerings from devotees. There are perpetual lights illuminating the statue.

Over the years, Hindus and other non-Catholic groups have been attracted to La Divina Pastora. When the railway line reached Siparia, making the south accessible to the Indians, they became devotees and developed their own name for her, Soparee Kay Mai, meaning Mother Kali.

The feast of La Divina Pastora is on the second Sunday after Easter, when the statue is carried in procession; a big day in the life of Siparians. The locals adorn themselves with new clothes, and feasting and celebrating are the order of the day.

After Siparia is Santa Flora and then Palo Seco, meaning dry wood. This is now oil territory. Just past is Rancho Quemado, meaning burning hut, the name no doubt connected with an Amerindian occurrence.

You should make a side trip to **Fyzabad** to see the statue of Uriah Butler, prominently placed where the oil workers' riots of June 1937 took place. With top hat, he is dressed in black as was Butler's wont. June 19 is celebrated as Labor Day with rallies and fiery speeches on this spot.

Leave Butler in Fyzabad and go onto the Siparia Erin Road, heading straight for the sea. **Erin** is a fishing village with liming fishermen and a generally slow pace. Here the sea is a bit muddy, but you can clearly see Venezuela, 7 or 8 miles (12 km) away. Venezuela parrots and pretty hammocks are

A buffalo-drawn cart near San Fernando.

sold in this town, and occasionally whales are washed up on the shore here.

Go back to San Fernando, by-passing Fyzabad, onto the Mosquito Creek. You will pass the mouth of the Oropouche River and on a tributary further on is a crematorium called the Shore of Peace. The Oropouche River goes inland through La Fortune and Woodland, where there is a mixture of both sugar and rice.

Nearer to San Fernando is the Godineau River. It is said that a Dr Singh killed his wife and disposed of her body by throwing it into the Godineau but the tide brought in her body and he was discovered.

On your way to San Fernando you will pass La Romain, a residential district, a new middle-class development called Gulf View. Take Lady Hailes Avenue with San Fernando main thoroughfare on your right. Turn off on the Rienzi Kirton Highway. This short link road was named after Mrs Gertrude Kirton, a former mayor of San Fernando, and Adrian Cola Rienzi, a former member of the Legislative Council and the founder of two trade unions – the Oilfield Workers Trade Union (OWTU) and the All Trinidad Sugar Estates and Factory Workers Trade Union (FWTU).

You will enter San Fernando, passing Naparima College, a prestigious boys school.

You come to **Harris Promenade**, commemorating Lord Harris, Governor of Trinidad from 1846 to 1854. The Roman Catholic church, Our Lady of Perpetual Help, was consecrated on May 29, 1849. The Town Hall and Council were established in 1846 and the wharf opened in 1842. It was then that San Fernando began assuming some importance. Now it is second only to Port of Spain.

On this promenade there are several churches of other denominations, Methodist and Anglican, and a statue of Mahatma Gandhi is prominent. There is also the engine of the last train which left Port of Spain for San Fernando, marking the end of railway service in Trinidad. An old calypso, "Last Train to San Fernando" said if you don't get this one, you'll never get another one, so on its last journey, people were crammed into the carriages, heads sticking out and some even managed to get onto the roof of the train, just to be on that last ride.

Take High Street, the main business street,

Worshippers of the Black Virgin of Siparia.

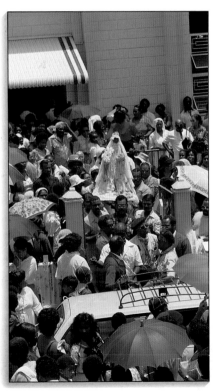

and ask for "Ali's Doubles." This is an Indian delicacy, a bite in the taste. Try it with a cold drink.

High Street and Harris Promenade join at the Library Corner, a popular meeting point in San Fernando with its non-functioning clock. "Meet me at the Library Corner," is what most people say about an appointment in San Fernando. The library is a well-appointed red brick building recently restored. Just on the left of the Library Corner is the Naparima Girls' School, and off on the right on Harris Promenade is the Catholic-run St Joseph's Convent, another girls' school. On Circular Road is the headquarters of one of the country's most powerful trade unions, the Oilfield Workers Trade Union (OWTU), formed in 1937 just after the Butler riots.

San Fernando is built around a hill, the lower portions of which were privately owned and provided house builders with a high grade gravel. So for years, landowners operated successful quarries before they were stopped by the government. The hill has been beautified with benches and trees and, affords a wonderful view over San Fernando.

Return to Port of Spain by driving back through Marabella past the old Union Park Race Course and onto the Solomon Hochoy Highway. Sir Solomon was the first Trinidad and Tobago citizen to be made a governor of Trinidad and Tobago.

Stay on the Solomon Hochoy Highway, and at Claxton Bay's turn-off. On the second hill after the bridge there is a statue of a headless woman. Countless stories surround this statue. The most popular tells that the daughter of an overseer had been seeing a laborer on the estate. One day the father tried to keep his daughter at home and placed a snake at the meeting point to scare away her lover. The girl ran away to meet her boyfriend and was herself bitten by the snake. The father built this statue for her.

Motorists swear that on nights they see the young girl walking along the highway, standing before their cars. There certainly have been many accidents in the immediate area. Others say that the statue is just one of the Virgin Mary.

Continue onto the Butler Highway turning left onto the Churchill Roosevelt. You will find your way easily to the Savannah.

Intricate fretwork of an old estate house, Siparia.

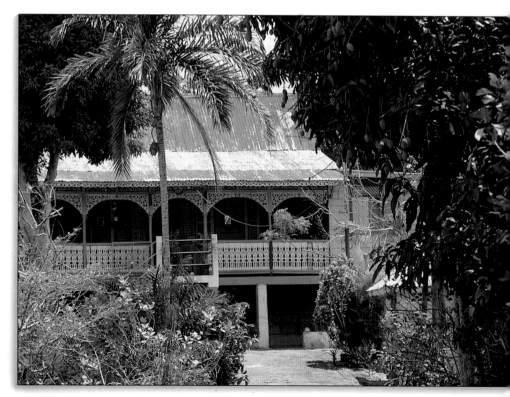

226

To Icacos Point and La Brea: The deep south is the peninsula of land stretching out from the southwest corner of Trinidad toward the west and South America. It is like a bigger shadow of the northern peninsula which contains part of Port of Spain and her suburbs. The La Brea tar pits are located there, as are a number of fishing villages, lookout points and beaches.

It is about three hours' drive to the furthest point on this tour, so if you plan to see a number of sights and return to Port of Spain the same evening, begin your journey early. Also keep in mind that in Trinidad on a weekday there can be traffic jams as early as 7am on the major highways.

Take the now-familiar Butler Highway onto the Solomon Hochoy Highway, which intersects Butler at about Chaguanas. Bypass San Fernando and go into Mosquito Creek. Gulf City is on the right and La Romain on the left.

You will pass through a heavily-wooded area, past the Chatham Youth Camp to Chatham Junction. The ward of Cedros begins here. There are several small villages along the way and some forested areas until Bonasse, way out towards the furthest point.

There is a good place to swim near Mammohansingh Park. Turn left onto Perseverance Road, driving through fields of coconut trees, into the village of **Fullarton**.

This is a "ribbon line village," as are most of the towns in Cedros, where the road is in the middle and houses strung out along the side. People from Fullarton often use the beach in preference to the road, walking along the sand that connects Fullarton with Bonasse when returning from the movies in the latter town.

The two main means of livelihood in this area are fishing and coconuts. Today the coconuts are being affected by red ring disease, which dries the palm.

Ask for Kelman, who owns the village inn and has a lot of ideas on how to spend time usefully. He'll tell you how to make good fish broth in the open and regale you with stories of the village in the old days, though he himself may only be in his late 30s.

Leaving Fullarton bear right at a fork in the road to **Columbus Bay**, again driving through a private coconut estate, and through the village of Los Gallos. It is believed that

Hills of San Fernando.

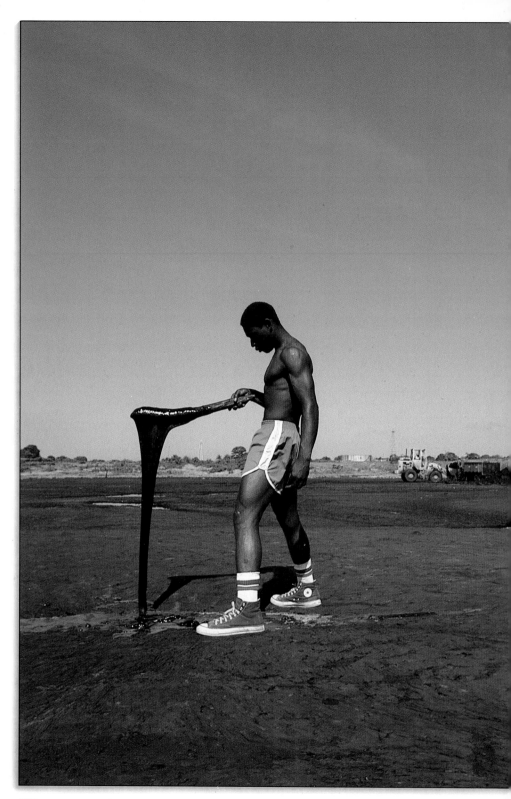

Columbus dropped anchor here on his third voyage to the West Indies. Columbus Bay is a crowded beach on holidays and most weekends, but if the tide is low you can drive another 2 miles (3 km) along the secluded beach or walk all the way to **Icacos Point**.

Icacos is another fishing village, the furthest point on the southwestern peninsula, and 7 miles (11 km) across the Serpent's Mouth from Venezuela.

An old lighthouse for fishermen is fast receding into the sea from erosion. From Columbus Bay or anywhere along that beach you can see **Soldado Rock** and three other small rocks. The negotiations over Patos concerning the boundaries landed Trinidad with Soldado. That was all the importance attached to the very small rock, until about 12 years ago when the zealous coastguard from Venezuela (La Guardia Nacionale) began patrolling the waters around Soldado and roping in fishermen for the Venezuelan jails near the Orinoco. If any fisherman offers you a boat ride, as they are wont to do, insist that he doesn't go past Soldado or pray that your Spanish is adequate.

On the way back, turn sharp left at the gas station at **Cap-de-Ville Junction**. Cape-de-Ville is a growing town on the outskirts of Point Fortin, a small fishing port and a town which is said to breathe: its wide streets permit sea breezes to blow freely. This town was built around the oil industry, its growth closely related to the Shell refinery, nationalized in the mid-1970s and renamed Trintoc (Petrotrin). There is an old section of the town called Teschier Village, occupied by the semi-skilled workers of the refinery who live in nearby semi-detached houses.

The playground at Mahaica saw the birth of some fine national footballers and one of the country's leading football teams, Point Fortin Civic Centre, has its home ground here. There are special housing quarters for Petrotrin's senior staff at Clifton Hill, a beautifully landscaped area with a golf course.

You will leave Point Fortin and come to **Vessigny Beach Camp**. This small beach with changing facilities is in a calm area, but in the rainy season the water is quite dirty.

Five minutes north is **La Brea** and the pitch lake. This is one of three pitch lakes in the world, the others being in Los Angeles (Rancho La Brea) and Venezuela (Guanaco).

Go to the restaurant near the lake or the newly-open visitors facilities and ask for an official guide. Ignore those who pester you on the road.

A good guide and perhaps a witty one will tell you where on the lake you can find a cure for your ailments, most probaby your sinus or aching joints. He might even explain how you can bathe in this lake, but not how you might sail on it as a popular publisher of British romance stories once claimed. The lake is big and black and you can walk on it and at times feel yourself sinking. Don't wear high heeled shoes.

In the late 16th century Sir Walter Raleigh came to the south of Trinidad, mentioning in his notes that he used some pitch from the lake to caulk his ships. He claimed it was better than anything else he had used. José Maria Chacon tried to encourage the pitch industry at La Brea, opening a factory to prepare pitch for export at a rate of 700 barrels a year. The first shipment went to the Royal Arsenal in Spain. Today pitch is exported to European countries and most of the Caribbean, and paves roads in New York City and Paris, amongst other places.

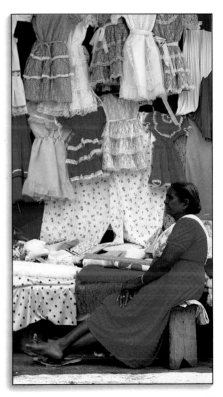

Left, "black gold" at La Brea Pitch Lake. **Right**, a roadside shop in Princes Town.

The village – which is how it should be described – the court house and post office seem to relate closely to the surrounding pitch. When the sun is very hot, the street and the houses seem to move in the shimmering light. Romme St Laurent refers to two pitch lakes in La Brea and perhaps the village was built on one of the two. A drive through La Brea calls for a cushioned bottom.

Brighton, the local port, has a long jetty for tankers to come alongside and receive buckets of asphalt or oil from Petrotrin. People say that "You pass me like a Brighton bucket." In other words, as if you didn't see me, you went by so quickly.

Pass the town of Rousillac and, on reaching Silver Stream River, you come to the end of the swamp. There are lots of mosquitoes and sandflies in this area, as well as Otaheite, a fishing village. There are several ghost towns in the south, but to spot them you will need an oil expert or a southerner in the know to be your guide. There are pumps just pumping away or you may see an oil rig covered with vines. Oil wells that once produced but have been capped are called ghosts.

The Atlantic Coast: Our next tour will be to Central Trinidad, and will take the form of a round trip to the East Coast, passing through sugarcane farms to the flat beaches of the East. The County of Caroni is synonymous with sugarcane and the rolling greenery of the Caroni Plains.

The cane arrows (flowers) are a beautiful sight just before harvest. A cane field then looks like a green wall with a steep of white tops going on for miles.

Turn right at the Uriah Butler Highway. Time and again you will come across French family names like de Gannes, de Verteuil, Lange, Rostant and Melizan, families who received land grants from the crown in the 18th century.

There is an interesting book written by Anthony de Verteuil about his family between 1800 and 1900, giving an excellent insight into this family which intermarried with the other French families that came to the island after the Royal Cedula of Population. If you find there are not as many Spanish names, it is because they headed "down the main" to South America in search of the legendary El Dorado, never finding the gold.

Turn off at Chaguanas, left through

Nariva River and Cocos Bay.

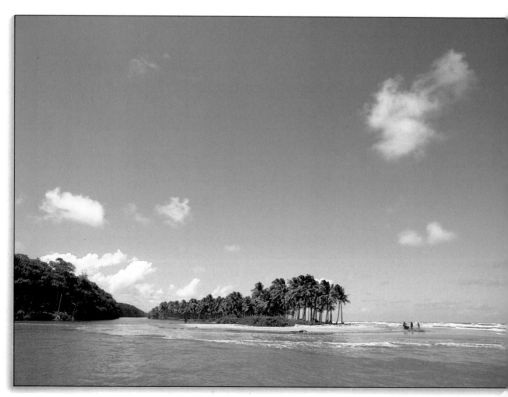

Montrose, past Longdenville, named after a governor from 1870–74. The people of these areas are mainly East Indian descendants of indentured laborers, now small sugarcane farmers or employees in the sugar industry. They were brought here after the abolition of slavery, first arriving on the *Fatel Rozack*, a passenger boat in 1845. To date their children have maintained most of their customs, cooking, dress, music, religion and some form of speech, which is why Indian movies are so popular in Trinidad today.

The **Caroni Plains** mean miles and miles of sugar. These plantations too were once held by the British company Tate and Lyle but were bought by the government in the mid-'70s. You will skirt the Montserrat Hill, surrounded by huge cocoa estates. You can ask to visit the San Salvador Estate, owned by Robert Montano, a businessman who has decided to explore the agricultural potential of the Central Range. Montserrat soil is said to be one of the very best for planting.

It is a delightful drive through Central Trinidad, with clean air, the smell of orange blossoms and beautiful scenery between the Caroni and Naparima Plains. From the town of Todd's Road, originally a railway station, the scenery is ever changing. At moments the forests seem to close in on you, creating an arbor. Note Hindu temples, mosques and an occasional Catholic or Anglican church. The Hindu homes are identifiable by flags planted on bamboo poles in the yards. These flags are up whenever there is a *puja* (prayer meeting) at the home. If you hear the sound of a conch shell it means one is in progress.

Turn right at the sign reading Tabaquite. On the hill is a luxurious round house, with two smaller houses next to it. This is the Lakeside Farm for cattle farming, with a lake at the back.

To visit the **Navet Reservoir** take the Carry–Nariva Road on your left into Brasso Venado (Arm of a Deer). The Reservoir is in the heart of Tabaquite, and supplies water to most of South Trinidad. To visit the water works itself you will have to make arrangements through your hotel with the Water and Sewerage Authority. On the outside of the secured area, however, is a minidam in cool surroundings where you can picnic.

In the 1970s, when the minidam burst, throwing 2 million gallons of water all around

Activities at Mayaro Beach.

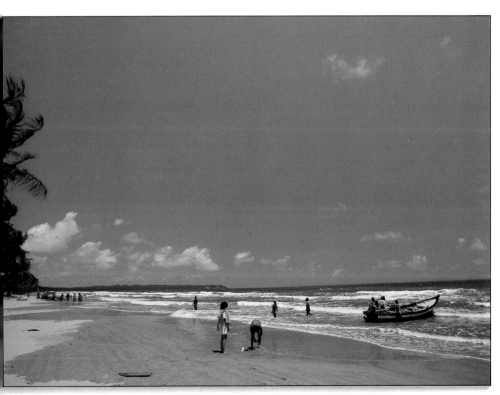

it, people came from all over Trinidad to camp on its banks, catching and cooking cascadura, a freshwater fish with a hard arrowed shell back. There is an old tale about the cascadura which has been written into poetry. Those who eat the cascadura will, the native legend says, wheresover they may wander, end their days in Trinidad. In the Brasso Venado Forest there is a hunter's trail for the adventurous. The wild meat is said to be good here, but you need a license from the Game Warden to hunt.

You will drive through a teak forest said to be the largest in the Western Hemisphere, an awesome sight in an area where habitation is at a minimum. Teak is a durable timber which doesn't warp or shrink and so is used for shipbuilding, furniture and houses. At Brasso Caparo River there are the remnants of a cocoa estate, and men with cutlasses and donkey carts walk the roads looking much the way they did 100 years ago.

Turn right for **Rio Claro**, a town that could be called the capital of Nariva County, as it is the seat of the local government. The town has a heavy Spanish influence and boasts a good parang group. It is a busy town, about 50 miles (80 km) from the city. Big banks and stores have branches here.

The words of the songs by the Paranderos concern the Virgin, St Joseph and the birth of Christ. The Amerindians were taught to make and play Spanish string instruments, to sing and venerate important Catholic feasts. The Capuchins were all for this and today there are good parang bands from Arima, Santa Cruz and the Palo Seco, Santa Flora area. The music is gay, and the singers wear pretty flowered clothing.

Leave Rio Claro on the Mayaro Road and soon you will see wide expanses of coconut trees, indicating that you are approaching the sea. Before the seaside town of Plaisance you will go over two wooden bridges over the Ortoire River. Turning left will take you north and eventually to Manzanilla.

Long ago, to get to Mayaro from Manzanilla there were two car ferries. There was a shop at the first ferry owned by a Chinese merchant, for there was not much to be had in these out-of-the-way places. Then the shops in what were known as outposts were owned and run by Chinese. Chinese immigrants were also brought in as laborers, **Coconut trees at Cocos Bay...**

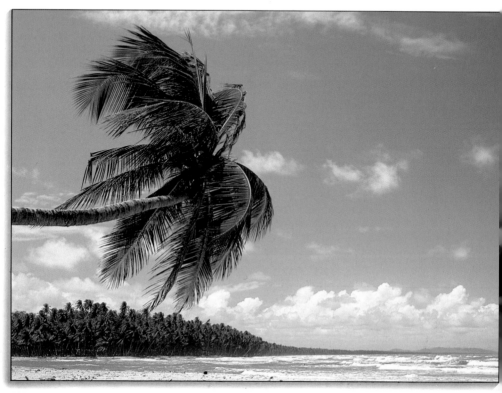

mainly from Canton, the first group arriving on the *Clarendon* in the 1850s.

The ferries were soon replaced by wooden bridges known as Bailey bridges, built by the US Armed Forces to facilitate movement in that part of the island.

The trade winds keep this coast refreshed year round. Across the East Coast, as the crow flies, will take you straight to Africa, and according to Romme St Laurent, coconuts arrived here when an African ship transporting the nuts ran aground.

For years on the Sunday before Easter there was a tub race from the first Bailey bridge to the mouth of the river after Point Radix about a mile and a half away, even though the Ortoire is noted for alligators and water snakes called anacondas. These species have been washed into the river from the Orinoco in Venezuela when it overflows its banks. The tubs were made with plastic buckets, old bath tubs or any old containers, and filled with drinks. To qualify the racers must have consumed all by the end.

Manzanilla is divided into two coconut estates, or cocals as they are called. The first as you are driving south to north belongs to the Bovell family. You will see many buffalypsoes (a buffalo used for beef herd) grazing on the estate. The second cocal is owned by the Huggins family, one of the big landowners.

Swimming along this coast is pleasant and late afternoon at sunset is delightful. On moonlit nights the beach is a silvery white. If taking a tour strictly to swim in Manzanilla, bring along your hamper, or you might find the villages are great at whipping up sandwiches and drinks at short notice. Some will even make a cook-up of pigeon peas and rice with some morsels of chicken thrown in with pumpkin.

On one of these swimming tours take time to stop at the Sou-Sou Land La Mariquita Estate. On the Manzanilla Road, about 4 miles (6 km) from the beach, you will see the Cocoa Village townhouses on one side and across the street the sign saying "La Mariquita."

It was until recently a cocoa estate owned by the same family which built the cocoa houses. However, with high land taxes and low prices for cocoa, many owners were willing to dispose of their land. One of the

. and at layaro.

big purchasers has been Sou-Sou Land Limited, a company which has been buying land and developing on behalf of the landless for housing. Sou-Sou is a patois word meaning penny by penny, and is a traditional form of banking among low income groups in Trinidad. Participants in these projects contribute any surpluses in income to purchasing their land.

The La Mariquita Estate is spread over 148 acres (60 hectares), of which 120 plots, each of 10,000 sq. feet (930 sq. meters), are allocated to housing. The estate is a mixture of cocoa, citrus, bananas and some pineapple, and is one of the few estates in the country open to visitors. The estate house was built in the mid-1970s but is old-fashioned with wooden floors and a rolling roof patterned after the cocoa drying houses. The founder of Sou-Sou Land, John Humphrey, hopes one day to make this estate into a showpiece for Trinidadians, Tobagonians and tourists alike.

Moruga and Guayaguayare: The last tour will take you to two distant points on the island: Moruga in the county of Victoria and Guayaguayare in the county of Mayaro. Prepare yourself for an entire day.

The route is the usual one down the Uriah Butler and Solomon Hochoy Highways to the San Fernando by-pass. Turn left at the Furness Watson Building midway on the by-pass, into Cocoyea. About 5 miles (8 km) out you will see the sugar refinery. **Usine Ste Madeleine**, a part of Caroni Limited, its beauty surpassing that of the rolling fields of Brechin Castle in Caroni. The road to the refinery is lined with royal palms as at Brechin Castle.

Ste Madeleine is one of those areas in Trinidad where the class contrast is quite apparent. On the one hand there are the company homes of senior staff at the refinery overlooking the Ste Madeleine pond, the sprawling yards, and the well-maintained golf course.

On the other, there are the simple, sometimes ramshackle homes of the estate laborers, whose children play their Sunday cricket on the unkempt roadside playgrounds. There are the railway lines on which the carriages roll in with company cane, but you will also see long lines of buffalo-drawn carts, the animals drooping in the midday heat waiting for the cane to be weighed.

A colorful home of a sugarworker in Guayaguayare.

234

More information on the sugar industry can be obtained from the Public Relations department of Caroni Limited who will organize a tour of their operations for you, including a visit to a distillery in the north. Molasses is one by-product of the refining process whose production can be observed.

Continue along the Manahambre Road past other sugar villages – Jordan Hill, Cedar Hill and Manahambre – into **Princes Town**. As you enter you will see the Anglican Church where two poui trees were planted by Prince Albert and Prince George, who later became King George VI. They visited Trinidad in 1880, arriving on the *HMS Bacchante* and were guests of Governor Sir Henry Turner Irving. When they visited the south, what was known as "the Mission" was renamed Princes Town, in their honor.

On the left past the church is the police station and court house which from its fret work is known to be of French influence. Leave Princes Town and take the Moruga Road past villages called First, Third, Fourth, Fifth and Sixth Company. These villages housed disbanded Anglican soldiers from the American Civil War who were sent to Trinidad to make their fortunes. The Second Company was lost at sea, hence no mention of its name. Each company village has its own cemetery and church.

In this part of Trinidad there are typical old houses and rolling savannahs. You are going through flat lands and the area is called precisely that in French, Basse Terre. The road goes straight into the fishing village of **Moruga** with its one main street. Many residents of Moruga are Spiritual Baptists and numerous houses on Indian Walk Road are Baptist shrines.

Moruga is also a center for the African derived belief system called obeah. People from all over Trinidad come to the small villages around Moruga to visit the obeah men and women. Obeah folk practice uses the "bush bath" to wash out evil or affliction; candles can be used to do evil or cast spells. For the bush bath herbs are selected and boiled according to the problem, but it is difficult to say what these selections are.

Like magicians, obeah men never tell. You can go to the obeah man if you want to get a job, if you want to persuade your young man to marry you, if you want to keep a

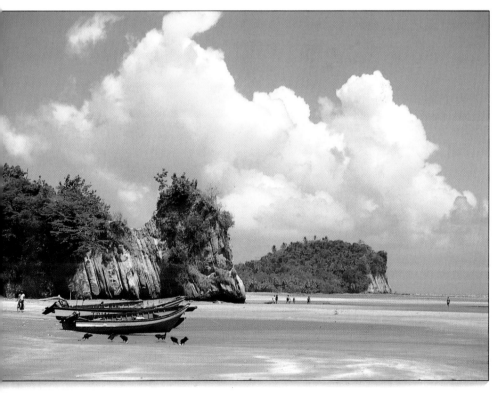

Blue skies over Moruga

delinquent husband at home or even to heal you of some kinds of sickness.

The beach in Moruga is extraordinary at low tide. You have to walk at least a mile and a half on the seabed of sand before you reach the water. If you walk a considerable way out you will appreciate a delightful scene of the fishing boats stuck in the sea bed, waiting to rise again when the tide comes in with sheer cliffs behind you.

You will also see the church, the old plantation house on high ground and this seabed of sand extending for miles on your left and right. To swim means a long walk to the water unless the tide is high. This is where Christopher Columbus spotted the three hills (those of the southern range) which led him to call the island Trinidad. To have a clear view of the three hills you need to be out on a boat like Columbus, closer to the Guayaguayare area.

Though Discovery Day (first Monday in August) has been renamed Emancipation Day, villagers continue to celebrate the grand occasion, complete with the arrival of Christopher Columbus in 15th-century garb who moves onto land, kissing the sand and lying flat as Roman Catholic priests do on ordination, claiming it in the name of the King and Queen of Spain. He is usually accompanied by his fleet. If you are near on this day, don't miss the opportunity to take part in the festivities.

Look at Moruga on your map. It is on the southern coast about one-third distance from the southeastern tip. As the crow flies north you will come to Arima, the center of the county of St George, at the foot of the Northern Range. Return by the road leading into New Grant, Tableland and Fonrose, into Rio Claro and onto the Mayaro Road.

Mayaro is in the county with the same name and on the Mayaro beach road you will see the built-up residential area where employees of Amoco (American Oil Company) live. A number of local families have beach houses here and there are two coconut plantations owned by the de Meillacs, another of the French families. You can stop anywhere along this beach for a good refreshing swim. Two major currents meet here, creating a crisscross effect in the waves. If you're not in any real hurry, you may want to stay here quite a while, taking in the fresh sea breeze from the Atlantic.

The beaches here are strewn with chip-chip shells and during chip-chip gathering season many a delicious dish can be made of the shell fish. But be prepare to wash them over and over to be rid of the sand.

Drive south to **Guayaguayare**, an Indian-sounding name like Chacachacare. In the same manner, people fondly refer to it as "Guaya." At Galeota Point on the very tip of the coast, you will see the oil rigs, out at sea.

From Upper Manzanilla to Rushville in Guaya is about 44 miles (73 km) of flat sandy beach lined by endless, tall straight coconut trees.

Return to Port of Spain along the Mayaro Road into Manzanilla over the Ortoire River. From Manzanilla drive on to Sangre Chiquito, Sangre Grande and Valencia. Then take the turn-off for the Churchill Roosevelt Highway which will bring you straight into the Beetham Highway and Port of Spain.

You have covered the length and breadth of Trinidad; you have traveled to the four points. Time and again you have entered the Northern Range which is most beautiful, because it is the heart of the Trinidad rain forest and a special paradise for nature lovers.

Left, a basket case (or "straw man"). Right, drying the laundry Caribbean-style.

Tobago

1300 m / 0,8 miles

Tourist attractions:

1 Kariwak Hotel
2 Sandy Point
   Beach Club
3 Tropikist Hotel
4 Crown Reef Hotel
5 Mt. Irvine Hotel
6 Back Bay
7 Turtle Beach Hotel
8 Arnos Vale Hotel
9 Blue Waters Inn
10 King's Bay Waterfall
11 Richmond Great House

Caribbean

Castara
Castara Bay

Mount Dillo

King Peter's Bay

Woodlands
Runnemede

Culloden

Moriah
Mount Thomas
Golden Lane
Indian Walk

St. David
Nutmeg Grove

Les Coteaux

Vale Rd.

Arnos Vale

Easterfie

Plymouth
Les Coteaux
Mason Hall

Courland Pt.
Adventure

Franklyn's
Concordia
Belmont

Great Courland Bay
Plymouth Rd.
Courland

St. George
Adelphi

Black Rock
Lower Quarter or Roselle
Mary's Hill

The Whim
Providence

Northside Rd.
Mesopotamia

Mt. Irvine or Little Courland Bay
Grange

Orange
Hill Rd.
Orange Hill

Calder Hall

Friendsfield
Mo
St. Geo

Booby Pt.
Buccoo
Bethel
Patience Hill
Lower Town
Morne Quiton
Hillsbo
Bay

Buccoo Coral Reef
Buccoo Bay
Buccoo Rd.
Prospect

St. Andrew
Bacolet

Scarborough

Carnbee Village
Lambeau
Rockly Bay
Minister Bay
Minister P

Golden Grove
Diamond

St. Patrick
Shirvan
Auchenskloch
Little Rockly Bay
Bacolet Pt.

Milford or Sandy Bay
Bon Accord Lagoon
Canaan
Mt. Pleasant

Bon Accord Village

Tyson Hall
Kilgwyn

Friendship

Brown's or Crown's Pt.
Robinson Crusoe's Cave
Canoe Bay
Cove

Columbus or Kennedy's Pt.

240

S e a

North Pt.

Corvo Pt.

Charlotteville

Starwood

Man of War Bay

St. John

Cambleton

Belmont

Anse Fourmi

Hermitage

Bloody Bay

Parlatuvier

Bloody Bay

⑨

Parlatuvier Bay

St. John

Tyrell's Bay

man's

Parrot Hall

Speyside

nan's

Trois Rivieres

Roxborough Parlatuvier Rd.

King's Bay

Merchiston

Tobago Forest Reserve

St. Paul

Windward Rd.

⑩

Delaford

Morne D'or

Pulteney Hill

Kendal Place

King's Bay

Shore Park

Roxborough

Pedro Pt.

Louis D'or

⑪

Prince's Bay

St. Mary

Carapuse Bay

The Lure

Cardiff

Belle Garden

Hillsborough

Pembroke

Glamorgan

Richmond I.

Windsor

Goldsborough

eld

Goodwood

Goldsborough Bay

A t l a n t i c   O c e a n

Hill

Montrose

Studley Park

Windward Rd.

ados Bay

Ganby Pt.

St. Giles or Melville Islands

Charlotteville

Starwood

Cambleton

Belmont

Little Tobago or Bird of Paradise Island

Goat I.

Speyside

Tyrell's Bay

241

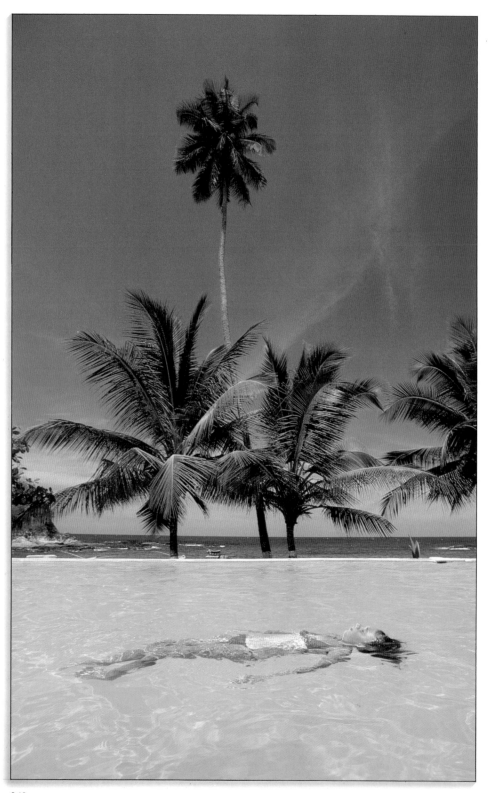

WELCOME TO TOBAGO

Like a Caribbean island of 50 years ago, Tobago stands relatively un-marked by international tourism. Though this is changing, picturesque bumpy roads winding past palm groves, tiny hamlets and locals waiting for a "drop," small hotels frequented by Trinidadian vacationers, a place where an outsider can still be an interesting anomaly and not simply an oppressive necessity. The traditional Tobago of unspoiled beaches, friendly fishermen will remain for some time. The question is: for how long?

From the cosmopolitan snap of Port of Spain to the rural languor of Tobago seems a far longer distance than the mere 20-minute ride on an Air Caribbean flight. Though they are indeed united in more than just economic and political ways, there are subtle (and not so subtle) differences between Trinidad and Tobago. Where Trinidad presents a surprising mixture of African, East Indian, Oriental and European culture and people, almost 90 percent of Tobagonians are of black African descent. And while Trinis tend to be a cosmopolitan bunch, even Scarborough, Tobago's largest town, is more of an enlarged market village than a real city.

But Trinidad and Tobago were of the same piece of South American land, and so Tobago offers the same diverse geography and plant and animal life. Twenty-six miles (42 km) long but only 3 miles (5 km) wide, Tobago is a constant feast for the eyes, as even interior roads are usually only 15 or so minutes from glimpses of the sea, and a route through the mountainous interior passes stands of enormous creaking bamboo and dense jungly growth before suddenly giving way to vistas of sparkling white palm-fringed beach, or open pastures grazed by placid cattle and scruffy goats.

The fish-shaped island is circumnavigated by two main coastal roads. However, the "head" and "tail" are beyond the reach of this circle, and north of Charlotteville there are only paths. Any point on the island is reachable in a few hours' drive at most, and most drives are a good day trip, with as much to see along the way as there is at the final destination.

Preceding pages: Tobagonians take a lime near the Windward Road. **Left**, rhapsody in blue at Arnos Vale Hotel.

TOURING TOBAGO

From the air, Tobago appears like a travel brochure picture, with bright blue water sparkling around a rolling green land, stretches of pale beach and frothy waves defining the perimeter. The mountains of the interior loom deep green and dusky purple.

Tobago is rumored to be Robinson Crusoe's island, and some guides would happily show you his exact cave, though the caves of the southeast tip could have been formed by wave action or man. More important than the verifiability of this claim though, is the truth that Crusoe could have subsisted happily here. Tobago is a self-contained paradise, a verdant island where the visitor could well imagine himself housed in a palm-frond cottage, sustained on the fruits of land and ocean, eternally entertained by the mutable beauty of the landscape of sand, sea, sky, and mountain.

Most place names reflect the recent European history of the island – Studley Park, Les Coteaux, Roxborough, Auken-skeoch, Courland – and the ubiquitous bright orange immortelle, imported as shade for cocoa trees, is as much a reminder of the colonial past as are the crumbling sugar mills hidden here and there in the forests. This is still an agricultural place where almost everyone on the island makes at least a part, if not all, of his living from farming or fishing.

An increasing number of tourists, from Europe in particular, are discovering Tobago. More hotels are being built and accommodation is becoming more exclusive. But the individualism of the island still survives, and each beach has its own personality, with fishermen's nets drying on one and goats grazing the edges of another.

Crown Point and Crusoe: Most visitors to Tobago fly into **Crown Point Airport**, at the southwestern tip of the island, though some still take the ferry from Port of Spain direct to Scarborough, the island's capital. The airport, renovated in late 1985, is a comfortable blend of the modern, the tropical and the touristy. A warm gusty wind blows scents of the sea through the hangar-like building and across the driveway is a pleasant, inviting open-air snack bar where

An aerial view of an island paradise.

travelers can take a moment to unwind before moving on to their hotels.

Out front, taxi drivers jostle for passengers, but don't choose one until you've investigated the options. A number of hotels provide minibus transport to and from the airport, and if you're staying at one of the nearby hotels like Sandy Point or Kariwak you can pretty much walk there. Car rentals are also available at the airport. Taxis are expensive, particularly for the further ends of the island (*see Travel Tips, page 266*), and a taxi driver can be your best guide. But be sure to agree on the charge before you begin; the rates drivers quote often depend on whether they can expect to have you again as their customer in the future.

Right next to Crown Point are a number of modern hotels. Air traffic noise doesn't seem to be a major problem, and the hotels are convenient to the major tourist attraction of **Buccoo Reef**, but this corner of the island is basically flatlands, so don't miss the rest of the island even if you do stay here.

The **Sandy Point Beach Club** and **Crown Point Condominiums** offer apartment-type accommodations in modern, air-conditioned buildings, as does the **Tropikist Beach Hotel**. Also nearby is **Kariwak Village**, worth a trip for dinner and drinks just to see what owner/manager Allan Clovis is up to.

One of the most knowledgeable and helpful hoteliers on Tobago, he presents art and photography shows of local artists, can find you a good taxi driver/guide, or point you toward a secluded beach where pre-Columbian arrowheads and potsherds can still be found. He is a storehouse of local intelligence and tourist advice.

Though the **Bon Accord Road** to the airport is little used past the airport turn-off, it does lead to some quiet shallow bays. This is the area Robinson Crusoe is said to have inhabited. Continue around the runway, past Sandy Point Beach Club all the way to the end of the road. You'll have completed a horseshoe. Through the low-growing sea grapes is a lovely half-mile double curve of sand, a flat, narrow and deserted beach only occasionally disturbed by the planes landing at the airport nearby.

Canoe Bay's waters are clear, shallow and calm, and seldom visited by more than the infrequent local fisherman or jogger.

You can poke around in the clay banks for remnants of earlier inhabitants.

Buccoo boat ride: Return along the airport road to reach **Store Bay**, whose name is an Anglicization of its first Dutch settler, Stoer. This is a jump-off point for trips to the Buccoo Reef. The Bay can be approached by the Pigeon Point Road further on, or more quickly from a small side road across from the airport.

The beach itself is merely pleasant, a protected cove nestling against low rocky ledges. On the right is the modern **Coco Reef Hotel**, formerly the Crown Reef Hotel, which underwent a multi-million dollar refurbishment and reopened in 1995. The bathing facilities are extensive here, with changing rooms, showers and toilets, and a number of red-rooted cement pagodas with picnic tables and benches. Throughout the island, the T&T Tourist Board has built extensive beach facilities, which can be used for a small charge.

Some of the best food shacks on the island have taken advantage of the tourist trade here, and delicious crab curry, turtle and conch roti, and fresh fruit are all for sale at little stands, many adorned with colorful paintings and slogans.

The trip to the reef is the closest thing to a tourist attraction Tobago can boast, and is worth the TT$25 just to satisfy your curiosity. Its success depends on the quality of the boat you get. Unfortunately, it's hard to know beforehand what a boat will be like, since tickets are bought on shore and boats rest offshore until the moment they must pick up passengers. Most of the "glass" consists of a central plexiglass panel in varying stages of cloudiness, so check with friends or at your hotel reception about the best boatmen when you go.

It's a 20-minute boat ride to Buccoo Reef, but 10 minutes out is the equally renowned **Nylon Pool**, basically an offshore sandbar whose thigh-high pale turquoise waters and soft clean sand provide a sybaritic bath. Floating in the still lagoon with the deep ocean on one side and palm-fringed beaches on the other is an entrancing experience.

Out beyond the pool lies the reef, a coral fringe much destroyed by pollution, boats and both thoughtless tourists and locals (*see Above and Below the Water, page 145*). **Wild orchid.**

Boats remain here for about half an hour before returning to shore.

The boat may stop at **Pigeon Point** to let off passengers. This is the beach used in almost all of Trinidad and Tobago's travel ads for its intense aqua waters, graceful palms and picturesque thatch-roofed dock. But don't get off here unless you want to pay for a taxi back, because it's a long (half-hour) walk back to Store Bay.

Pigeon Point is the only private beach on Tobago, lying surprisingly enough, at the end of Pigeon Point Road. When driving, keep to the left at the major fork and at the end of the pavement continue down the dirt road to the guard. A small entrance fee is usually charged.

The beach is a long idyllic stretch, the vacationer's Platonic ideal of a Caribbean seashore. Along the way, food shacks and picnic tables are shaded by royal palms, while beyond, cattle graze the soft green grass of a coconut grove, like something out of a Rousseau painting.

All over the island there are areas reserved for grazing cattle. Until the 1960s these were generally coconut estates, when labor became expensive and scarce. The beach curves around into the **Bon Accord Lagoon**, a fisherman's harbor perfect for strolling and beachcombing.

This is probably the best place on the island for shells, laying as it does off the reef. The classic conch shells with their sunny pink and apricot insides are scattered here and there where fishermen have left them after removing the meat. At mid-morning or late afternoon a fisherman might return with his catch of yellow and pink snapper, hog fish, or conch. Not as perfectly groomed as Pigeon Point, this beach is scattered with palm fronds, coconut hulls and the more mundane rubbish of bottles and cans, but it is often uncrowded even when Pigeon Point is overrun.

Like Buccoo Reef, Pigeon Point is a tourist's necessity, although it is advisable to avoid it during the weekend, when it is likely to be crowded with visitors from a cruise ship offshore, eager to make the most of their 2 hour taste of Tobago.

Surf and turf: Along the Milford Road are the towns of **Canaan** and **Bon Accord**, small settlements named after the religious missions which originally occupied these sites. There are small shops and a couple of roti stands serving the concrete block homes. Further along, near the **Shirvan Road**, are government-funded housing areas of neatly similar concrete block houses.

Continue down the **Milford Road** to the Shirvan Road toward the northeast. You'll pass signs for **Buccoo Beach**, a rocky, littered and sometimes polluted public beach not worth a stop. The Shirvan Road is quietly pretty, and runs near the water through pale green groves of tall palm and squat banana.

Shirvan turns into the Grafton Road, with the **Mount Irvine Bay Hotel** marked by the pink, orange and purple bougainvillea that fringes its cottages and by the neatly clipped greens and towering palms of its famed golf course. Mount Irvine is built on the site of an old sugar plantation owned by Charles Irvine in the latter half of the 18th century. The golf course is open to anyone for a fee, and there is a restaurant built around the old stone sugar mill.

The **Museum of Tobago History** also began on the hotel grounds. A one-room display area tended by Edward Hernandez, passionate and learned when it comes to the history of his island, contains shells, pre-Columbian and European tools, buttons and tableware from pirate ships and colonials, potsherds and a host of other archaeological finds from all eras of Tobago's history. In 1989 agreement was reached in the Tobago House of Assembly to relocate the museum to a new building at Fort George.

The public beach just northeast of the hotel has some of the nicest and most complete facilities. A favored spot for surfers, there are good waves breaking about a quarter mile offshore. The changing room building is built next to the old site of the Mount Irvine Estate sugar depot, where ships from all over deposited their ballast of slate and bricks in exchange for sugar and, later, cocoa cultivated on the estate.

Now there are the usual locker rooms and showers, as well as a small bar where you can sit at a concrete table and drink Carib with a bake 'n' shark. Local parties are sometimes held here at night, featuring wild game and wild music.

The deep, clean beach is dotted with sea

Fishing boats at rest at Plymouth.

grape trees whose leafy canopy has been trained into sun umbrellas. The sea floor is rocky in places, and at low tide there are wonderful little pools caught in the declivities, swarming with sea roaches, crabs and tiny fish. Safest bathing spots are delineated by yellow and red flags.

Secluded sun spots: For a really secluded beach, walk a short way down the main highway to a rusted, rickety gate leading into a palm grove. Walk across the grove to the sea, past benign cattle to the cliff, and it should be easy to find a spot to climb down to deserted **Back Bay**. This is a favored beach for nude sunbathing but is usually deserted and the waves can be quite good for body surfing.

Continuing along the road toward **Black Rock** and **Plymouth**, keep to the high main road to the right, or take a turn a bit beyond the Back Bay entrance and take the shore road along **Grafton Beach**. This long, wide, usually empty stretch of beach is easily accessible from places along the road. It might be totally deserted, or there could be a couple of people running dogs and fishing for sea roaches, the tiny sand colored crustaceans which look exactly like their nickname and are used for bait for offshore fishing. It's a nice place for a swim as well, as there are often gentle waves, but there can be strong currents at times.

The Grafton Beach Resort – considered by some to be one of Tobago's best hotels – dominates this area, and offers its guests a lovely view of Grafton Bay and a quiet beach. Grafton beach is located just across the road from the hotel which stands on the old Grafton estate, which was once owned by the Smith family, who had a long history on the island. Although the house fell into disrepair the land was preserved as a bird sanctuary for many years and wildlife still flourishes here. It is not unusual to see cocricos, motmots and other birds flying around the resort and the surrounding area.

Just outside the small village of Black Rock is the unassuming **Mon Cheri Café** which often appears closed. Try it anyway, for their wonderful kingfish pelau and other inexpensive Creole dishes.

Of turtles and kings: Northeast of Black Rock is the **Turtle Beach Hotel** on **Great Courland Bay**, once the site of an early

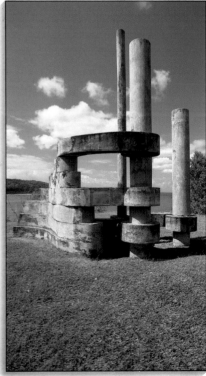

settlement and now famous for the immense sea turtles which come up on the beach at night to lay their eggs. Courlanders, more commonly known as Latvians, were some of the first Europeans to settle on Tobago, Lutherans looking for a place to emigrate after the Thirty Years' War.

The settlement was begun around 1659 by Duke Jekabs, a godson of James I of England. Eventually the Courlanders sent to Tobago by Jekabs were absorbed into other colonies on the island, some at Mount Irvine, or Little Courland Bay.

The bar at Turtle Beach is popular on the nights the hotel hosts its weekly steel band show. During egg-laying season in April and May, groups meet at night to observe the turtles on the beach, who seem unperturbed by the presence of humans.

Beyond Black Rock is Plymouth, the biggest town on the north side, but don't go looking for a town center. Plymouth is mostly a small residential village on a promontory overlooking Great Courland Bay, with small shops for local needs, a gas station and one tourist attraction: **Fort James**.

The fort was built by the British in 1768 as a barrack, and named after King James II. Now all that remains is a neatly kept low stone edifice, set amid clipped lawns and a few botanical plantings. Peering in through the window reveals the fort's present usage – as a tool shed. The view from the escarpment is nice, with vistas of curving Turtle Beach to the left and fishing boats at rest closer by.

The approach road to the fort passes a small concrete block School for the Deaf, the local grandstand and field, and another Tourist Board attraction mentioned in every guidebook. In the courtyard of a small stone church is the **mysterious tombstone**, whose inscription reads, "*She was a mother without knowing it and a wife without letting her husband know it except by her kind indulgences to him.*" (Betty Stiven 1783.) One can just imagine Betty's domestic situation.

Take Jager Road to the ocean, and if you can get around the fence you might find Carib and Arawak tear-drop axes in the freshwater rivers where they meet the sea.

The walk from the fort provides a charming, superficial picture of village life, with cocks crowing and schoolchildren in neat **Baby turtles on Turtle Beach.**

blue uniforms running about, and pastel houses with neat yards against wooden shacks overgrown with hibiscus, banana palms and other tropical plants.

North Road, one of the main streets in town, turns into a dirt lane and then ends in a narrow stretch of rough beach, good for a quick dip only, but refreshing if you're hot and a half hour's drive from the next beach!

The Mot-Mot Trail: The gently curving road out of Plymouth leads inland for some time, with **Arnos Vale Hotel** about a mile away. Terraced along a small hillside with winding paths through botanical plantings, Arnos Vale offers some of the best snorkeling and bird-watching on Tobago. Even if you don't stay there, it's worth the trip for those attractions.

The original English owners covered the hillside with scarlet ixora, pink oleander, pastel bougainvillea, rosy hibiscus, multicolored foliage bushes, many flamboyant trees with their deep green leaves and orange flowers, and other sweet-scented tropical plants. The stunted trees with rubbery leaves on the beach are Indian almonds. Take the Mot-Mot Trail early in the morning for bird-watching, or follow other little paths to their summits overlooking the bay.

Because the cove is so protected, with sharp rocky outcroppings stepping down into the water, there are myriad places for brilliant tropical fish to live and hide. Rent snorkeling equipment from the hotel, and swim out to see barracuda, brain coral, sea fans, the blue-green parrot fish, male stoplights, the multicolored angelfish with their pendant "whiskers," yellow and black rock beauties, hawkfish, electric blue tangs and surgeonfish, rays, trumpetfish and the waves of small silver blue grunts which miraculously surround you in shallow water.

Fishing off the rocks can yield Caribbean salmon, kingfish, bonita, or albacore, though offshore your chances are improved. To the left of the main beach, a short hike over the rocks or a brief swim, is a secluded triangle of sand; to the right, carved into rocky cliffs, are caves. There is even a very dark Indian man lying in one, and you can tell his particular cave by the Hindu flag outside!

Creole Coteaux: The Arnos Vale Road past the hotel continues to curve upwards through rolling countryside planted with the short,

Bovine bug epellent.

leafy banana palms which are, strictly speaking, large herbs. A half mile or so past the hotel is a sign on the right for Franklyn's Road, a hilly, bumpy track which eventually emerges in the hill town of **Les Coteaux**.

But just after the turn, on the right practically hidden by thick undergrowth, is the original **Arnos Vale water wheel**. Its deep red bricks now covered with creeping vines, the wheel dates back to colonial times.

The track leads past Franklyn's Estate, now a modern vacation home surrounded by a high pink wall and wrought-iron gate, with an unlikely stand of pine trees. Past that are small houses with neat yards, and many deep cuts.

The Arnos Vale Road continues through low dry hills reminiscent of Indonesia, or Africa, past the ubiquitous tethered livestock, and into the village of Les Coteaux, a crossroads of comparatively goodly size in this area of Tobago.

The sounds of crowing rooster and klaxon horns make every day sound like Sunday and the residents will happily offer directions, whether or not they know the way and, whether or not you can interpret the dialect.

The name of their home, an obvious leftover from the days of French colonization, is pronounced by locals as something more akin to "Leckito." If you give it a French pronunciation, you risk misunderstanding.

At Les Coteaux three roads meet: to the left the road leads up north along the shore; to the right down through lush hills and streams to Scarborough, and straight ahead (sort of) it twists off toward the Hillsborough Dam. Keep left to explore the northern shore.

A tropical Amalfi Coast: The bad mountain road leads over rocky terrain with ravines crowded with the immortelle, vivid orange in dry season, and terraced hillsides fringed by the pale green of bamboo stands. Little iridescent lizards, the baby dinosaurs, dart across the road, which is often washed out in places, and periwinkle-blue morning glories carpet the road banks.

For **Culloden Bay**, take the Culloden Road at the fork, leading south through the tiny hamlet of **Golden Lane**. There are beautiful vistas out to sea across hills dotted with palms and breadfruit trees. Take a sharp right at the Moriah/Arnos Vale junction in Golden Lane and an extremely rocky dirt

Ramshackle house near Les Coteaux, now demolished.

road leads to the bay. (Beware: the map can be confusing.)

Culloden Bay is a pebbly fisherman's cove with the charm of the utilitarian. The fishermen here catch redfish, bonito and albacore, among other things, and if you care to venture down (there are some amazing trees along the way) you might convince one of them to take you fishing some very early Sunday morning for a lot less than the organized tours will charge. The boats are fiberglass dinghies, and their methods uncomplicated – trolling with heavy line and massive hooks – but the fishermen know how to read the waters and skies for schooling fish.

Return the way you came, past the small settlements of pastel houses on stilts, some with flags that resemble those of the Hindus but signify a Shango house, and small grocers marked by Carib beer signs. North of **Moriah** the coastal road traverses steeper and steeper hills as it climbs toward the small fishing villages and perfect beaches of Castara and Parlatuvier.

Here are some of the most spectacular views and stunning shores on the island, glimpsed around hairpin turns, as the glittering navy sea shades into turquoise near the shore hundreds of feet below. At the height of the road you might simply dive into clouds like the unbroken expanse of sparkling water. **King Peter's Bay**, on the way, named for a Carib monarch, is not particularly good for swimming.

The **Sisters Rocks** appear offshore surrounded by white foam, right before the road spins down headily to Castara Bay. On the beach you might imagine yourself on the Amalfi Coast, with sharp, dark green cliffs enclosing the town and bay, and the blue water glittering like diamonds. **Castara**, like most of the north coast towns, is a fishing village, and most of the 500 or so residents support themselves by a combination of fishing, farming and government work, most notably road repair. It is a Tobago conundrum that a great number of island men work on the roads yet many still remain deeply potholed, although there has been a marked improvement in recent years.

Castara has the usual changing rooms, showers and toilets, but mostly you'll find fishermen liming in their shed while they

Subtle smiles of Tobago.

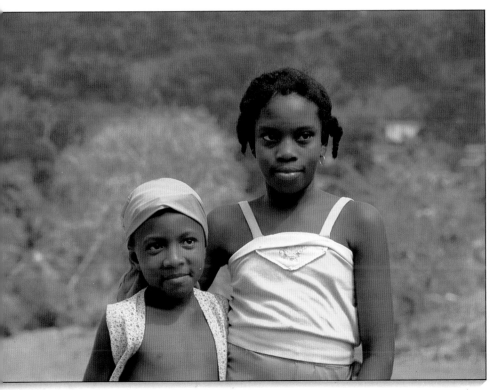

mend nets and wait for the tide to change. The long wide beach, edged by low thick palms, often has nets laid out to dry, and wooden dinghies float offshore with their bamboo rods balanced like insect antennae.

If you're hungry, visit Henry Jackson's "First and Last" roti stand just up the road from the beach, where he sells tasty goat, chicken and potato roti, cold drinks, liquor and such sundry items as bay rum, hard balls and toothpaste. Sit on the shaded bench and watch shy smiling children pass while friendly bony dogs beg at your feet for scraps. Or there's the "No Problem" food supply store nearby.

North of Castara the views are equally stunning, as the road winds inward through jungle, up and down steep hills and back out toward the coast. The second rocky bay past Castara is **Englishman's**, below the railing on the coastal side. Drive down to where the road is straight and then find the path to this secluded beach.

Next is **Parlatuvier**, about a leisurely 30-minute drive from Castara. Parlatuvier has a perfect crescent beach curving away toward pretty pastel houses and palm-fringed hills,

a little elementary school shaking with the noise and concentration of children, a tiny store or two, and not much else. Teenage boys lounge under palm trees, burly fishermen drag in their seines, and the sea rolls quietly on the sand. Parlatuvier is village life at its simplest.

Beyond the beach, the North Road crosses a small bridge over a reedy estuary and heads up the hill toward the left. Beyond, the road is often impassable but it does provide quiet green views and perhaps motmots or cocricos in roadside bushes until the lane peters off entirely on a curve above a mossy green ravine.

The right fork leads to a crossroad, after a bumpy ride on a wide dirt road, and a right at the cross leads to **Roxborough**, over the top of the mountain.

Beyond Parlatuvier is Charlotteville and the south side, traveling along the road between the two towns is a beautiful drive through jungle past **Bloody Bay**, the site of a long-ago battle which stained the waters red, and **Man of War**, where pirates secreted their booty.

Interior idyll: There are a number of over-

A fisherman brings in his seine.

land routes to the south side. The Parlatuvier-Roxborough road is about a half-hour drive through jungle above steep ravines filled with bamboo and birds, until a low cocoa grove and a school signal that you have reached the Windward Road.

Another overland route is via the **Hillsborough Dam**, in the heart of the **Tobago Forest Reserve**. This is a much longer and rougher journey, which can take almost two hours to complete. At the north end of Les Coteaux, continue straight on to the **Mason Hall Road**. After the bridge bear right down a dirt road and you're on your way south.

This area, like much of Tobago, was for years cocoa and coffee estates and is still cultivated for those crops, though on a much smaller scale. You can still see coffee-drying houses with their corrugated roofs that slide on rafters to expose the beans when it's sunny and cover them when it rains. The huge iron pots in some yards used to be (and still sometimes are) used for boiling sugar. Neighborhood dogs were allowed to lick them clean and so are called "pot hounds."

The bumpy dirt road passes soft hills and isolated houses where young girls walk three miles a day just to fetch water and do the family laundry. At the pavement, take a left, past neatly tended gardens and small glades and you are at the dam.

A surprising mixture of pines and palms surround the quiet lake, and if you walk out across the dam you might see a cayman alligator nosing about the reeds. The dam is a good place to begin a hike or a hunt, but don't set out without a guide who knows the area well. Check with your hotel reception before setting out, or the tourism office (TIDCO) in Scarborough for recommendations and permits required.

The road from the dam down to the **Windward Road** at **Studley Park** takes about an hour. First pass the lush growth of palms and bamboo supported by streams trickling through mossy beds, and stop the car to listen to the loud noise of balisier leaves rubbing together. Pass a gravel quarry and then wind down through the small town of Studley Park, situated just five minutes above the water.

Back to civilization: The interior on the west side of the island is more populated and less

View from Moriah to King Peter's Bay.

wild, situated as it is between Plymouth and Scarborough. Near **Patience Hill** is the **National Fine Arts Center**, a small stucco building housing a permanent exhibition of old maps of Tobago alongside changing modern exhibits by Tobagonians or about Tobago. The ride between the two towns is only 20 minutes or so, providing you don't stop to pick up hitchhikers or have a roti and beer along the way.

Scarborough is Tobago's largest and most important town, a market center and port where 17,000 of the island's 40,000 inhabitants live. Compared to some of the more European cities in the Caribbean, Scarborough still has an essentially rustic appearance, although it has been spruced up. The port is a regular cruise ship stop and tourists come ashore at her deep water harbor and head immediately for the beach. As a center for island life, it's certainly worth an afternoon's perusal.

Ranged up and down a steep hill overlooking **Rockley Bay**, Scarborough became the capital in 1779. The town is divided into Upper and Lower Scarborough, the latter having been a Dutch depot in the 17th cen-

tury. Nowadays, the ferry from Port of Spain docks here, as do fishing and cargo boats, though over the years ship captains have cursed the sharp red rocks of the harbor which give the bay its name. The town consists largely of tin-roofed shops, shacks selling a variety of clothing and local produce, and some more solid cement buildings housing several well-known larger stores.

A diminutive town square sits below government buildings and the Tourist Bureau on Jerningham Street, and the narrow streets crawl with slow moving traffic, schoolchildren and professional limers. On Friday and Sunday, an open fruit and vegetable market brings villagers to town.

Any number of undistinguished and sometimes unnamed bars and restaurants serve fried chicken, beer, roti, and fish and chips. **The Old Donkey Cart House** restaurant, on the road east toward Bacolet, has more expensive Creole food and a relatively expensive German wine list. In an old Victorian house overlooking Bacolet and Rockley bays, the restaurant is gussied up with Christmas lights and taped music.

In Lower Scarborough there is a modern

Scarborough from Rockley Bay.

mall encompassing a school and the local library, among other buildings, and though the brick and concrete modern architecture seems out of keeping with the rest of town, it houses a number of useful resources.

The library offers a periodical section on the main floor with a wide selection of Caribbean magazines and newspapers. The Caribbean book section upstairs contains many British and American books on Trinidad and Tobago, some impossible to find elsewhere, as well as all monographs and books written by T&Ters on Tobago. This is a cool, quiet (until school lets out and kids come here to flirt) and different place to spend the hot midday hours.

Scarborough also boasts a **Botanic Garden**, near the approach highway, where you can stroll amid cultivated versions of plants and trees which grow wild on the island, but are sometimes difficult to find.

Fort King George, high above Scarborough, was built by the English in 1779 to protect the town, and was later captured by the French. Like Tobago, it changed hands a number of times, and now lies in partial ruins above the hospital, surrounded by palms, ferns and lawns. The views, particularly at sunset, are breathtaking.

Bacolet and coconuts: From the Fort, continue on the Windward Road, past the Old Donkey Cart House between low hedges and neat palm groves, a tropical version of rural England, to within 100 yards (91 meters) of the Windward Road junction, at the Bacolet River. Continue down a small paved lane on the right and at the intersection take a left, then another left to the end of the road. Walk 50 feet (15 meters) toward the sparkling water, and you are on beautiful **Bacolet Beach**, one of Tobago's most famous.

A long, rough, beautiful crescent fringed with tall palms and littered with coconut husks and tree trunks, Bacolet was the setting for the movie version of "The Swiss Family Robinson." The dark sand beach is set in a residential area of large seaside homes with well-groomed yards, though a deep coconut grove separates it from nearby houses. Pounding surf creates a misty spray of rainbows and haze around the palms, and the beach is often deserted.

In the grove you might see coconut pickers and their rickety ladders balanced on the

Below, Scarborough schoolboys at recess. Right, wood sculpture "The Jig" by Luise Kimme on exhibit at the National Fine Arts Center.

beds of old rounded-line, pickup trucks. Their ability to launch themselves into the fronds 40 feet (12 meters) above an absolutely straight trunk is astounding and rare. Coconut sellers used to climb the trees in search of the best fruit, but now, lament old-timers, most wait until the nuts drop of their own accord.

Winding up the Windward: The drive from Buccoo to Charlotteville at the far end of the Windward Road would probably take three or four hours without stops. But as it passes some of the most enchanting beaches in the Caribbean on the way, there's little chance you'll make the trip in three hours.

Ideally, one could take two or three days and take the road in stretches, returning home each night by a slightly different route, or staying at one of the hotels or guesthouses on the Windward Road.

The Windward is also one of the most used roads on the island, much more so than the northside road, and so you may encounter mild inter-village traffic which, combined with hair-raising turns over breathtaking prospects, slows one's progress considerably yet pleasurably. East of Scarborough,

it is a tropical combination of California's Highway One and Italy's Amalfi Coast.

Beyond Bacolet, the Windward Road curves to and from the shoreline, offering glimpses of long misty beaches or sparkling water, with coconut and cocoa groves and watery estuaries between the road and the beaches.

You can swim pretty much anywhere and if you spot an inviting beach, be assured that there is at least a footpath leading to it. **Hillsborough** and **Barbadoes Bay** offer many bathing sites.

There are only a few lodging places up this end, and all are small, and most, unassuming. Village life reigns supreme here, and the roads are traversed by strong Tobago women, renowned for their broad shoulders and ample girth, with bundles on their heads or umbrellas unfurled against the sun and passing showers.

The ubiquitous schoolchildren are sassier here and boys may shout unintelligible but highly amusing remarks to the sightseer passing through. In time-honored Tobagonian (and African) tradition, these light-hearted verbal assaults are meant as **King's Bay Waterfall.**

much for amusement as energy releasers and an acceptable means of criticism. Though the *picong* may make the visitor feel slightly uncomfortable, generally it's not meant terribly seriously.

Towns are small and perched precariously on cliffs overlooking stunning seascapes, and on those days when light rain comes and goes, there may be three or four rainbows at once, stretching from slope to sea, from treetop to pastel house. There are few roti stands or restaurants, and those that exist are closed on the weekend after 4pm or any other time that the owner would rather be elsewhere.

Richmond restored: Just outside the hamlet of **Belle Garden**, keep an eye out for the wooden sign to **Richmond Great House**. One of many old estate houses, Richmond Great House is one of the few to have been restored. A typical 18th-century plantation house, it was bought in a state of great disrepair by a Professor Lynch of Columbia University in New York City. After extensive restoration, the house opened as a guesthouse offering a sense of history and local atmosphere for a small number of visitors.

The square whitewashed brick house sits on top of a knoll overlooking rolling land to the sea, with mountains behind and palm trees and jungle as far as the eye can see. The Great House's chief charms are its location – isolated yet civilized, and a short ride or 15 minutes' walk from the beach; its design, which permits cool breezes to blow through the rooms even on the hottest of days; and for visitors interested in African art, the professor's extensive collection of objects. It is also a good place for nature lovers, with an abundance of birds and plant life all around.

Continue on to the village of **Delaford**, and right outside look for a sandy parking lot on the left side of the road. This is the entrance to the **King's Bay Waterfall**. One hundred feet high, the highest in the Republic, in the rainy season the falls are full and active with rain and stream water, and it can be excitingly treacherous to climb the ledges above the main pool.

In the dry season, it is much calmer and somewhat tame. The Tourism office (TIDCO) provides changing rooms and a neat path to the falls, alongside a cocoa grove. High

Bird of Paradise Island from the Windward Road.

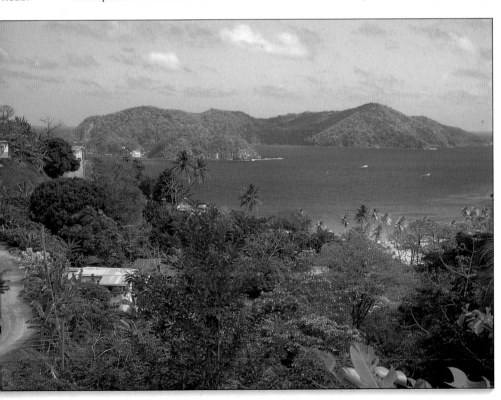

overhead, in the branches of some tall trees, look for the pendant nests, resembling socks filled with sand, of the crested orapendula. These birds permit rice grackles to live in the nests alongside them, as they eat parasitic insects off the chicks' bodies.

Royal sands and Birds of Paradise: Down the road (the King's Bay Depot Road) is the approach to **King Bay Beach**. This sheltered beach has deep gray sand and a soft pebbly bottom. The usual facilities are provided, though most beachcombers are townspeople from Delaford, or local fishermen.

A small rstaurant next to the beach is a comfortable place for an informal meal – when it's open. Private sailboats sometimes dock offshore for a week or so to avail themselves of the protected harbor and peaceful, verdant scenery. Enclosed by the jungle-covered hills as it is, King's Bay seems cooler and wilder than more westerly beaches.

After King's Bay, the Windward Road turns inland until **Speyside**, the home of locally favored **Jemma's Restaurant**, and the jumping off point for trips to **Bird of Paradise Island**. This small, almost barren little island a mile or so off the coast is the only place in the western hemisphere where Birds of Paradise can be seen, as they are indigenous to New Guinea and were brought to this island at the beginning of the 20th century, when they were threatened with extinction in their native habitat (*see Above and Below the Water, page 145*).

Recent hurricanes have diminished the bird population so that it is unclear how many birds remain. You might want to check with the game warden about the bird count, since tour boatmen will all tell you there are plenty to be seen. It's a 20-minute boat ride to any of the three offshore islands, and you can swim at the beach in front of the playing field before and after you go.

Blue Waters at Batteaux Bay: Beyond Speyside, toward the tiny enclave of **Lucyville**, is the remote and romantic **Blue Waters Inn**, a small hotel on its own bay, across from **Goat Island**. After climbing a side road for a few hundred feet, you'll see on your right the entrance to the Inn, a small dirt lane. Drive toward it and you'll think you're about to fly off into the blue, the declivity is so steep. It is a thrilling vista, and

An old water wheel in the grounds of an abandoned estate in Speyside.

one that can make you want to jump right into the ocean once you arrive.

It consists of 11 rooms, really separate cottages along the small beach, and an airy, open dining room for meals and drinks. The narrow beach is confined by sea grapes like natural cabanas, and bird-watching is almost unavoidable.

The end of the road: Between Speyside and Charlotteville the road winds across the mountains through dense, wet, deep green jungle. Curving and mountainous, it can be treacherous during sudden heavy downpours, and though it is only about 4 miles (6 km) between the two towns, the drive takes a good half hour. Midway is a scenic vista from a metal lookout tower placed at Tobago's highest point. Bird of Paradise Island is distinctly visible across forest and water.

Charlotteville is the most picturesque of many picturesque towns on Tobago. Isolated by the mountains to the south and the impassable road to the west, it sleeps undisturbed on sharp, steep cliffs above a deep blue bay. Some of the best fishing on the island can be found offshore, and most male inhabitants are fishermen. There are beach facilities and a beach club offering local music at night, and you may rent cabins on the beach, with simple interiors and porches from which to watch the sunset.

More extensive than it seems at first, Charlotteville is made up of numerous dirt and paved lanes winding back and up along the mountainside. Beyond and to the west is the continuation of the north road, a dirt lane impassable after a few miles. But it's worth a bumpy ride for its sheer fecundity.

Everything is covered in a carpet of soft green vegetation, with orchids and bromeliads growing from trees, guy wires, telephone poles or anything else that provides a small foothold. Tree frogs chirp ceaselessly and small perfect waterfalls edge the roadside here and there. You might even see parrots flying above, or hear a cocrico, one of Trinidad and Tobago's national birds. The effect is of being in an enormous misty terrarium. It makes the south end of the island seem positively arid!

If there are too many deep muddy potholes, do turn back, because it might be hours until someone else passes. And days before a tow truck can come.

Charlotteville tumbles down the hill to Man of War Bay.

INSIGHT GUIDES
Travel Tips

Your vacation.

Your vacation after losing your wallet in the ocean.

Lose your cash and it's lost forever. Lose American Express® Travelers Cheques and get them replaced. They can mean the difference between the vacation of your dreams and your worst nightmare. And, they are accepted like cash worldwide. Available at participating banks, credit unions, AAA offices and American Express Travel locations. *Don't take chances. Take American Express Travelers Cheques.*

do more

Travelers Cheques

Getting Acquainted

Area: 1,980 sq. miles (5,128 sq. km).
Trinidad – 1,864 sq. miles (4,828 sq. km). **Tobago** – 116 sq. miles (300 sq. km).
Capital: Port of Spain (Trinidad); Scarborough (Tobago).
Population: 1,270,000.
Language: English.
Religion: Roman Catholic 32 percent; Protestant 29 percent; Hindu 25 percent and Muslim 6 percent.
Time Zone: GMT minus 4 hours; one hour ahead of Eastern Standard Time.
Currency: Trinidad and Tobago dollar (TT$).
Weights and measures: imperial.
Electricity: 110 volts.
International dailing code: 1 868.

Orientation

Of all Caribbean islands, Trinidad is furthest south, just 7 miles (11 km) from the coast of Venezuela across the Gulf of Paria. Roughly triangular in shape, the island is about 50 miles (80 km) long and almost 40 miles (64 km) wide, with three mountain ranges traversing the interior. These areas remain heavily forested and rich in wildlife. The east and west coasts tend to be swampy; the most popular beaches are in the north, over the mountains from Port of Spain. The south is very different, with its famous pitch lake, oilfields and several mud volcanos.

Fish-shaped Tobago is 26 miles (41 km) long, 7 miles (11 km) wide and lies 21 miles (32 km) northeast of Trinidad. A central range of mountains forms a spine through the Tobago Forest Reserve in the north. Coral reefs surround much of the southern tip of the island. Several smaller islands lying off the coasts are wildlife sanctuaries.

Climate

The weather is almost always perfect. Because of the trade winds, the sun's heat is mitigated by sea breezes. Average temperatures are 74°F (23°C) at night and 84°F (28°C) during the day. There are two seasons: the Wet and the Dry, from December to May and June to November respectively. All this means – except in late October and November, when hurricanes further north can create stormy weather – is that from June to December it rains briefly in the afternoon. June is the wettest month; February and March the driest. It never rains during Carnival.

The People

As a nation, the population of Trinidad and Tobago is divided between roughly equal numbers of African and East Indian descendants, and much smaller percentages of Chinese, Europeans and Syrians. This diversity is mainly confined to Trinidad, however; in Tobago, over 90 percent of the people are of African descent.

Culture

The ambience on both islands is pleasantly relaxed, but good manners are important in Trinidad and Tobago. Visitors are expected to act like guests: to say "please" and "thank you," and to ask permission before taking anyone's picture. And although Trinidadians, in particular, have a disarming way of getting straight to the point in conversation, it's still inappropriate to launch right into a request for service or directions without a proper greeting – "hello, good morning," "good afternoon," or "good evening."

In T&T time tends to be enlarged. If your Trini friends say they'll pick you up at 8, they'll probably come closer to 9. Don't be insulted and don't worry about other appointments because the whole country is on the same schedule. "He's coming just now" may mean he'll be here any second or in the next day or two – often the latter. Slow down; it'll happen when it happens; "no problem." If you really need something done in a hurry, be polite and be persistent.

Economy

Diversification of the economy away from dependence on oil and gas has been given high priority by successive governments. Tourism in particular is expected to make a much greater contribution to growth and employment in the years ahead.

See the "History and People" section of this book for background on Trinidad and Tobago's complex political and economic history.

Government

Trinidad and Tobago became fully independent from Britain in 1962, and declared the Republic into being in 1976, when the President replaced the British Monarch as head of state. The presidential role is largely ceremonial and symbolic. Executive power resides with the elected government, headed by the Prime Minister. Tobago's legislative body, the House of Assembly, sets domestic policy for that island.

The democratic system has functioned well in Trinidad and Tobago since independence, with two hiccups. One was in 1970, when dissident army officers tried to break out of their camp at Chaguaramas, with the intention of heading into Port of Spain to unseat the government. They eventually surrendered.

The more serious challenge to democracy came 20 years later, in 1990, when a fanatical Muslim group, the Jamaat-al-Muslimeen, stormed Parliament, holding the then Prime Minister, A.N.R. Robinson, and several of his ministers, hostage for five days. They were eventually persuaded to give up by the army. Over 20 people died in the assault on Parliament and the fire-bombing of the nearby police headquarters, including one MP. The Prime Minister himself was injured, though not seriously.

Planning The Trip

Don't forget your radio, especially as Carnival approaches, you won't want to turn it off. Also bring paperbacks, sunscreens, cosmetics, and any sporting goods you plan to use. Import duties raise the price of these goods, so it's probably better to bring them from home. If you plan to do much walking, either in the nature centers (bring insect repellent!) or to avoid the high private taxi fares, a pair of good tennis shoes will come in handy.

Electricity

Trinidad and Tobago operates on 110 volts and 60 cycles of electric current. If you need a transformer, most hotels can supply one.

What To Wear

Casual clothes in lightweight fabrics are most comfortable for touring the countryside. In town, most men wear dark trousers and shirt-jacs, or more formal business suits. Women wear dresses or skirts and blouses for work and shopping. Note that skimpy clothing, particularly on women, will attract attention and probably occasion comment.

Even at the best restaurants there's not much call for evening wear. Casual clothes in lush colors and lavish fabrics prevail: in fashionable Trinidad a sense of style is what counts. On the beaches, anything goes. But, especially in Tobago, keep in mind that this is a small-town society, so the rules of small town propriety should be observed. Wear bathing suits on the beach only.

Entry Regulations
Visas & Passports

All visitors must have a return or ongoing ticket and a valid passport for entry into Trinidad and Tobago. Entry visas are not required for citizens of Commonwealth countries with some exceptions, including Australia and New Zealand. US citizens are also exempt. About 30 other countries have visa abolition agreements with Trinidad and Tobago. Those entering on business for 30 days or less, do not need work permits. A departure tax of TT$75 is levied on all travellers leaving by air and sea.

Animal Quarantine

It is better not to try to bring pets. Regulations are very strict regarding the entry of animals, requiring a 6-month period of quarantine.

Customs

What you can bring in: Personal effects are duty free. Adult visitors are allowed 50 cigars or 200 cigarettes or 1 lb. (250 g) of tobacco plus ½ quarts (1½ liters) of wines or spirits, free of duty. Gifts valued up to TT$1,200 are also duty free.

What you can take home: US Customs regulations allow each resident to take home purchases totaling US$400 without paying duty, provided that the resident has been out of the country at least 48 hours and has not claimed the exemption within the past 30 days. Family members living in the same household can pool their exemptions. You may also mail home any number of gifts worth up to $50 each, as long as one person doesn't receive more than $50 in one day. But these gifts may not include spirits, perfume or tobacco. For more information, write for the booklet *Know Before You Go* from the US Customs Service, Washington, DC 20229.

Returning residents of Canada who have been out of the country over 48 hours may bring back CAD$100 worth of merchandise without paying duty. The merchandise must accompany the resident, and the exemption, claimed in writing, may be taken no more than once per quarter. Canadians who have been abroad more than 7 days may also bring home duty-free goods worth up to $300 once each calendar year.

These goods may be shipped separately, but must be declared when the traveler reaches Canada. Canadians are eligible to take *both* the $100 and $300 exemptions on separate trips, but the two cannot be combined. The duty-free totals may include up to 200 cigarettes, 50 cigars, 2 pounds of tobacco for residents over 16, 40 ounces of wine or liquor, or 24 cans of beer, if you meet the age regulations of the province where you arrive.

The total exemption for residents returning to the United Kingdom from outside the EU is L32. This may include 9 fluid ounces (225 grammes) of toilet water, 2 fluid ounces of perfume (50 grammes), and for persons over 17, ½ lb. (250 grammes) of tobacco, or 200 cigarettes, or 100 cigarillos, or 50 cigars. For visitors living outside Europe, double the tobacco limits. Duty-free alcohol is a liter of spirits or 2 liters of sparkling wine, plus 2 liters of still table wine.

Health

Vaccinations for smallpox and yellow fever are not required for entry into T&T unless you have just passed through an infected area.

Throughout the Republic, the water is safe to drink and even street food is generally tasty and fresh for most of the year. However, during Carnival it's probably best to avoid the seafood and meat specials sold from numerous shanties around the Savannah. Often the food is cooked at the vendor's home in the morning, and stored without refrigeration throughout the day.

The National Aids Program of Trinidad and Tobago also issues a timely remind for Carnival and all year round: "Aids is preventable; don't give it to yourself." Avoid casual sex, any procedures which pierce the skin, and remember that alcohol abuse can affect your judgement.

The sun shines with dangerous intensity all year round. Wear ample sunscreen, built tanning time slowly up from 15 minutes in the early morning and late afternoon, and bring a hat or buy one.

Currency

The TT dollar is the basic unit of currency in Trinidad and Tobago. It was declared freely convertible in April 1993, with rates being set by the market. The pre-flotation rate was TT$4.25 = US$1. There was an immediate 26 percent depreciation in the rate, to TT$5.77. The rate has fluctuated since then, reaching TT$6.30 = US$1 by 1997. Visitors arriving in Trinidad and Tobago with more than TT$20,000 or US$20,000 in their possession are required to declare it to a customs officer upon arrival.

First Citizens Bank has a convenient foreign exchange booth at Piarco airport (tel: 669-2489), to facilitate visitors on arrival and departure.

Most of the major credit cards are now accepted almost everywhere in Trinidad and Tobago. Two local banks issue Visa cards and international cards are welcome at most locations such as shops, hotels and restaurants. International cards can access the holder's account in his or her home country and provide local currency through automated banking machines.

Public Holidays

Public holidays, when offices, banks and most shops closed, are: **New Year's Day, Good Friday, Spiritual Baptists Day** (March 30), **Easter Monday, Corpus Christi, Indian Arrival Day** (May 30), **Labor Day** (June 19), **Emancipation Day** (August 1), **Eid-Ul-Fitr** (as decreed), **Independence Day** (August 31), **Divali** (as decreed), **Christmas Day** (December 25), **Boxing Day** (December 26).

Whit Monday is no longer an official holiday, it was replaced by Arrival Day, later renamed Indian Arrival Day. Carnival Monday and Tuesday have never been official holidays but are observed as such, anyway. Even government offices, and all banks, are closed. Everybody is too busy participating in the festival to notice.

Getting There

By Air

Piarco airport in Trinidad is 5½ hours flying time from New York, 3½ hours from Miami, 5 hours from Toronto and 9½ hours from London. **Crown Point** airport in Tobago is just 12 minutes away by air from Trinidad.

Tourism in Tobago has grown quickly in recent years and several regular charter flights are now laid on from various countries to bring visitors to Crown Point directly.

Caledonian Airways offer charters from the UK, Trans Air from the US, Holasun Airways from Toronto, Lauder Air from Italy, Aerotuy from Caracas and Air Mustique from Martinque.

The Trinidad–Tobago domestic air route is now operated by the locally-owned airline, Air Caribbean. It flies eight round trips a day.

BWIA International, formerly 100 percent owned by the government but now privately managed and majority privately owned, flies to Piarco from London five times a week, from New York daily, from Miami daily, from Caracas daily, from Toronto five times a week, and from Guyana daily. Connections to Trinidad from other Caribbean islands are also possible through LIAT, and BWIA itself.

The number of airlines serving Trinidad on a scheduled basis has been reduced in recent years. British Airways no longer services the country, nor does KLM Royal Dutch Airlines. Besides BWIA itself, the following companies provide a service:
American Airlines, 63 Independence Square, Port of Spain, tel: (868) 623-5008.
Air Canada, Independence Square, Port of Spain, tel: (868) 625-2195.
Air Caribbean, 90 Independence Square, Port of Spain, tel: (868) 623-2500.
BWIA, 30 Edward Street, Port of Spain, tel: (868) 625-2295.
Guyana Airways, 13 Pembroke Street, Port of Spain, tel: (868) 627-2753.
LIAT, 122 Frederick Street, Port of Spain, tel: (868) 624-8211.
Linea Aeropostal Venzolana, 13 Pembroke Street, Port of Spain, tel: (868) 623-8243.
Suriname Airways, Cruise Ship Complex, Port of Spain, tel: (868) 627-4747.

By Sea

Trinidad and Tobago is developing its assets as a cruise destination. A dedicated cruise ship berth and associated shopping area has been established at the Port of Spain port and Scarborough has been upgraded to be able to handle two cruise ships simultaneously. This, combined with a boom in the cruise industry, means new options for travelers and more cruise lines with one or both islands on their routes. Check with a specialist travel agent before booking.

The main problem with taking the sea route is the difficulty in extending your stay beyond the few hours the ship is docked. Most cruise ship tickets are sold for complete voyages and you'll probably want to avoid the logistical manoeuvring involved in a change.

The ships from the following cruise lines stop at Trinidad and/or Tobago. **Cunard Cruise Lines**, tel: 800-327-9501.
Epirotiki Lines Inc. (World Renaissance), tel: 800-221-2470.
Princess Cruises, tel: 800-421-0522.
Windjammer Cruises, tel: 800-245-6338.

Useful Addresses

Tourism Offices

The former Tourism Development Authority (TDA) and other government promotional agencies have been merged to form TIDCO. It does not yet have its own offices abroad but works through private marketing and PR firms.
Trinidad: TIDCO, 12–14 Phillips Street, Port of Spain, tel: (868) 623-6022, 623-1932; fax: (868) 625-7548.
Tobago: TIDCO, Unit 12, IDC Mall, Sangster's Hill, Scarborough, tel: (868) 639-4333; fax: (868) 639-4514.
Canada: The RMR Group Inc., Taurus House, 512 Duplex Avenue, Toronto M4R 2E3, tel: (416) 485-8224; fax: 485-8256.
Europe: Morris Kevan International, International House, 47 Chase Side, Enfield, Middlesex, United Kingdom, tel: 0144 (181) 367-3752; fax: 367-9949.
US: Travel Trade, tel: 1-888-595 4TNT or Hotline tel: 1-800-748-4224.

Practical Tips

Security & Crime

Wherever you travel, use common sense. Leave your hotel key at the desk when you go out, stay off deserted streets especially after dark, don't leave valuables unattended on the beach or in your room, and avoid conspicuously displaying money: a TT$20 bill may be a flashy sum when it's handed to a street vendor but not in a hotel restaurant.

Port of Spain is a big city, and big city precautions should be observed. Do not under any circumstances cross the Savannah at night, except during Carnival (and then only if it is well lit and full of people), watch out for pickpockets, and compare taxi and other prices before you commit yourself. Certain areas of Port of Spain are safer than others.

The Independence Square area has been re-born as the Brian Lara Promenade and is now drawing crowds back to the city center after dark but streets east of Henry Street should, generally speaking, be avoided. Policemen and security personnel are now more visible in the main urban centers of Port of Spain and San Fernando and this should give comfort to locals and visitors alike.

TRINIDAD

Police: 999
Fire: 990
Ambulance: 990

TOBAGO (SCARBOROUGH)

Police: 639-1200
Fire: 639-2222
Ambulance: 639-2108

Medical Services

For minor illnesses and cuts or bruises, some of the larger chain hotels have doctors or nurses on call. Major illnesses can be handled by specialists, most of whom are in or near Port of Spain. You might want to check with your hotel or embassy for recommendations.

Outlying areas are served by local Health Centers which offer a free service to members of the public during specified hours.

Major hospitals include Port of Spain General Hospital, San Fernando General Hospital, Eric Williams Medical Sciences Complex (Mount Hope), Community Hospital of Seventh Day Adventists and St Clair Medical Center.

T&T uses the metric system. Given below are some standard equivalents of metric units:

1 inch = 2.54 centimeters
1 foot = 0.305 meters
1 mile = 1.609 kilometers
1 square mile = 2.69 square kilometers
1 gallon = 3.785 liters
1 ounce = 28.35 grams
1 pound = 0.434 kilograms

Monday through Friday, most shops and offices are open from 8am until 4 or 5pm. Most supermarkets stay open until 8pm. Saturday noon is closing time for shops in the urban centers but the suburban malls, like Long Circular, West Mall and Gulf City outside San Fernando, stay open late.

All banks open from 8am–2pm or 8am–noon and 3–5pm on Friday. They close on Saturday, with the exception of the First Citizens Bank's foreign exchange bureau at Piarco.

Many world religions and numerous denominations are represented in Trinidad and Tobago. The selection of religious groups and worship services below comes from a list compiled for visitor information by the Tourism Development Authority.

Anglican

All Saints, 13 Queens Park West, Port of Spain. Tel: 627-7004. Sunday 6 and 7.30am, 6pm, daily 6am.
St Andrew's Tobago, Scarborough. Tel: 639-2485. Sunday 7.30am.

St Paul's, Harris Promenade, San Fernando. Tel: 652-2182. Sunday 6am and 7.30am.
Trinity Cathedral, Abercromby Street, Port of Spain. Tel: 623-7217. Sunday 6, 7.30 and 9am, 6pm.

Baha'i

Baha'i Meeting, Petra Street, Woodbrook. Sunday 8am.

Baptist

Patna Baptist Church, Diego Martin. Sunday 10.30am, 5.30pm.

Buddhist

Community Prayer, Methuen Street, Woodbrook. Sunday 10am.

Roman Catholic

Assumption, Long Circular Road, Maraval. Tel: 622-5728. Saturday 6pm, Sunday 7 and 9am, daily 6.30am.
Cathedral of the Immaculate Conception, Independence Square, Port of Spain. Tel: 623-5232. Saturday 7am and 7pm, Sunday 6.30, 8 and 9.15am, 6.30pm.
Notre Dame de Bon Secous, Harris Promenade, San Fernando. Tel: 652-2269. Saturday 7pm, Sunday 6, 7.30 and 9am, 6pm, daily 6.15am.

Hindu

Krishna Mandir, Todd Street, San Fernando. Sunday 7.30am.
Port of Spain Mandir, Ethel Street, St James. Sunday 8am, 6pm.

Methodist

Hanover, corner of Duke and Abercromby streets, Port of Spain. Sunday 9am and 6pm.

Moravian

Belmont, St Barbs Road. Sunday 8am.

Mormon

47 Tragarete Road, Port of Spain. Sunday 9am.

Muslim

The Anjuman, Sunnat-Ul-Jamaat Assoc. Inc., Headquarters Jama Masjid, 2 Queen Street, Port of Spain. Tel: 623-8963, 657-8373.

Pentacostal

Chaguanas, Cumberbatch Street. Sunday 9.30am.

Faith Center, 3–5 Prince of Wales Street, San Fernando. Sunday 8am and 6pm.

Pentacostal Cathedral, 29–31 Duke Street, Port of Spain. Tel: 623-4335.

Presbyterian

Church of Scotland, 50 Frederick Street, Port of Spain. Sunday 8am.

Church of Scotland, Scarborough, Tobago. Sunday 9am and 6.30pm.

Media
Press

There are four daily papers published in Port of Spain and distributed throughout Trinidad and Tobago. They are the *Trinidad Guardian*, *Daily Express*, *Newsday* and *The Independent*.

A number of weekly tabloids are also available and popular. Though prone to lurid stories and bathing beauty photos, some also feature lively investigations and political debates. They include the *Bomb*, *Blast*, *Heat* and *The TNT Mirror* with its companion paper, *The Sunday Punch*. The Trinidad and Tobago Roman Catholic Church publishes *The Catholic News*.

The *Tobago News* is published weekly in Scarborough, and is entirely devoted to local events.

Magazines & Books

Magazines devoted to local themes are not readily available these days. If you travel by BWIA, you will find on board the BWIA *Caribbean Beat* magazine, revised every two months, which contains well-written articles on various aspects of Trinidad and Tobago and Caribbean life. *Panache*, a woman's magazine published in Barbados, is also available locally, with some Trinidad and Tobago material in it.

Carnival Countdown, published by Media and Editorial Projects Limited, the same company that produces the BWIA magazine, appears at Carnival time each year, with topical information on that year's festivities. TIDCO has now begun putting material about Trinidad and Tobago out on the Internet.

The main bookstores in Port of Spain and San Fernando all stock local reading material, including *The Book of Trinidad*, (Paria Publishing Co., 1992) and *Birds of Trinidad and Tobago* (Media and Editorial Projects, 1994). For bookshops, try **Metropolitan** in the Colsort Mall, Frederick Street, **RIK Services Limited** in Queen Street, **Charran's** in Independence Square and **St Aubyn's Book Services** at Royal Palm Plaza, Maraval.

In Tobago, the Scarborough public library has a wide book selection.

Radio & Television

There are 13 radio stations and three television stations. Only Trinidad and Tobago Television (TTT) broadcasts throughout the day. Cable services are also available. Direct broadcasting services by satellite, using digital technology, became available to Trinidad and Tobago homes in 1996.

Postal Services

Located throughout the islands, Post Offices are open from 8am–4pm Monday through Friday.

Telecommunications

Telecommunications Services of Trinidad and Tobago Television (TSTT) provides local and overseas telephone, fax and other services. Visitors can make calls or send faxes from the company's offices at 54 Frederick Street and 1 Edward Street in Port of Spain. International direct distance dialling is available throughout the country. A cellular (mobile) phone service is now also offered by TTT.

Charges for operator-assisted overseas calls are based on three minutes minimum for station-to-station. For person-to-person or collect calls, 3 minutes minimum plus a one-minute surcharge.

Local operator: 0
Overseas operator: 0
Directory enquiries: 6411
Enquiries for sending faxes, cables, etc. can be made at hotel front desks.

Embassies

USA: 15 Queens Park West, Port of Spain, tel: 622-6371.

Venezuela: 16 Victoria Avenue, Port of Spain, tel: 627-9821.

Consulates

Barbados: Eastern Main Road, Mount D'Or Road, tel: 662-2271.

Dominican Republic: 5 Norman Terrace, Cascade, tel: 624-3667.

Guyana: Park Plaza, Port of Spain, tel: 627-1692.

Suriname: Cruise Ship Complex of Port of Spain, tel: 627-4747.

High Commissions

Canada: 3 Sweet Briar Road, St Clair, tel: 622-6232.

Jamaica: 2 Newbold Street, Port of Spain, tel: 627-7480.

United Kingdom: 19 St Clair Avenue, Port of Spain, tel: 622-2748.

Getting Around
Orientation

For advice before your trip, you may consult one of the TIDCO marketing agents abroad. The TIDCO office at Piarco airport is open every day, 8am–midnight. TIDCO staff also meet all cruise ships and arrange special activities, like tours and calypso performances for the passengers. The Trinidad and Tobago Hotel and Tourism Association will also provide brochures on member hotels and information about facilities and services. For details write to PO Box 243, c/o Travel Center, Uptown Mall, Edward Street, Port of Spain, tel/fax: (868) 624 3928.

On Arrival

On the plane or ship, just before you arrive, you will be asked to fill out an immigration form. Immigration officials collect one copy as you enter the country. Save the duplicate, you will need it for departure. Also be prepared to show your return ticket and give the address were you will be staying in Trinidad and Tobago. If you do not have a T&T address, TIDCO staff meet all flights and can provide information on accommodation available.

From The Airport

Trinidad

Piarco Airport is located about 12 miles from Port of Spain. You can take a taxi into town; go by bus, which may involve carrying your bags some distance; or arrange to pick up a rental car, which will probably take a good bit of prior arranging. If you are traveling alone on a weekend, when the business districts of Port of Spain are fairly deserted, it is better to take taxi.

Go to the taxi dispatcher by the door of the Arrivals area, check the fare – it will probably be about TT$115 (US$20) – and beware of the many drivers who rush up to offer their services; some are not above grossly overcharging. Driving time from the airport to the Savannah is about 30 minutes with minimal traffic; during rush hour it can take over an hour.

Tobago

When you make your reservation, find out whether your hotel has an airport transfer service and approximately how long the drive is from the airport. Several of the hotels near Store Bay and Crown Point are in easy walking distance if you travel light. Others are a long and costly taxi ride away. Here too, if you take a taxi, consult the dispatcher, check the posted rates, and agree on the fare with the driver before setting out. Most of the drivers are well informed guides who will gladly take you on a tour later.

Public Transport

Bus

The Public Transport Service Corporation (PTSC) runs the national bus service. Buses go to all parts of both islands and are reasonably priced. Buses assigned to the main trunk routes (from Port of Spain to San Fernando, Chaguanas, Arima, Sangre Grande and back) are now air-conditioned. They are boarded at the City Gate terminus on South Quay.

Maxi-Taxis

These color-coded mini-buses follow particular routes on both islands. In Tobago, ask directions to the nearest stop.

Route Taxis

These cars carry up to 5 passengers along set routes from fixed stands to various destinations, but are rapidly being replaced by the Maxi-taxis (see previous listing). Sometimes drivers will digress slightly for visitors if the car isn't crowded. Unless they render special services, drivers do not expect tips. In Scarborough, Tobago, route taxi stands are located across from the bus terminal and central shopping plaza.

Private Transport

Hire Taxis

Like route taxis, hire taxis have an H on their licence plates, but they are essentially private taxis, carrying only you and your companions exactly where you want to. Hire taxis do not have meters and are rather expensive. In Tobago the fare from the airport to Speyside is approximately TT$100, to Scarborough TT$30. Usually rates are equivalent between drivers, but you can sometimes strike a bargain if you use the same driver for a number of trips or as a guide for a narrated tour: something most do with enthusiasm. Always agree on fares in advance. Also note fares in Tobago double after 9pm.

Hire taxis wait near most large hotels. Below are a few taxi services:
Bacchus Rental and Car Service, 37 Tragarete Road, Port of Spain, tel: 622-5588.
Ice House Taxi Service, Brian Lara Promenade, Independence Square, tel: 627-6984.
Independence Square Taxi Service, Independence Square, tel: 625-3032.
St Christopher's Taxi Co-op Society Ltd, tel: 624-3560 (Hilton hotel – head office), tel: 625-4531 ext. 1541 (Holiday Inn).
Tobago Taxi Cab Co-op Society Ltd, tel: tel: 639-2707, tel: 639-2659 (Carrington Street), tel: 639-2742 (Milford Road), tel: 639-8252 (Store Bay).
Tobago Taxi Owners and Drivers Association, tel: 639-2692 (Scarborough).

Driving Regulations

Citizens of Commonwealth countries may drive for up to three months with a valid license issued in their respective countries. If your stay exceeds this limit, apply to the Licensing Division on Wrightson Road. International driving licenses are accepted from other countries. Check with the Licensing Division, tel: 625-1031.

Rental Cars

Car rental in Trinidad and Tobago is handled by numerous local fleets. Many take credit cards for both rental fees and the substantial deposit (up to TT$1,000) that is often required. Day rates for non-air-conditioned cars with manual transmission begin at about TT$150; weekly rates from TT$1,000.

TRINIDAD

Auto Rentals, Uptown Mall, Edward Street, Port of Spain, tel: 623-7364.
Econo-Car Rentals, 191-193 Western Main Road, Coconite, Port of Spain, tel: 622-8074.
Himraj Rent-a-Car, Piarco airport, Piarco, tel: 669-0980.
Singh's Auto Rentals, 7–9 Wrightson Road, Port of Spain, tel: 625-4247.
Tragarete Car Rentals, 75 Tragarete Road, Port of Spain, tel: 622-3025.

TOBAGO

Auto Rentals, Crown Point airport, tel: 629-0644.
Rattan's Car Rental, Crown Point airport, tel: 639-8271.
Store Bay Road, Crown Point, tel: 639-8778.
Sweet Jeeps, Sandy Point hotel, tel: 639-8533.
Tobago Travel Limited, PO Box 163.

Scooters

You must be certified to ride a motor cycle or scooter on your driver's license in order to rent one. Call **Island Bikes** at Ben Accord, tel: 639-8587.

Water Transport

Two ferries ply between Port of Spain and Scarborough, the *M.V. Tobago* and the *M.F. Panorama*, but only the latter is now authorized to carry passengers. The trip takes five hours, and food and drinks are available on board. Cabins are available for one way double occupancy. Tickets are sold only at the Port of Spain and Scarborough offices; passenger ticket sales close two hours before sailing time. For more information call 625-4906 in Port of Spain or 639-2417 in Tobago.

If you are leaving by plane, you must arrive at the airport 2 hours before your flight is due to depart. Last minute schedule changes are not unheard of, so reconfirm your reservation 24 hours in advance, and make sure the flight is on time before leaving for the airport. Traffic between Port of Spain and Piarco now flows much more smoothly than before, thanks to the extension of the four-lane highway network but it is still wise to leave about an hour before check-in time, if you are catching a plane during the afternoon rush-hour period (3.30–6pm). During the morning rush hour, the highway is relatively clear going in the direction of the airport.

On leaving Trinidad and Tobago, the carbon copy of the immigration form you filled out on arrival, will be collected by the airline clerk. There is no longer any outgoing immigration check, though there is the usual security check. The departure tax has been increased to TT$75 per person.

Hitchhiking

When driving in the country, you might see hitchhikers, particularly in Tobago. Everyone from schoolchildren to grandmothers hitch (though visitors shouldn't) and it's only friendly to "give a drop" to children, the elderly, and mothers with babies. Exercise more caution with young men.

Where to Stay

Accommodation

Trinidad has a limited number of hotels, compared to the Caribbean's resort islands, and nothing that could be called a resort, American-style. As beautiful as the beaches are here, visitors come for music, culture, business, and Carnival, then retire to Tobago for relaxation. Many business travelers stay at the **Hilton** or the **Holiday Inn**, which have good facilities. The **Kapok Hotel** and **Hotel Normandie** also have a substantial business clientele and popular restaurants.

The prices given below are for a double room based on the European plan:

Inexpensive	=	up to US$70
Moderate	=	US$70–US$90
Expensive	=	over US$90

Hotels
Trinidad

INEXPENSIVE

Moniques, 114 Saddle Road, Maraval, tel: 628-3334, 6282351. Good food, homely atmosphere, run by husband and wife team.

Pelican Inn Resorts, 2–3 Coblenz Avenue, Cascade, tel: 627-6271. Best known for the bohemian atmosphere of its bar.

Tradewinds, 38 London Street, St Joseph Village, San Fernando, tel: 652-9463. Sparse but comfortable facilities.

Tropical, 6 Rookery Nook, tel: 622-5815. Hidden away from city bustle in burgeoning middle class suburb.

MODERATE

Bel Air International, Piarco airport, tel: 664-4771/3. Ideal for short-term or in-transit visitors. Good service.

Hosanna Hotel, 2 Santa Margarita Circular Road, St Augustine, tel: 662-5449. Popular with those seeking a "spiritual" atmosphere.

TJ's by the Sea, South Trunk Road, La Romain, South Trinidad, tel: 657-9278. Good view of Gulf of Paria.

EXPENSIVE

Chaconia Inn, 106 Saddle Road, Maraval, tel: 628-8603/5. Now restructured as "apartment-type" hotel.

Holiday Inn, Wrightson Road, Port of Spain, tel: 625-3361. Conveniently situated right in the heart of Port of Spain. Best suited to business visitors.

Kapok Hotel, 16-18 Cotton Hill, St Clair, Port of Spain, tel: 622-6441. Within easy jogging distance of the Savannah. Good Chinese food.

Normandie Hotel, 10 Nook Avenue, St Anns, tel: 624-1181. In the same area as the Hilton but less expensive.

Royal Hotel, 46–54 Royal Road, San Fernando, tel: 652-4881. Useful for business visitors going south.

Royal Palm Suite Hotel, 7 Saddle Road, Maraval. Caters to a growing preference among visitors for self-contained accommodation.

Trinidad Hilton, Lady Young Road, Belmont, Port of Spain, tel: 624-3111. The world's only "upside down" hotel offers what you would expect from a famous international chain.

Valley Vue, 67 Ariapita Road, St Anns, tel: 624-0940. Popular for conferences, because of its hillside location.

Tobago

INEXPENSIVE

Arthur's By The Sea, Crown Point, tel: 639-0196. Owners have a reputation for being helpful.

Belleviste Apartments, Sandy Point, tel: 639-9351. Another example of the self-help trend.

Cocrico Inn, North and Commissioner Streets, Plymouth, tel: 639-2961. Restaurant and self-catering plans.

Jetway Holiday Resorts, Crown Point, tel: 639-8504. Tobago version of the apartment-type hotel.

Jimmy's Holiday Resort, Crown Point, tel: 639-8084. Similar to above.

Old Grange Inn, corner Buccoo and Auchenskeoch Road, Mount Irvine, tel: 639-0275. Typical olde worlde atmosphere of the established Tobago hotelry.

Ocean Point Holiday Resort, Milford Road, Lowlands, tel: 639-0973. Swimming pool on the premises if you don't fancy the sea.

Rainbow Resorts, Crown Point, c/o Bon Accord Post Office, tel: 639-8271. The only hotel advertising rooms specially adapted for wheelchair users.

Sandy Point Beach Club, Crown Point, tel: 639-8539. Restful atmosphere, within striking distance of airport.

Viola's Place, Lowlands, tel: 639-9441. Another effort to cash in on the growing preference for apartment-type accommodation.

MODERATE

Blue Horizon Resort, Jacamar Drive, Mount Irvine, tel: 639-0432. Surrounded by expensive competitors but manages to hold its own.

Bougainvillaea Inn, Studly Park, tel: 660-2075. Kitchenette facilities and nature trails nearby.

Crown Point Beach Hotel, Crown Point, tel: 639-8781. Studio and cabin-type arrangements. Pool available.

Conrado Beach Resort, Milford Extensin Road, Pigeon Point, tel: 639-0145. Family-run hotel, right on beach. The local fishermen are next-door neighbours.

Speyside Inn, Windware Road, Speyside, tel: 660-4852. On the outskirts of the attractive Speyside village.

EXPENSIVE

Arnos Vale, Scarborough, tel: 639-2881. About 10 minutes drive from the capital, friendly atmosphere.

Blue Waters Inn, Batteaux Bay, Speyside, tel: 660-4341, 660-4077. Isolated, with a certain rustic charm.

Coco Reef Resort, Crown Point, tel: 639-8571. Formerly the Crown Reef hotel. Reopened in 1995, under new name, after US$27 million re-fit.

Footprints Eco Resort, Culloden Bay, tel: 660-0118. Tobago's first eco-hotel, set in a 61-acre property with Culloden reef offshore.

Grafton Beach Resort, Black Rock, tel: 639-0191. Probably the Tobago hotel most recommended internationally but somewhat pricey.

Le Grand Courland, Black Rock, tel: 639-8871. Has attracted mixed reviews from visitors. Only hotel with its own golf course.

Manta Lodge, Windward Road, Speyside, tel: 660-5268. Favored by dive enthusiasts, who can frolic with the giant Manta Ray offshore.

Mount Irvine Bay Hotel, Mount Irvine, tel: 639-8871. One of the first 'up-market' hotels in Tobago. Facilities include its own golf course.

Kariwak Village, Crown Point, tel: 639-8442. No beach but restaurant with good food.

Palm Tree Village, Little Rockley Bay, Milford Road, tel: 639-4347. Kitchenette attached to cabins. So-so beach but better one nearby.

Plantation Beach Villas, Stonehaven Bay, Black Rock, tel: 639-9377. At the upper end of the expensive category. Six villas, pool.

Rex Turtle Beach Hotel, Courland Bay, tel: 639-2851. Been having trouble with some local fishermen, who do not want to move. Varied facilities.

Tropikist Beach Hotel, Crown Point, tel: 639-8512. Air-conditioned rooms, with balcony, but beach a bit rocky.

Woods Castle Holiday Resort, Crown Point. New entrant on the scene. Trying hard to please.

Guest Houses
Trinidad

Alicia's House, 7 Coblentz Gardens, St Ann's, Port of Spain. Tel: 623-8560. Reasonable.

Carnetta's, 28 Scotland Terrace, Andalusia, Maraval, tel: 628-2732.

Fabienne's, 15 Belle Smythe Street, Woodbrook, tel: 622-2753.

Halyconia Inn, 7 First Avenue, Cascade, tel: 623-0008.

Jireh's, 109 Long Circular Road, Maraval, tel: 628-2337.

Nadens Court, 32 St Augustine Circular Road, Tunapuna, tel: 645-2937.

Par-May-La's Inn, 53 Picton Street, Port of Spain, tel: 628-2008.

Zollna House, 12 Ramlogan Development, La Seiva, Maraval. Tel: 628-3731. Reasonable.

Tobago

Coral Inn, Store Bay, Crown Point, tel: 639-0967.

Coral Reef, Milford Road, Scarborough. Tel: 639-2536.

Della Mira, Bacolet Street, Scarborough. Tel: 639-2531.

Mount Marie Co-operative Holiday Resort, Mount Marie, Scarborough, tel: 639-2014.

Richmond Great House, Belle Garden. Tel: 660-4467.

Serenity, Centre Street, Canaan, tel: 639-0753.

Bed & Breakfast

The Trinidad and Tobago Bed & Breakfast Co-operative Society has about 100 rooms on its books which have been inspected and approved. Rates range from US$50–US$75 per day for a double room, with children under 12 being allowed a 12 percent discount in some homes. The Society's address is Cruise Ship Complex, 1 Wrightson Road, Port of Spain, tel: 627-2337 **or** PO Box 3231, Diego Martin, Trinidad.

Special Accommodations

Asa Wright Nature Center and Lodge, Blanchisseuse Road, Arima, tel: 667-4655 or write PO Box 4710, Arima Post Office. Designed for bird watchers. Has featured in wildlife shows on BBC TV.

Pax Guest House, Mount St Benedict, Tunapuna. Operates on the Modified American Plan (room, breakfast and dinner). Stunning view of Port of Spain and central Trinidad. Part of a Benedictine monastry complex.

Reservations

Reservations will make your travels here run smoother. But you can probably find a room without advance reservations in Port of Spain or Tobago, though you may not get your first choice. The exception to this is Carnival season when reserving a room far in advance is essential, especially if you want to stay near to the Savannah.

Eating Out

Travelers from the budget conscious student to the business executive can find food to suit their tastes and pockets, though food prices on the whole are relatively high. The more expensive hotels tend to serve a kind of bland continental cuisine, but some offer special creole meals.

Restaurants run the gamut from roti shops frequented by work people to sophisticated restaurants housed in restored Victorian mansions, serving the best French, creole, Indian, and Asian cuisines. Roadside stands proliferate, as do American fast-food outlets, like McDonalds, Pizza Hut and Kentucky Fried Chicken (KFC).

Prices are categorized as follows:

$	=	TT$5–TT$30
$$	=	TT$30–TT$60
$$$	=	TT$60–TT$100
$$$$	=	TT$100 +

Where To Eat

Port of Spain & Vicinity

Ali Baba, Royal Palm Plaza, Saddle Road, Maraval, tel: 627-5557. Arabic food served in verandah-type setting. Seats 120. $$–$$$

Anchorage, Chaguaramas, tel: 634-4334. Overlooks Chaguaramas Bay – naturally specializes in sea food. $$$–$$$$

Apsara, City of Grand Bazaar, Valsayn, tel: 662-1013. Claims to employ qualified Indian chefs from New Delhi. $$$–$$$$

Botticelli's, City of Grand Bazaar, Valsayn, tel: 645-8733. A chance to sample Italian. $$$–$$$$.

Buccoo Rouge, West Mall, Westmoorings, tel: 632-4072. Claims to be Trinidad's only authentic French restaurant. $$$–$$$$

La Boucan, Hilton Hotel, tel: 624-3111. International and West Indian specialities. $$$

Le Château de Poisson, 38 Ariapita Avenue, Woodbrook, tel: 622-6087. If sea food is your taste, 'see' them. $$$–$$$$

China Palace, Ellerslie Plaza, Maraval, tel: 622-5866. Chinese food with a difference. $$$–$$$$

The Eatery, upstairs Town Center Mall, Frederick Street, tel: 627-2922. Large open area for dining. Open 7am–5pm. Indian, Chinese, Arabian and creole food available. $

Fantasie, Hotel Normandie. Tel: 624-1181/4. International.

Flags, 141 Long Circular Road, Maraval. International menu. $$$–$$$$

Gourmet Club, Ellerslie Plaza, Maraval, tel: 628-5113. Specializes in Italian food. Seats 95. Open for lunch and dinner. $$–$$$$

Hong Kong City, Cor Tragarete and Maraval Roads, Port of Spain, tel: 622-3949. Eat in or takeaway. $$–$$$

Il Colesso, 47 Ariapita Avenue, Woodbrook, tel: 623-3654. One of a group of Italian restuarants sprouting up in and around Port of Spain. $$$$

Lychee Gardens, Upper Level, West Mall, Westmoorings, tel: 637-2668. Chinese food, in oriental-style restaurant. $–$$

Monsoon, 72 Tragerete Road, Port of Spain, tel: 628-7684. Sit down or takeaway service. Indian specialities. $

Olympia, Holiday Inn, Wrightson Road, tel: 625-3361/8. Offers buffet breakfast and lunch and a la carte dinner. $$–$$$

Pavio's, Shoppes of Maraval, Saddle Road, Maraval, tel: 622-7026. Italian food, soft ambiance, good service. $$-$$$

Pelican Inn Restaurant (pub upstairs), 2–4 Coblentz Avenue, Cascade, Port of Spain, tel: 627-6271. Try the garlic shrimp and other sea food specialties. $$-$$$

Pier 1, Williams Bay, Chaguaramas, tel: 634-4426. The Watch Tower restaurant specializes in international cuisine. $$$–$$$$

Rafters, 6a Warner Street, Newtown, Port of Spain. Tel: 628-9258. General menu but serves seafood some nights. $$$–$$$

La Ronde, Holiday Inn. Tel: 625-3361. A la carte continental food. $$–$$$

Singho, Long Circular Mall, St James. Chinese dishes. $$–$$$

Solimar, 6 Nook Avenue, St Anns, tel: 624-62267. International cuisine. $$–$$$

Tiki Village, Kapok Hotel, Maraval, tel: 622-6441. Chinese food at its best. $$–$$$

Valpark Chinese Restaurant, Valpark Shopping Plaza, Valsayn, tel: 662-4540. Offers Cantonese cooking in soothing atmosphere. $$–$$$$

Veni Mange, 67A Ariapita Avenue, Woodbrook, tel: 624-4597. Creole cooking, with homely touch. $$–$$$

Wok N Roll, Highland Plaza, Glencoe, tel: 637-6858. Highly-rated Chinese cuisine. Can be delivered to your door, if you're staying in the area.

Elsewhere In Trinidad

Horaces' Garden Restaurant, 6–8 Farah Street, San Fernando, tel: 657-8331. Long-established southern Chinese eatery. $$–$$$$

Mandarin Court, Mid Center Mall, Chaguanans. One of the main oriental restaurants in central Trinidad. $–$$

Pagoda, 59 Independence Avenue, San Fernando, tel: 657-6375. Relaxing atmosphere in an oriental setting. $–$$

Le Petit Bourg, Farrell House Hotel, Southern Main Road, Claxton Bay, tel: 659-2230. Continental and local food, with a view of the Gulf of Para. $$–$$$

Soong's Great Wall, 97 Circular Road, San Fernando, tel: 652-9255. The Soong family has been offering southerners Chinese cuisine for generations. This is their flagship outlet. $$$–$$$$

Surf's Country Inn, North Coast Road, Blanchisseuse, tel: 669-2475. Overlooks the Caribbean Sea, so its seafood speciality should not be surprising. $$–$$$

Tobago

Arnos Vale Hotel, Plymouth, tel: 639-8084. Local and international dishes. A bonus at teatime is the appearance of colorful Tobago birds. $$$–$$$$

Le Beau Rivage, Mount Irvine Golf Course, tel: 639–8871. Open-air restaurant, overlooking golf course. French cooking. $$$$+

The Best of Thymes, Ocean Point Condo, Lowlan, tel: 639-0973. Seafood, local and East Indian dishes in a garden atmosphere. $$–$$$

Blue Crab, Main and Robinson streets, Scarborough, tel: 639-2737. As name implies, seafood is one of its specialities. $$–$$$

Conrado Beach Hotel, Milford Extension Road, Pigeon Point, tel: 639-0145. Local food in air-conditioned comfort, with view of the sea. $$–$$$

Dillons Seafood Restaurant, Crown Point, tel: 639-8765. International dishes also thrown in for good measure. $$$–$$$$

East Ocean Restaurant, Breeze Hall, Lower Scarborough, tel: 639-4535. Chinese food. $

Eleven Degrees North, Shore Bay, tel: 639-0996. Caribbean, Mexican and Cajun food. $$$

The Fish Pot, Blue Waters Inn, Speyside, tel: 660-4341. Located on the beach. Local, international and seafood. $$$–$$$$

Golden Spoon, Crown Point, tel; 639-0873. Local and international. Dinner always served by candlelight. $–$$$

Gomes Sunrise, Lower Milford Road, Scarborough, tel: 639-3477. One of the few restaurants in Trinidad and Tobago specializing in Portuguese food. $$

Jatt's Harbor Wok, Milford Road, tel: 639-2745. Serves Chinese food in an island where seafood is the speciality. $–$$$

Jemma's Seafood Kitchen, Speyside, tel: 660-4066. Quaint setting, with a tree house. $$–$$$

Kariwak Village, Crown Point, tel: 639-8442. Caribbean seafood in rustic setting. Live entertainment at weekends. $–$$$

Kings Well Inn, Cor. Burnette and Carrington Streets, Scarborough, tel: 639-3883. Proprietors Kim and Cheryl's Bake and Buljol should not be missed. $–$$

The Kiskadee, Rex Turtle Beach, Courland Bay, tel: 639-2851. A mix of local and international dishes. $$–$$$$

Leandros Mediterranean Bistro, Le Gran Courlan, Black Rock, tel: 639-9667. Mediterranean dishes as well as local sea food. $$$$

Marcia's, Store Bay Local Road, Bon Accord. Local food. Reservations for lunch advisable. $$

Old Donkey Cart, Bacolet, tel: 639-3551. Local and international cuisine. Housed in an old-fashioned Tobago home. $$–$$$

Papillon, Old Grange Inn, Buccoo Junction. tel: 639-0275. Yet another seafood eatery. $$–$$$

Patinos, Shirvana Road, tel: 639-9481. Good food prepared by the son of the proprietor. Try the red snapper. $$–$$$$

Peacock Mill Restaurant and Garden, Friendship Estate, Milford Road, tel: 639-0503. International cuisine during the week, barbecue at weekends. $–$$$$

Rouselle's, Bacolet, tel: 639-4738. Seafood and local dishes in a cosy atmosphere. $$$–$$$$

The Seahorse Inn, Old Grafton Road, Black Rock, tel: 639-0686. The specialty is seafood but other local dishes are also served. $$$–$$$$

Seahorse Inn, Grafton Beach Resort, Grafton, tel: 639-0686. Highly recommended, extensive menu. $$$$

Sugar Mill, Mount Irvine Hotel, Mount Irvine, tel: 639-8871. A 200-year old converted mill. Relaxed atmosphere. $$–$$$$

Tamara's, Coco Reef Resort and Spa, Crown Point, tel: 639-8571. An international menu for the sophisticated palate. $$$$

La Tartaruga Cafe and Bar, Buccoo Bay Buccoo, tel: 639-0940. Specializes in Italian food, in response to increased Italian presence in Tobago. $–$$$

Drinking Notes

Mixed drink specialties in Trinidad and Tobago revolve around rum, and it's not hard to find a rum punch that will infuse any time of year with a bit of Carnival. Trinidad is also home to Angostura Bitters, a secret concoction that has been adding zest to mixed drinks for generations. Two popular brands of beer are Stag and Carib. And don't forget to sample local soft drink favorites like sorrel, ginger beer and mauby.

Attractions

Culture

In addition to Carnival and the indigenous arts of calypso and steelband, Trinidad and Tobago boasts a number of theaters, museums, art galleries and festivals. Trinidad and Tobago has also produced some of the region's best known and finest writers and performers, and much of the current crop of plays, verbal art and choreography is performed regularly. Check newspapers for special events.

Art Galleries & Museums

Agape Arts International, 56 Petra Street, Woodbrook, tel: 622-5134.

Aquarela Galleries, 1a Dere Street, Port of Spain, tel: 625-5982. Open Monday–Friday 9.30am–5.30pm; Saturday and Sunday 10am–2pm.

Art Creators, Flat # 402, 7 St Ann's Road, Port of Spain, tel: 624-4369. Open Monday–Friday 10am–1pm, 4–7pm; Saturday 10am–noon.

Chaguaramas Military History and Aviation Museum, Western Main Road, Chaguaramas, tel: 634-4391.

Gallery 101, 101 Tragarete Road, Woodbrook, Port of Spain.

The Gallery One Two Three Four, Normandie Hotel, St Anns, tel: 625-5502.

National Museum, 117 Frederick Street, Port of Spain, tel: 623-7166. Open Tuesday–Saturday 10am–6pm.

National Fine Arts Center, Orange Hill Road, Scarborough, tel: 639-6897.

Concerts

Queen's Hall, 1–3 St Ann's Road, St Ann's, Port of Spain, tel: 624-1284. Music, fashion shows and other events.

Hilton International, Port of Spain, tel: 624-3211, 624-3111. Check for periodic concerts in the Ballroom.

Naparima Bowl, 19 Paradise Pasture, San Fernando, tel: 652-4704.

Spektakula Forum, 111 Henry Street, Port of Spain, tel: 623-2870, 623-

0125, 625-0652. Venue for a number of leading calypsonians.

Theaters

Central Bank Auditorium, 1 St Vincent Street, Port of Spain, tel: 625-4921 ext. 2665.

Little Carib Theater, Corner Roberts and White streets, Woodbrook, Port of Spain, tel: 622-4644.

Space Comedy Theater, Bretton Hall, Victoria Avenue, Port of Spain, tel: 623-0732.

Music

For those who want to hear steelband music, panyards dot the city: open lots where the bands practice regularly – particularly in the weeks leading up to Carnival. They do not stage shows, since this is truly practice space, but there is something about hearing the sparkling sound of a steelband at night that is more thrilling than staged events. This way you can decide on your favorites before the competition begins. The following is a randomly selected list of panyards. Usually, the music starts around 7pm.

NORTH

Amoco Renegades, 17A Oxford Street, Port of Spain.
Blue Diamonds, George Street, Port of Spain.
Carib Tokyo, Plaisance Road, St John
Humming Birds Pan Groove, Fort George Road, St James.
Kool, 25–27 Baneres Road, St James.
Laventile Sound Specialists, Eastern Quarry, Laventile.
Neal & Massy All Stars, Duke Street, Port of Spain.
North Stars, 63 Bombay Street, St James.
Pandemonium, 3 Norfolk Street, Belmont.
Pan Vibes, St Francois Valley Road, Belmont.
Petrotrin Invaders, Tragarete Road, Port of Spain, opposite the oval.
Phase II Pan Grove, 13 Hamilton Holder, Woodbrook.
Starlift, 187 Tragarete Road, Port of Spain.
T & TEC Power Stars, 14 Western Main Road, St James.
Valley Harps, Morne Coco Road, Petit Valley.
Witco Desperados, Laventille Community Center, Laventille.

SOUTH

Antillean All Stars, 8–10 Carib Street, San Fernando.
Couva Joylanders, Railway Road, Couva.
Fonclaire, Dottin Street, San Fernando.
Hatters, Lady Hailes Avenue, San Fernando.
Jah Roots, Warden Road, Port Fortin.
Pan Patriots, Charlo Village, Penal.
Petrotrin Deltones, Railroad Road, Siparia.
Skiffle Bunch, (Pan Round Neck), Lambie Street, Vistabella, San Fernando.
T and TEC Motown, Navet Road, San Fernando.
Tropical Angel Harps, Enterprise Village, Chaguanas.

EAST

Birdsong, Cor Connel and St Vincent streets, Tunapuna.
Harmonites, Churchill Roosevelt Highway, Barataria.
Klondykes Pan Sounds, Macoya Road, Tunapuna.
Melodians, Bellamy Street, Cocorite Road, Arima.
National Quarries Cordettes, Moonoo Street, Sangre Grande.
Potential Symphony, Upper Sixth Avenue, Malick Bataria.
Scherzando, Evans Street, Curepe.
Textel Pantastic Sounds, Old Southern Main Road, Curepe.
Tunapuna All Stars, Railway Road, Tunapuna.

General

You'll find information and phone numbers for Trinidad and Tobago's main visitor attractions in the walking and driving tours that make up the "Places" section of this book.

Other Visits

If your main stop is Trinidad, don't leave without spending some time in Tobago – or vice versa. **Hibiscus Tours** in Colsort Mall, Frederick Street (tel: 625-0784) has one-day packages to Tobago, including air fare, airport pickup and a visit to several tourists sites.

Briko Air Services (Piarco, tel: 669-3915) can arrange plane and helicopter sightseeing trips within Trinidad and Tobago and to other islands.

Cruises

Trinidad and Tobago re-emerged as a Caribbean cruise ship destination once more after the Cruise Ship Complex was established at the Port of Spain port in 1989 and improvements made to the port of Scarborough in Tobago. About 100 ships call into Trinidad and Tobago's ports each year.

Trinidad has been developing special tours to encourage cruise visitors. There are currently three main tours for visitors, each lasting about four hours, leaving ample time for getting back to the ship before it sails.

The tours are normally pre-agreed between the local tour operators and individual lines, so it is advisable to check at the start of the cruise to find out what is available.

The three set tours are:

The Maracas Swim Tour: a short drive through Port of Spain, taking in the Botanical Gardens and the Magnificent Seven buildings, then to Maracas beach and back to the ship. About US$29.

City-Saddle Road-Maracas Tour: a short drive through Port of Spain, taking in the Botanical Gardens and the Magnificent Seven buildings, but turning around at Maracas without a swim stop and returning to the ship via the Santa Cruz Valley and a cocoa plantation. About US$31.

City-Cultural Tour: a drive through Port of Spain via the Botanical Gardens then to a cultural presentation, either at Queens Hall or at the Little Carib Theatre. Indian dancing, folk music, steelband, Carnival costumes etc. About US$33.

There is also an Eco-Tour, which is requested by nature lovers on board. It takes about twelve hours all told, and includes a day at the Asa Wright Nature Centre, lunch, then a visit by boat to see the Scarlet Ibis at the Caroni swamp. About US$40–50.

More tours are planned, including a deep-sea fishing tour (tourists will be transported by car to Chaguaramas and taken off shore by yacht), a golf tour, a visit to the Benedictine Monks at Mount St. Benedict and a tour of Trinidad's gas-based industrial heartland at Point Lisas.

Before or after touring visitors may want to do a bit of shopping. The complex has a 40-booth handicraft market attached to it and the following best buys are suggested:

- Hand-painted tee-shirts (US$20–25.)
- Earrings, steel pans, key chains, etc in copper (US$5.)
- Calabash handbags (US$5–10.)
- Ceramic pots (US$5–15.)
- Leather sandals (US$15–20.)
- Leather belts (US$10–15.)
- Straw hats (US$2.)

In the Cruise Ship Complex itself there are a number of souvenir stores, notably Stechers, which offers the famous Royal Oak rum at US$7 for 26-ounces and Cuban cigars. A box of 5 costs around US$30 and a box of 25 from US$80–200, depending on the brand.

Tour Operators

TRINIDAD

With the growth of cruise tourism, organized tours have increased substantially in Trinidad, most geared to eco-tourism. The following tour guides are among those listed by TIDCO:

Classic Tours, 7 Christina Court, Maracas, tel: 628-5714.

Executive Tours, 189 Gulf View, La Romain, tel: 657-9612.

Alstona Travel, 69 Independence Square, Port of Spain, tel: 625-2201.

Naipauls Tour and Travel Service, Holiday Inn, Port of Spain, tel: 623-5516.

The Travel Center, Level 2, Uptown Mall, Edward Street, Port of Spain, tel: 623-5096.

For visits specifically to the **Caroni Bird Sanctuary**, where one of the country's "national birds," the Scarlet Ibis, can be seen, contact Winston Nanan, **Nanan's Bird Santuary Tours**, 38 Bambook Settlement Number One, Uriah Butler Highway, Valsayn, tel: 645-1305.

TOBAGO

Tobago Travel Limited, Store Bay Road, tel: 63908778.

Ramrattan Services Limited, PO Box 112, Scarborough, tel: 639-1695.

Educatours, Carnbee, tel: 639-7422.

Pat's Nature Tours, Man-O-War Bay Cottages, Charlotteville, tel: 660-4327.

For tours specifically to the famous Buccoo Reef, contact:

Buccoo Ree Co-operative Society, Buccoo Point, tel: 639-8582.

Hew's Tours, 53 Coral Gardens, Buccoo, tel: 639-9058.

Nightlife

If an evening of theater or steelband music doesn't excite you, your best bet is probably dinner and dancing at one of the hotels, or a disco. At the Hilton's **Carnival Bar**, dancing and live music begin at 9pm. The **La Boucan Restaurant and Pool Terrace** at the Hilton also have music and entertainment various nights of the week. The **Chaconia Inn** has a DJ at weekends and is popular with the younger generation, as is the **Upper Level Club** at West Mall, Westmoorings. **Valley Vue Hotel** at Ariapita Road, St Anns, has DJ music, as well as a live band, on Friday and Saturday. The **Mas Camp Pub**, at the corner of French Street and Ariapita Avenue, offers calypso shows during the week and a band on weekends. **Attic Disco** at Shoppes of Maraval, Saddle Road, has different entertainment each night. **Pier One** at Chaguaramas has a varied program during the week – call 634-4472 for details. **La Fantasie Room** at Normandie Hotel has Ralph Davies on piano at the weekends.

For a pub-type night out, try **Smokey and Bunty** on the Western Main Road, St James, **Cocoa House** at Ariapita Avenue, **Pelican Inn** at Coblentz Avenue, **Wazo Deyzeel** at Sydenham Avenue, St Anns, **Moon Over Bourbon Street** at West Mall, **Anchorage** at Point Gourde Road, Chaguaramas, **Cricket Wicket** at 149 Tragarete Road, opposite the Oval Cricket ground and **Karaoke Lounge**, Carlton Center, San Fernando.

Tobago nights tend to have a heavy tropic darkness that calls for cool, rich sounds. You may find them when **Kariwak Village** follows its dinner buffet with a smooth and mellow brand of live music. The most sophisticated spots are the larger hotel bars at **Arnos Vale** and **Mount Irvine Bay**. As for drinking, try **Bonkers Inn**, Store Bay Local Road, **Black Rock Cafe**, Black Rock, **Starting Gate Pub**, Shirvan Road, **Pigeon Point Resort**, Pigeon Point, **Eleven Degrees North**, Store Bay and **Seahorse**, Grafton Road, Black Rock.

Festivals

General

Festivals include Carnival, the Steelband Music Festival (every two years), the annual Hindu festivals of Phagwah and Divali, the Muslim festivals of Eid ul-Fitr and Hosay, the Best Village Folk Festival (October–December), annual Flower and Orchid Shows (March and October), La Davina Pastora in Siparia (April), the Santa Rosa Festival, honoring the original Amerindian inhabitants of Trinidad. Tobago's Heritage Festivals (in July). For power boat lovers, there is the Du Maurier Great Race between Trinidad and Tobago (last weekend in July.)

See the "Festivals" chapter for a closer look at T&T's many celebrations.

Shopping

What To Buy

The Trinidad and Tobago mix of ethnic backgrounds provides a wide variety of shopping possibilities, particularly in Asian and East Indian goods. Silver filigree is an Indian specialty sold at Piarco as well as in Port of Spain and San Fernando at large stores. Fine silks and fabrics are widely available, particularly in Chaguanas in central

Trinidad, a half hour's drive from Port of Spain. Also try **Vanis** and **Chandinis** in the Valpark Shopping Plaza. African prints can be purchased from **Nayankahs** in the Colsort Mall, Frederick Street or **Olayinka** in Long Circular Mall, St James.

For local leathercraft – shoes, handbags, etc. – try the **United Craft Workers Drag Brothers Co-op** at Piccadilly Street, east Port of Spain. **The Trinidad and Tobago Blind Welfare League** shop at 118 Duke Street has a large selection of wicker craft.

The People's Mall at the corner of Frederick and Queen streets offers local T-shirts, jewelry, calabash handbags and other items. At **East Side Plaza** on Charlotte Street, you can find handicraft, batik clothes, local condimetns and even a man selling local herbs which he claims can "cure everything"..

Feelings at 100 Frederick Street sells local gifts and handicrafts. Other outlets for jewelry are **Glen's Jewelry** at 195d Western Main Road, Cocorite. The traditional Port of Spain jewelry stores, **Stechers** and **Y de Lima**, are still going strong on Frederick Street. The more recent souvenir shops in the Cruise Ship Complex, on Wrightson Road, should not be overlooked. Uptown, there is **Boutique Cybele** and **Boutique Begum** at the Hilton Hotel, which both offer oriental garments, batik and tie-dye clothes, jewelry and handbags. At the Normandie Hotel in St Anns, **The Market** contains about seven craft and fashion shops, including **The Craft Shop**, **Aquerias**, **Newly New**, **Tee Shirt**, **Brians** and **Zolton**. If you are in to pottery, try **Ajoupa** at Ellerslie Plaza in Boissiere Village, Maraval. On your way to or from the airport try **Preetanjali's** at Trincity Mall, for East Indian clothes.

Steelpans are expensive and cumbersome but if you are a serious musician, the real thing is available at **Trinidad and Tobago Instruments Ltd**, 144 Old St Joseph Road, Laventille, tel: 627-0185. Or take home a miniature version, to display in your living room.

Sports

Participant Sports

With the perfect climate and diverse geography of the islands it would be difficult to avoid participating in some form of physical activity, whether it's joining the parade of morning joggers circling the Savannah or cycling over back roads in Tobago. Golf, fishing, tennis and running are a few of the sports featured in special tournaments and competitive events; check with TIDCO for more information. The following list notes some facilities for the more popular sports.

Deep Sea Fishing

TOBAGO

Stanley Dillon, c/o Bon Accord Post Office, Crown Point, tel: 639-8765.
Go Ran Quarsordt, Viking Dive, Crown Point, tel: 639-9202.

Golf

TRINIDAD

St Andrews Golf Club, Moka, Maravali. Tel: 629-2314.
Chaguaramas Public Golf Course, Bellerand Road, Chaguaramas, tel: 634-4227.

TOBAGO

Mount Irvine Bay Hotel, Mount Irving, tel: 639-8871.

Scuba Diving

TOBAGO

Sean Robinson, Tobago Dive Experience, Speyside, tel: 660-5258.
Grafton Beach Resort, Grafton, Black Rock, tel: 639-0191.
Ray Hinds, Sun Island Divers, Lambeau.

Snorkeling

TOBAGO

John Darwent, Tobago Marine sports, PO Box 300, Scarborough, tel: 639-0291.
Blue Waters Inn, Speyside, tel: 660-4341.
Crown Point Beach Hotel, Crown Point, tel: 639-8781/3.

Squash

TRINIDAD

Long Circular Mall, tel: 622-3470. Advance bookings required.
Pelican Inn, Cascade, tel: 632-4888.
Valley Vue Squash Courts, St Anns, tel: 627-8046.

Tennis

TRINIDAD

Hilton Hotel.
Tranqulitiy Square Lawn Tennis Club, Victoria Avenue, Port of Spain, tel: 625-4182.

TOBAGO

Arnos Vale.
Mount Irvine Hotel.
Turtle Beach Hotel.

Spectator Sports

Trinidadians love to play games of all sorts, especially cricket, and there are numerous opportunities to watch a game on a neighborhood or international level. Horseracing has now been centralized at Santa Rosa Park on the Churchill Roosevelt Highway, Arima and takes place every weekend. For information about spectator events, check the newspaper or call the **Jean Pierre Sports Complex** (tel: 623-0305) and **Queen's Park Cricket Club** (tel: 622-3787).

Further Reading

General

Anthony, Michael and Andrew Carr. *David Frost Introduces Trinidad & Tobago*. London: Andre Deutsch, 1975.

Anthony, Michael. *Towns and Villages of Trinidad and Tobago*. Circle Press, Trinidad, 1988.

Besson, Gerard and Brereton, Bridget. *The Book of Trinidad*. Paria Publishing, Co. Trinidad, 1992.

Boomert, Arie. "*The Arawak Indians of Trinidad and Coastal Guyana, ca 1500–1650*." Journal of Caribbean History 19:2. University of the West Indies, 1986.

Borde, Pierre Gustav. *History of the Island of Trinidad under the Spanish Government*. Vols. I & II. Port of Spain: Paria Publishing Co., 1982.

Brereton, Bridget. *Race Relations in Colonial Trinidad 1870–1900*. Cambridge: Cambridge University Press, 1979.

Brereton, Bridget. *A History of Modern Trinidad 1783–1962*. London: Heinemann, 1981.

Calder-Marshall, Arthur. *Glory Dead*. London: Michael Joseph, 1939.

Carmichael, Gertrude. *The History of the West Indian Islands of Trinidad and Tobago*. Port of Spain: Columbus Publishers, 1986.

Ffrench, Richard and Peter Bacon. *Nature Trails of Trinidad*. Trinidad & Tobago: S.M. Publications, 1982.

Gomes, Albert. *Through a Maze of Colour*. Port of Spain: Key Caribbean Publications, 1974.

Hargreaves, Dorothy and Bob. *Tropical Tree*. Kailva, Hawaii: Hargreaves Co., 1965.

Jacobs, Richard. *Butler Versus the King*. Port of Spain: Key Caribbean Publications, 1975.

James, C.L.R. *Life of A.A. Cipriani*. Lancashire: Nelson, 1932.

James, C.L.R. *Beyond a Boundary*. Jamaica: Sangsters, 1963.

Jones, Anthony, Mark. *The Winston "Spree" Simon Story*. Port of Spain: Educo Press, 1982.

Lewis, Gordon K. *The Growth of the Modern West Indies*. New York: Monthly Review Press, 1968.

Lewis, W.A. *Labour in the West Indies*. London: New Beacon Books, 1977.

Martin, Tony. *The Pan African Connection: From Slavery to Garvey and Beyond*. Massachussets: The Majority Press, 1983.

Naipaul, V.S. *The Middle Passage*. Harmondsworth: Penguin Books, 1962.

Naipaul, V.S. *The Loss of El Dorado*. Harmondsworth: Penguin Books, 1973.

Naipaul, V.S. *Finding the Centre*. London: Andre Deutsch, 1984.

Newson, Linda. *Aboriginal and Spanish Colonial Trinidad*. London: Academic Press, 1976.

Nunley, John W. *Caribbean Festival Arts: Each and Every Bit of Difference*. London and Seattle: Saint Louis Art Museum in association with The University of Washington Press, 1988.

Quevedo, Raymond. *Atilla's Kaiso: A Short History of Trinidad calypso*. St Augustine: University of the West Indies, 1983.

Ramdin, Ron. *From Chattel Slave to Wage Earner*. London: Martin Brian & O'Keefe, 1982.

Robinson, Arthur N.R. *Mechanics of Independence*.

Ryan, Selwyn. *Race and Nationalism in Trinidad and Tobago*. Toronto: University of Toronto Press, 1972.

Ryan, Selwyn. *The Politics of Succession*. St Augustine: University of the West Indies, 1979.

Sander, Reinhard W., ed. *From Trinidad: An Anthology of early West Indian Writing*. London: Hodder & Stoughton, 1978.

Warner, Keith. *The Trinidad Calypso*. London: Heinemann, 1982.

Williams, Eric. *History of the Peoples of Trinidad and Tobago*. Port of Spain: PNM Publishing Co., 1962.

Williams, Eric. *Inward Hunger: The Education of a Prime Minister*. London: Andre Deutsch, 1969.

Williams, Eric. *Forged From the Love of Liberty: Selected Speeches*. Port of Spain: Longmans Caribbean, 1982.

The books listed above are non-fiction, historical or biographical accounts. By themselves they will give the reader a general outline of the facts of Trinidad and Tobago's history.

However, to get a feel for the experience of that history, the reader must turn to the country's creative writers, for only they can transform knowledge into understanding. A short list must include:

Boissiere, Ralph de. *Crown Jewel*. London: Pan Books, 1981.

Burnett, Paula, ed. *The Penguin Book of Caribbean Verse in English*. Harmondsworth: Penguin Books, 1986.

Lovelace, Earl. *The Dragon Can't Dance*. London: Andre Deutsch, 1979; *Salt*. Faber and Faber, 1996.

Mittelholzer, Edgar. *A Morning at the Office*. London: Heinemann Educational Books, 1974.

Naipaul, V.S. *The Mystic Masseur*. Harmondsworth: Penguin Books, 1964.

Naipaul, V.S. *The Suffrage of Elvira*. Harmondsworth: Penguin Books, 1969.

Naipaul, V.S. *A House for Mr Biswas*. Harmondsworth: Penguin Books, 1969.

Naipaul, V.S. *The Mimic Men*. Harmondsworth: Penguin Books, 1969.

Resistance, Brother. *Rapso Explosion*. London: Karia Press, 1986.

Selvon, Samuel. *A Brighter Sun*. London: Longman Books Ltd., 1979.

Walcott Derek. *Sea Grapes*. London: Jonathan Cape Ltd., 1976.

Walcott, Derek. *The Star Apple Kingdom*. London: Jonathan Cape Ltd., 1980.

Walcott, Derek. *The Fortunate Traveller*. London: Jonathan Cape Ltd., 1983.

Finally, the reader should listen to the wit and wisdom of Trinidad and Tobago's calypsonians. Their oral history and poetry, social commentary and bawdiness, nonsense rhyme and satire, scandal mongering and fantasy has no parallel in any other art form.

Other Insight Guides

There are over 340 *Insight Guides*, *Compact Guides and Pocket Guides*, including 15 on the Caribbean region. Companions to this book include *Insight Guides* to *Caribbean*, *Barbados*, *Bahamas*, *Bermuda*, *Jamaica* and *Cuba*.

Index

The Insight Approach

The book you are holding is part of the world's largest range of guidebooks. Its purpose is to help you have the most valuable travel experience possible, and we try to achieve this by providing not only information about countries, regions and cities but also genuine insight into their history, culture, institutions and people.

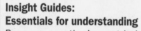

Since the first Insight Guide – to Bali – was published in 1970, the series has been dedicated to the proposition that, with insight into a country's people and culture, visitors can both enhance their own experience and be accepted more easily by their hosts. Now, in a world where ethnic hostilities and nationalist conflicts are all too common, such attempts to increase understanding between peoples are more important than ever.

Insight Guides:
Essentials for understanding

Because a nation's past holds the key to its present, each Insight Guide kicks off with lively history chapters. These are followed by magazine-style essays on culture and daily life. This essential background information gives readers the necessary context for using the main Places section, with its comprehensive run-down on things worth seeing and doing. Finally, a listings section contains all the information you'll need on travel, hotels, restaurants and opening times.

As far as possible, we rely on local writers and specialists to ensure that the information is authoritative. The pictures, for which Insight Guides have become so celebrated, are just as important. Our photojournalistic approach aims not only to illustrate a destination but also to communicate visually and directly to readers life as it is lived by the locals.

Compact Guides
The "great little guides"

As invaluable as such background information is, it isn't always fun to carry an Insight Guide through a crowded souk or up a church tower. Could we, readers asked, distil the key reference material into a slim volume for on-the-spot use?

Our response was to design Compact Guides as an entirely new series, with original text carefully cross-referenced to detailed maps and more than 200 photographs. In essence, they're miniature encyclopedias, concise and comprehensive, displaying reliable and up-to-date information in an accessible way.

Pocket Guides:
A local host in book form

However wide-ranging the information in a book, human beings still value the personal touch. Our editors are often asked the same questions. Where do *you* go to eat? What do *you* think is the best beach? What would you recommend if I have only three days? We invited our local correspondents to act as "substitute hosts" by revealing their preferred walks and trips, listing the restaurants they go to and structuring a visit into a series of timed itineraries.

The result is our Pocket Guides, complete with full-size fold-out maps. These 100-plus titles help readers plan a trip precisely, particularly if their time is short.

Exploring with Insight:
A valuable travel experience

In conjunction with co-publishers all over the world, we print in up to 10 languages, from German to Chinese, from Danish to Russian. But our aim remains simple: to enhance your travel experience by combining our expertise in guidebook publishing with the on-the-spot knowledge of our correspondents.